ON THE EDGE AND IN CONTROL

A Proven 8-Step Program for Taking Charge of Your Life

Dr. Deborah Bright

McGraw-Hill

New York   San Francisco   Washington, D.C.   Auckland   Bogotá
Caracas   Lisbon   London   Madrid   Mexico City   Milan
Montreal   New Delhi   San Juan   Singapore
Sydney   Tokyo   Toronto

Library of Congress Cataloging-in-Publication Data

Bright, Deborah.
   On the edge and in control : a proven 8-step program for taking
charge of your life / Deborah Bright.
       p.   cm.
   Includes index.
   ISBN 0-07-007916-1 (alk. paper)
   1. Self-control.   2. Self-management (Psychology)   I. Title.
BF632.B66   1999
   158.1—dc21
                                                              98-24777
                                                                 CIP

McGraw-Hill

A Division of The McGraw·Hill Companies

1 2 3 4 5 6 7 8 9 0   DOC/DOC   9 0 3 2 1 0 9 8

ISBN 0-07-007916-1

Printed and bound by R. R. Donnelley & Sons Company.

This publication is designed to provide accurate and authoritative information in regard to the subject matter covered. It is sold with the understanding that the publisher is not engaged in rendering legal, accounting, or
other professional service. If legal advice or other expert assistance is
required, the services of a competent professional person should be sought.
   —*From a declaration of principles jointly adopted by a committee
   of the American Bar Association and a committee of publishers.*

 This book is printed on recycled, acid-free paper containing a
minimum of 50% recycled, de-inked paper.

McGraw-Hill books are available at special quantity discounts to use as pre-
miums and sales promotions, or for use in corporate training programs. For
more information, please write to the Director of Special Sales, McGraw-Hill,
11 West 19th Street, New York, NY 10011. Or contact your local bookstore.

To my mother and father, whose support was always there when I was on the edge, and to my husband, Paul, who helped me to find control, and whom I love dearly.

Contents

CONTENTS

Preface

*Great men are little men expanded; great
lives are ordinary lives intensified.*

—Wilfred A. Peterson

Every young athlete dreams at least once of making the Olympic team. As a platform and springboard diver, I spent 11 years in training, practicing four to five hours every day, to reach the point where that dream was close to becoming a reality. In 1968 I had just qualified for the Olympic trials—the first step toward fulfilling my vision of representing the United States. During a routine workout, I noticed that my ability to focus my left eye was failing, and my coach commented that the eye "looked funny." I was rushed to a doctor, who concluded that both of my eyes had been seriously damaged as a result of my diving. The problem was a detached retina, and if I did not undergo immediate surgery—and give up diving forever—I would become totally blind. While I was being wheeled into the operating room, reality set in . . . my life-long dream of making the Olympic team was shattered forever.

While recovering from eye surgery, I felt a total loss of control. Physically, I was getting better, but emotionally I couldn't get past feeling cheated and angry over having been deprived of something I had worked so hard to achieve. I rejected people's attempts to get me involved in other activities. One day while snuggled half-asleep in the back seat of my father's Mercury, I vividly recall being awakened by the sounds of crushing pebbles as the car rolled into a parking lot. I don't know why the sounds were so vivid.

It was almost as if they were a metaphor for the painful turbulence that I felt within myself, because no one, not even my parents, could help me with a new direction for my life. Those crushing pebbles were like a clarion call from some distant guardian angel that alerted me to look to myself as the one to shape my future.

At that moment I made the choice to take control of my life. But accepting control was only the beginning—now I faced the challenge of rebuilding my life, since everything up to then had been centered on diving. I wasn't a natural athlete. I had picked up a number of skills to help me perform exceptionally when faced with high-pressure, competitive situations. Now I worked hard to transfer those skills to my everyday life . . . I became a student of control.

Over the years I have continued to sharpen these skills, and have taught them to thousands of people, ranging from small entrepreneurs and heads of family-owned businesses to Fortune 100 companies. In addition, a less-publicized aspect of my work that brings me great joy is using these skills to help professional and amateur athletes move closer to their own dreams. These same skills have been articulated for you in this book. May they help you gain control and bring out the best of your abilities. This is your personal challenge.

Deborah Bright

Introduction

*Every job is a self-portrait of the person
who did it. Autograph your work with
excellence.*

—Anonymous

oes this describe your life? Today's frantic pace can make climbing out of bed seem like breaking through a racetrack starting gate. After scurrying around to get yourself together, you run out the door to join the millions of people like yourself who are heading off to work. After racing to work, you plow through a slew of e-mail and voice mail messages that all seem to demand an instant reply. You're swamped by the variety of ways to communicate, overwhelmed by trying to keep up with all the technological changes taking place today—and trying to anticipate how they'll impact what you do tomorrow. Your thoughts of the future, though, quickly get diverted to issues at hand as your work piles up and the reality sets in that getting everything done by the end of the day is simply impossible. You try to finish as much as you can, knowing that once you leave, there are other responsibilities to fulfill: kids need rides to soccer practice or music lessons or the doctor; aging parents need help with household chores or just some company; there are groceries to buy, meals to prepare, errands to run. The race keeps pushing you along at a pace dictated by others. There is no finish line to strive for as one day skips into the next without a rest.

At the same time, the cultural fabric that used to cover all aspects of American life seems to be unraveling at an alarming rate. At work, loyalty to the organization and "an honest day's work" no longer get you by. Even going beyond what is expected of you is not enough to get you ahead. The rules that were once clearly understood at work and well entrenched in society are crumbling. Some have been replaced with new ones, but others are yet to be determined. Our lives are filled with uncertainty, insecurity, and unpredictability. It's as if we are being pushed to the edge, and our stress tolerance levels stretched to the max. With each passing day, many of us are beginning to equate survival with success.

I've had firsthand experiences with what it takes to look to yourself to make something happen. Like many of my clients, I had to learn tough lessons, and to this day I keep working on them. My understanding of control dates back to my college years, when I was competing as a diver. The first college coach I had was a young, top-ranked diver himself, who shared my dream of one day going to the Olympics. The way he thought I should get there, however, was by doing everything he said. He told me what major to pursue, what courses to take, what I could eat, and how long I should train each day. He even watched over my social life. He was always concerned about who I was dating and how often we went out. Because he was a well-known diver in his own right, and shared my dream, I willingly followed everything he said. We were together much of the time. It wasn't unusual for us to train four to six hours a day, and when we traveled to diving meets, we spent even more time together. The diving team was so small that we often ate together and engaged in casual conversation afterward. Besides having tremendous support, I had someone who was going to make me a champion. Then the unexpected happened.

My coach of almost three years was offered a wonderful coaching position at a men's college. He wanted me to follow him, but it meant my transferring to a women's school, and one that I had never heard of before. Not knowing what to do, I talked it over with my parents. Finally, we decided that I should not follow him, but transfer to a top diving school instead. I now had to face not only new classmates but a new coach—one who was even more well known nationally than my former coach. That was only a minor difference. The big difference had to do with their style of coaching. My new, highly seasoned coach believed strongly in creating "independent blue-ribbon winners." Those are the athletes who can rely on themselves to work through problems and perform at the highest level when the situation demands it. The blue ribbon has to do with the belief that even though only one athlete will capture the gold medal and be in first place, every athlete can be a blue-ribbon winner, or a solid citizen, both on and off the diving board. Learning to adapt to his style of coaching was extremely painful. In workout sessions, he would ask me what I thought I had done wrong, instead of telling me what my errors were and how to correct them. At meets, he would sometimes not show up. The first time that happened, I totally panicked. The divers in the competition were extremely good, and I felt insecure and alone. My horror was very similar to the feeling you get when you're supposed to be somewhere at a certain time, and you're lost in your car. I was so angry when I finally saw him! I'll never forget what he said to explain his not showing up: "You're the one who's winning the medals, not me." After that experience, I felt like leaving him, but instinct told me to stay. In the years that followed, I had to make a 180-degree shift from relying totally on someone else to relying on myself. The contrast from one coach to the other was my personal introduction to understanding control, and my accepting it.

On the Edge and in Control is about how to create order and at the same time build the momentum to achieve. But this requires going beyond the traditional time management and goal-setting techniques that most of us have been taught. You need to look deeper and adopt a more complete and integrated approach in which you simply learn to engage in keeping promises to yourself.

To help you accomplish your goals, this book offers a road map:

Take Control + Keep Promises to Yourself and Others + Become a Pro-Achiever + 8 Steps to Take Charge of Your Life = On the Edge and in Control.

Emerging above the level of mere survival requires more than understanding control; you need to view it as an integral part of your life. It's absolutely something you *can* do.

TAKE CONTROL

Taking control involves more than simply thinking in terms of being in control or out of control. This narrow view can lead to disappointment. First you need to rethink your view of what control is: Control is not the end result; it's a vehicle for getting there. Taking control requires looking at things from a number of different angles, while at the same time never losing sight of both long- and short-term goals.

By learning how best to direct your energies, you can unlock the chains that once held you back. By reexamining situations where you once felt limited and powerless, you'll discover new options. At the same time, you'll realize a renewed sense of confidence that will propel you to move forward and make things happen. No longer will you experience the "victim mentality." As a matter of fact, you'll experience quite the opposite. By accepting control, you cross a new threshold and start to look to yourself to make things happen. You'll begin to understand how to distinguish between the kind of responsibilities we all face as adults and the kind of inner-driven responsibility that operates from the motto "It's up to me to make things happen—unless circumstances are absolutely beyond my control." This type of self-commitment is called *personal responsibleness*.

KEEP PROMISES TO YOURSELF AND OTHERS

Do you have personal responsibleness? When things don't go as planned, do you feel exonerated by blaming others? In conversation, do you often say things you later regret? Personal responsibleness goes beyond what you do. Through the self-scoring questionnaires that touch on both home and work habits, you will have a chance to look at yourself in a new way, one that will allow you to assess your own degree of personal responsibleness.

When you accept personal responsibleness, you take on a new-found energy and sense of fulfillment. You don't perform tasks or engage in conversations simply to please others—you are fulfilling obligations to yourself. Personal responsibleness is the all-important and intangible quality necessary for leveraging yourself to get results, and for creating your own personal success momentum. It's also an attitudinal maturity that serves as the foundation for perfecting the art of achievement.

BECOME A PRO-ACHIEVER

Achieving in today's complex times, where uncertainty is common-place, requires adopting a different kind of attitude set—one that is rooted in reality. Unknowingly, in maintaining the long-cherished positive attitude, you may sabotage your efforts to reach desired out-comes, because positiveness tends to foster the illusion of control, blinding you from the realities and complexities of many situations. What is this different kind of attitude set that is compatible with today's business environment, in which leaders want employees to help move an organization forward in addition to simply completing tasks? This different attitude set is the *achieving attitude*. It emerges from *personal responsibleness*. In other words, attempts to improve our lives by adopting or pasting on an attitude set take too surface an approach, and are ultimately short-lived. The upbeat attitude comes and goes, much like a faucet that gets turned on and off. Incorporating an attitude set that will stick, and one that is aligned with our complex times, is actually not a pursuit. Rather, it emerges when we accept control and integrate personal responsibleness. The achieving attitude stemming from personal responsibleness is a self-developing guidance system that operates with duality of purpose: performing at exceptional levels and ensuring that our efforts result in a valuable difference being realized.

By describing the achieving attitude in everyday language, this book will give managers the terms they have been looking for to express what they want from employees. Likewise, employees will better understand what managers have probably been trying to tell them for some time. This different kind of attitude set is suited for today's complex world because it seeks out problems (just as a negative attitude does) and views them not as obstacles that can't be overcome, but rather as challenges that need to be dealt with in an overall strategy for achieving desired outcomes.

The strategic process introduced in Chapters 1 to 4 of this book is essential. It builds the intangible skills that position you to interact effectively with others, resolve daily problems, and successfully complete tasks. *On the Edge and in Control* demonstrates how to operate with an achieving attitude. Achieving individuals are experienced and realistic enough to know that reaching desired outcomes consistently requires the utilization of a number of optional skills. Here's where the books you've read on negotiating, listening skills, goal setting, and time management are of value.

EIGHT STEPS TO TAKING CHARGE OF YOUR LIFE

The eight steps you will be introduced to in Chapters 5 to 12 are compatible with achieving individuals who have accepted control. These skills deal with how you think, feel, and process information, rather than with what you should say or do. For instance, you'll learn how to read between the lines and see things as they really are. If you don't, you can fall off track and flirt with the illusion of control, because you lack the information to figure out how things really operate or because you have misinterpreted information and drawn faulty conclusions. Typically, the need to "read between the lines," to "see things as they really are," or "play the political game" refers to the need to recognize and deal with "unspokens." Unspoken expectations exist in every relationship, whether at work or at home. When things are unclear and you are swimming in a sea of unspokens, you feel as if you don't have control—and that's an accurate feeling. You're guessing every step of the way.

Likewise, lots of stress and frustation are created when what you understand doesn't match with what others think. Now you're faced with mismatched expectations. Think about the emotions you feel when you want to go out for dinner and your mate wants to stay home, or when you want to make your own decisions at work and your boss keeps insisting that you get approval on everything first. The issues and situations vary in importance, but one thing remains constant: Much of the frustration that arises at work or at home comes from mismatched and unclear expectations between people. Blaming these problems on communications is superficial. In Chapter 5 you'll have a chance to complete questionnaires that will help you to determine if you are paying attention to unspoken expectations, and if your relationships with the people around you have clear and matched sets of expectations.

Most managers do a good job of explaining what they expect from their employees. But when the spotlight shifts from the boss to the employee, bosses often feel as if they are in the dark. They know more about their products and customers than they do about their employees and what makes them tick. Rather than try to pin blame, Chapter 6 sheds light on how managers, employees, and team members can go about building matched expectations packages.

Operating with duality of purpose doesn't require forgoing personal interests for the sake of the "team." Rather, you need to expand your focus to include the team as well and, as situations arise, make the necessary adjustments to keep both in alignment. Chapter 7 demonstrates how to gain alignment among team members and how to equip people with a likeness of thought, as opposed to a sameness of thought. A team operates with likeness of thought when all members of the team internalize the six maxims of interdependent team thought described in the chapter.

In your effort to be a good team player, consider the following situation. You want to help Dave, one of your peers. You offer some advice, but Dave immediately becomes defensive and argumentative. You try a second time, and the same thing happens. Will you go back for a third try? Probably not. At that point you think to yourself, "I don't need the hassle, and I don't need a confrontation." Who loses out? Obviously, Dave does. Most likely, no one will tell him that he is ineffective at receiving criticism. Dave's defensiveness barricades him from others and leads to blockage of information—information that could be valuable in helping him achieve certain desired outcomes. No one likes to be criticized, and like most of us, Dave has received little or no training on how to benefit from being on the receiving end of criticism. Chapter 8 reveals that criticism is the most powerful form of communication you have at your disposal. Who has control during the criticism exchange and how to avoid responding defensively are just two of the issues examined. Chapter 8 also introduces a receiver reaction chart that offers a new understanding of Eleanor Roosevelt's famous words of advice: "No one can make you feel inferior without your consent."

It's easy to lose your focus in today's chaotic environment, which makes you feel like you're in a popcorn bag with every kernel popping at once. When you lose your focus, you become susceptible to the illusory zones of control and your energies can easily be misdirected. To help you stay at your best and keep your focus when situations demand it, Chapter 9 introduces you to a secret weapon for combating this problem—the 2M simultaneous focus. The first M refers to the macro, and the second to the micro. Today, the big-picture focus, or macro, is not enough. Nor is it effective to limit your view to the micro. You'll learn in this chapter how to simultaneously zoom in on both in order to take control of everyday demands when priorities change and there is too much to do and too little direction from others.

In tough situations, your energies can easily be misdirected unless you have learned specific skills for greater self-control. Years ago, when I was competing 34 feet above the water in platform diving, I developed a number of techniques that I call quick charges to sharpen my focus and regain my confidence. That's just what quick charges are: skills that you can use in high-pressure situations—instantly and without detection from others. There are quick charges for letting go of negative thoughts, for handling intimidation, and for calming yourself. The quick charges introduced in Chapter 10 give you the control you need to appear cool, calm, and collected. To onlookers, your confident demeanor looks totally natural—only you know otherwise.

An insidious energy drainer is being your own worst enemy. You may have heard the expression "If you had a friend who talked to you the way you talk to yourself, she wouldn't be a friend for long." What's unique about self-criticism is that you are simultaneously the giver and the receiver of the criticism. Interestingly, you can exert your energies to destroy yourself, or you can redirect them to empower yourself by creating your own "honesty forum," where you use your control to examine what you are saying to yourself. Learning the dynamics of self-criticism and using the steps described in Chapter 11 will help you engage in an honest, healthy, and stimulating dialogue with yourself that will leave you feeling stronger and more confident.

Do you reach the end of your workday feeling exhausted and

lacking energy to spend quality time with the people you care about most? What about re-energizing yourself so you don't have to collapse on your days off? The belief that having to do more with less would be a temporary phenomenon is fading. The issue of *Newsweek* reported that "fatigue is now among the top five reasons people call their doctor. Chapter 12 shows you how to stop long enough to experience personal quiet time and re-energize yourself. Many people find that personal quiet time has an additional benefit: By giving them an opportunity to reflect on where they're going and what is important to them, it helps them put their lives in balance. Again, the key to putting balance into your life lies with you, because you know how to operate on the edge and stay in control.

HOW TO READ THIS BOOK

Think of reading this book as having a meaningful conversation with a friend. Everything your friend says has your best interest in mind, but it's still up to you to think about your friend's words and believe in them for yourself. Otherwise, you won't take action and your friend will have given you good ideas and nothing more. Similarly, it doesn't really matter that others have benefited from the skills and concepts introduced in this book. What is important is that *you* believe in them and are committed to integrating them into your style and your repertoire of skills.

ACKNOWLEDGMENTS

I would not have been able to write a book while at the same time keeping a business running smoothly without the great help of Michael Jackson, who tirelessly worked with me through numerous edits; Marianne Laren, who ensured that concepts and ideas in the book held together; and John Feloni, who helped to refine the focus of the book. I will be forever grateful to Penelope Boehm for both her constant support in running the business and her friendship over the years, and to Timothy Hill, who keeps picking up the pieces at work, where there's always too much to do and never enough time. I wish to thank John Britton, who keeps the company technologically on the edge, so we can be more efficient.

Thank you to Dr. Harry Croft, to whom I refer often in the book. In addition to providing his professional expertise on a number of mental health issues, Dr. Croft, through many hours of discussion, helped me to keep my ideas on a professional track.

A special thanks to Dr. Robert Levit for his friendship, advice, and encouragement.

This book never would have been possible without the involvement of three outstanding people to whom I am most grateful: Bert Davis, who was not only encouraging and insistent about this manuscript becoming a book, he even helped me find the best publisher for it; Betsy Brown, whose focus and charm blend to make what I consider to be the ideal editor; and Bob Tabian, my agent who never lets me down. A sincere thank you to the great team at McGraw-Hill. To Pattie Amoroso, whose editorial skills helped to make the book more understandable; and to everyone else at McGraw-Hill who helped so much in promoting and advancing the message of this book to the public: Kurt Nelson, Lynda Luppino, Sharon Lane, Claudia Riemer-Boutote, Elizabeth Aviles, Lydia Rinaldi, Evan Boorstyn, and the rest of the publicity team at McGraw-Hill.

I would also like to thank the following people for their time and help in solidifying the concepts and ideas presented in this book:

Acunto, Carole	Dabal, Jan
Anderson, Willard	Daseke, Don R.
Angelino, Mark	Davidson, Jim
Annunziata, Bob	Davis, Bert
Badger, Mark	Davis, Bill
Bailer, Tom	Davis, Harriet
Barnes, Al	Davison, Pete
Bates, Paul	Daza, Joyce
Beaver, Bob	DeCesaris, Geaton, Jr.
Bell Karen	Delano, June
Blades, Judy	DeMatteo, Patricia
Bolstad, Randy	DiOrio, Tom
Bridges, Clayton	Ditman, Terri
Burlingame, Harold	Ellig, Bruce
Burns, Liz	Esposito, Jim
Burrus, Daniel	Eyles, Mary
Cerow, Bob	Fisher, Ann
Cintron, Marlene	Friedman, Victor
Clark, Nancy	Geller, Bob
Corseman, Sarah	Gilpin, Jan
Cosgrove, John	Gilson, Chris
Couture, Sue	Glenz, David
Critzos, Arlene	Goeken, Sandra
Croft, Harry	Gormely, Dennis
Cupp, Durene	Grant, Gwendolyn
Curfiss, Larry	Gray, John

Greenberg, Eric
Hannaford, Lonnie
Hanson, Laurel
Harford, Jan
Harris, Barbara
Hartley, Duncan
Heinze, Ken
Hill, Leonard
Holmes, Becky
Holmes, Bill
Howard, Karen
Hoy, Frank
Hughes, Linda
Ingber, Alan
Killoyne, Don
Kirn, Steve
Knopf, Lewis
Komsa, Kathryn
Kostere, Kim
LaSalle, Christine
Leeds, Dorothy
Lehrer, Bill
Levit, Robert
Louenberger, Connie
Lowe, Paula
Macauley, Clark
Mack, Linda
Malloy, Danielle
Medina, Ellie
Meng, Matthew
Michmerhuizen, Brian
Molinaro, Lou
Moore, Jim

Morley, Mike
Nobis, Melody
Noble, Karen
Opler, Susan
Owens, LaVerne
Paino, Phil
Patton, Jean
Pawloski, Terri
Peale, Ruth
Pilka, Jody
Powers, John
Predpall, Dan
Price, Linda
Putré, Bill
Quattrini, Nancy
Reese, Ann
Rivers, Ron
Robespierre, Eric
Rohlen, Ann
Rosenblatt, Nat
Ross, Jennifer
Runko, Paul
Schiffman, Ed
Schneiderman, Mark
Small, Eric
Stiles, Art
Stierwalt, Rick
Titus, Joan
Totin, Wayne
Turrell, Bob
Twardy, Claudia
Vandeberg, John T.
Varlotta, Gerard

ACKNOWLEDGMENTS

Vernikovsky, Dalia
Voight, John

Wachtelle, Dick
Walker, Rick

About the Author

Dr. Deborah Bright, author of the best-selling *Creative Relaxation,* regularly coaches professionals from all fields on how to thrive—not just to survive—in the demanding arenas of today's high-energy offices and two-career households. A former Olympic diver, Dr. Bright is a consultant to professional golfers as well as to tennis and baseball players and America's top corporations. She has shared her insights on national television, including appearances on the *Phil Donahue Show* and *Regis and Kathy Lee,* and is frequently quoted in *The Wall Street Journal, Fortune, Cosmopolitan,* and *USA Today.*

The current address to Bright Enterprises' Website is:

http://www.drbright.com

FIRST
STEPS

1 TAKE CONTROL

Get action. Seize the moment.
Man was never intended to become an oyster.

—Theodore Roosevelt

"I just got off the phone with my mother. Every time I talk to her, she ends up complaining that I never see my family any more, and every time I end up feeling guilty. Why do I let her do it to me?"

"My boss left the office again today without telling me whether I would get next weekend off. She knows I'm waiting for an answer, and she has to have made her decision by now. Why am I always left hanging like this?"

"I know I could have a better job than I have now, but I just don't have the skills or the time to get them on my own. I've tried taking classes after work, but something always comes up that interferes. I just couldn't juggle both at once. The pressure just got to me. I'm afraid I'll be stuck in this job for a long time before something changes for me."

"As the demands of my job increase, so does the pressure. I'm constantly worrying about whether things got done, and if I'll get a call on my pager. My wife complains that all I think about is work. She tells me to stop thinking about it. If only I could . . ."

"My boss is always running around. We spend so little time together. I really don't know if he's pleased with the job I'm doing. If only he wouldn't leave me in the dark, I'd feel a lot better."

On the surface, it appears as though these people are all concerned with very different problems. But there is one solution for all of them: They need to take *control*.

By taking control, you will no longer feel overwhelmed, boxed in, and unable to do anything about a situation. You've probably heard this before—what's been missing, however, is a clear understanding of *how* to do it. To get started, it's important to take a moment to define what is meant by control.

IN SEARCH OF CONTROL

When I speak of control, am I referring to having power over others and getting them to do things against their will, or dominating situations to get my own way? No. The kind of control I am referring to is personal control—control over yourself and over your situation. More specifically, control is the process of isolating key factors that, when put to use, will result in achieving a desired outcome. At the heart of control is action directed at:

- Clearly identifying the desired outcome
- Isolating the key factors that can determine the outcome
- Propelling yourself into action

Desired outcomes are typically the intermediary milestones you want to reach as part of an overall effort to accomplish a goal. Desired outcomes include such micro things as having a good discussion with your boss, delivering a well-received presentation, and spending a fun evening with your family. The accumulation of desired outcomes produces a forward momentum that is energizing because it signifies that you are making something positive happen. That realization in and of itself instills a sense of self-confidence.

In most situations, there are many factors that can determine an outcome. The *key factors* are the specific ones that you can draw upon and put into action with the belief that they will increase your chances of attaining a desired outcome. The more clearly you can identify these key factors in a given situation, the greater your chances of achieving what you want.

The third area, *taking action*, is what separates those who obtain their desired outcomes—and stay on the edge—from those who keep thinking of how good things could be if they were there. We are always trying to persuade ourselves to do something in order to reach a desired outcome. What's important is isolating the *key factors* and then taking action. Let's look first at an example of taking control that's so simple you likely wouldn't give it much thought: You want to safely move a heavy flower pot to another part of the room. Here, control entails having the ability to consider the key factors involved in achieving this desired outcome. Can you lift the pot and carry it for a sustained period of time? To check out the ease of carrying the pot, you can practice lifting it before actually setting yourself in motion. Another key factor worth noting is the pathway: Can you find a path across the room that avoids any obstacles? Once you have determined that you have the ability to carry the pot and that you know the best path, you are ready to take action. By safely moving the pot to another part of the room, you have exercised full control. The key factors identified can involve the consideration of little things, as this example demonstrates.

Now let's consider another example: Your desired outcome is to reward yourself at the end of the day—something many of us overlook. If you select the key factors of taking a warm bath and reading a book, then you have full control and can achieve your desired outcome. But if you choose instead to go out with your mate and "have a fun evening," the situation becomes more complex. Your ability to have full control is questionable, because your mate (or any other person) is an unpredictable and uncontrollable factor. If he or she is not in the mood to go out, your plans for the evening are spoiled. This example illustrates that as situations increase in complexity (such as when other people are involved), your ability to influence key factors and determine outcomes wanes.

What's important is to place yourself in the *pivotal position* in order to make best use of the key factors. By assuming the pivotal position, you are deciding to take charge of what's going on around you, rather than just allowing things to happen. Think of the pivotal position as being on the edge: From this vantage point, you have a wide-angle view of surrounding circumstances as well as the leverage to impact the situation.

TAKING CONTROL VS. SETTING GOALS

As you have probably determined, taking control is not to be confused with setting goals. When setting goals, you decide what you want and then map out a plan to reach your goal. Thus, goal setting gives you direction. Taking control is what keeps you on track and working within the legitimate parameters of your plan.

> *Taking control is not the same as setting goals.*

Control involves understanding the key factors that can bring about a desired outcome and lead you closer to your goals. It also involves putting the key factors into action. Control ensures achieving the desired outcome, which can result in the satisfaction of needs, drives, and goals.

Let's look at a quick example. Lynn is a young mother who wants to make some improvements in her life and her career. Her goal is to find a more rewarding job. Her plan is to get a college degree by completing several courses. She has enrolled at the university, bought her books, and made plans to study for three hours every weeknight. Her goal and plan of action are now in place.

Now, put yourself in Lynn's place. Could you stick to the plan? You could start out studying each night, but after a few weeks you might end up skipping a night or two when you were in a bad mood, facing a lot of unrelated pressure, or simply feeling sorry for yourself. When you fail to keep your resolve repeatedly, your goals stand in danger of becoming merely dreams.

With an understanding of control, you can achieve your goals. Taking control involves figuring out which key factors you must isolate and work with to ensure that you reach the outcomes you desire. As a situation changes, the key factors also change, so continuous reevaluation is an integral part of taking control. You can get fooled into thinking you have control when you don't.

An investor in the stock market finds that every time he buys and sells certain stocks, he makes a profit, so he thinks his model is working and he has isolated the key factors that yield the desired outcome. But when he experiences a few losses, he knows his model is ruined. Or a golfer has a couple of great rounds then says, "I've finally got my swing"; in other words, the golfer has isolated the key factors and has sequenced them properly so that she can swing consistently. But the next time out on the golf course, she finds that when she puts her swing into motion, she doesn't get the same results. No player has complete control of his or her swing. Even professional golfers are always trying to "find" their swing. Like them, we are all seeking out the things we need to do or the key factors we can work with to help us to achieve a desired outcome.

Thinking we have it all figured out, then finding that we don't and that we need to go back to the drawing board, is part of what makes us human. It's also the reason control is a constant pursuit.

TOTAL CONTROL VS. TRUE SENSE OF CONTROL

Can you ever have total control? "When considering the larger picture," says Dr. Harry Croft, psychiatrist and director of professional and community education at San Antonio Regional Hospital, "it's not possible to have *total* control . . . it's not even possible to determine whether or not you will be alive tomorrow. There are too many variables that you cannot predict or have any influence over. What about people who have done nothing wrong, who have worked hard for years, and now find themselves in a position to lose their jobs through no fault of their own? In our effort to introduce some predictability into our lives and to create a feeling of order, it is more realistic to strive for a true *sense* of control."

> *It's not possible to have* **total** *control.*
> *Seek to realize a true sense of control.*

Understanding what we can and cannot control is an essential part of taking control. These parameters of control are discussed fully in Chapter 2. For now it is enough to recognize that there will always be some things that we cannot control. Total control implies full control of both self and situation, but neither is possible. For example, when it comes to self, we cannot control our getting older; regarding situation, we cannot control the weather.

By striving for a true sense of control rather than total control, explains Dr. Croft, you are setting out on a reasonable pursuit. You can realize a true sense of control in handling everyday situations. *Sense* is an appropriate word, because you can *feel* when you have achieved it. There is a balance between feeling comfortable and feeling challenged, between enjoying where you are and making progress toward where you want to be. When your investment of energies to isolate and work with certain factors regularly yields desired outcomes *and* your efforts lead you closer to your goals, then you have realized a true sense of control.

> *Short-term desired outcomes need to be consistent with long-term goals.*

The two elements of this description are equally important: Short-term desired outcomes must be consistent with longer term goals. Consider again the inevitable process of aging. When you have a true sense of control, you accept that you cannot stop your body from aging, but you also realize that you can improve your odds for living a long life by exercising, eating well, and seeing a doctor regularly. These same tactics improve the quality of your life day by day, so there is consistency over the short and long term.

Some strategies that work well in the short term can produce future problems. For example, when Kevin started a new job several years ago, he wanted to feel more relaxed throughout the day. He found that smoking cigarettes did the trick for him. But his chronic cough finally drove him to see a doctor, who discovered polyps in his throat—likely caused by smoking. So in the long term, this variable did not serve him well.

Another example strikes close to home for many of us who face increased work demands. Melanie, who works for a major tire company on the East Coast, wanted to ensure that everything got done on time and at the proper level of quality, so she tapped the most obvious variable—the hours she put in at the office. This strategy worked for a while, but then she started to notice that she was more tired than usual and her mind was dull. The feeling of being constantly under pressure began to lessen her enthusiasm for her job. Working longer hours helped Melanie get through some rough spots, but in the long run she found that she needed to identify and use other key factors.

Keep in mind that in any given situation, you are already operating with a sense of control. An example is preparing dinner for guests. You have learned which dishes work the best with dinner guests, and you have devised a system for preparing the dinner with the least expenditure of energy. You also know just when to accept offers of help from guests, so you can serve a delightful meal while still enjoying the party yourself. Another example is leaving work at the end of the day. Whether you are aware of it or not, you have already established your routine. A routine such as clearing all completed files from your desk or building a to-do list before leaving the office serves you well because it closes out the day, while at the same time preparing you for the next morning. In each case, you operate with a true sense of control because you have an understanding of what you need to do or the key factors you need to work with in order to reach a desired outcome. The challenge is to take your understanding of control and apply it to a wider range of circumstances.

TRAPS THAT RESULT IN A FALSE SENSE OF CONTROL

It all seems so obvious. But it's not uncommon for us to find ourselves losing focus, falling off track, and not realizing desired results. When we misdirect our energies at any point along the way, we end up operating under a false sense of control. With a false sense of control, we let our focus slip and isolate faulty factors that jeopardize the achievement of desired outcomes. All of us at some point have felt we are on the right track, only to find that our investment of energies resulted in a disappointment. To steer clear of the peril of illusionary traps of control, you will want to familiarize yourself with the perception-warping zones of control. Learning about these zones will help you avoid misdirecting your energies and falling into the trap of thinking you are operating with a sense of control, when in fact you are heading for disappointment.

> *While in the pursuit of control, you can get off track and gain a false sense of control.*

There are three primary perception-warping zones that can ensnare individuals seeking control. The *rigid zone* is a trap of restrictive behavior patterns; the *dependency zone* is the pitfall of reliance on something or someone other than yourself; and the *blind zone* is an ambush of misinformation. Since operating with a false sense of control is insidious, these zones can best be seen through examples from real life.

THE RIGID ZONE

You stray down a common path into the rigid zone when you adopt rules or schedules in an effort to achieve a desired outcome, but then allow those rules or schedules to become your central focus—and a false indicator of control. Take David, a CEO determined to be healthy and to have a lot of energy to get through the tough days. He gets up very early in the morning and meditates, then goes jogging for 20 minutes, then eats fruits and cereal for breakfast while he reads the paper, all before going to work. To feel in control of his day, David must religiously follow this routine for a "healthy start." If any of the steps are left out or not executed precisely as planned, he gets upset and is unable to get through his day with the kind of energy he needs. The disruption of his set plan forces the false sense of control to surface.

> *In the rigid zone, rules and schedules become your central focus.*

Whether by self-imposed rules or by an insistence (conscious or not) on following a script that has worked in the past, people can become trapped in the rigid zone when they permit external factors to become their central focus. When rigid adherence to the pattern is disrupted, their inflexibility becomes apparent. Outwardly visible signs of being flustered or uncomfortable reveal the false sense of control.

People can also fall into the rigid zone when they don't have a cadre of skills to rely on. Few members of an audience will answer no when asked the obvious question, "Is there anyone here who hasn't made a mistake?" But what's not so obvious are the particular skills that people can draw upon to quickly recover from mistakes. We all face tough daily situations, and many that arise are not our doing. But the more skills you have, the greater your chances are of achieving your desired outcomes. Think of it this way: If you were riding a bike up a mountainside, you'd be glad the bike had more than one gear!

THE DEPENDENCY ZONE

> *The dependency zone means reliance on some-one or something other than yourself.*

The second area that can lull people into a false sense of control is the dependency zone. Here people see themselves as making things happen, but the results are attributable to something other than the investment of their energies. The dependency zone has three aspects: personal, situational, and chemical.

Let's consider an example of someone trapped by the personal aspect of the dependency zone. Curt was the first in his family to attend college. After earning a bachelor's degree in business, Curt joined the family enterprise, a successful retail furniture store built up over the years by Curt's grandfather and father. Curt took over management of the books and put into practice some of the business principles that he learned in college; he let his dad take care of the customers and the newspaper ads. In the first two years Curt worked in the furniture business, the store had recordbreaking sales, and Curt attributed that success to his innovations. When his father suddenly became seriously ill, Curt was left to run the store by himself. He fired the top salesman and made other changes, with the unintended result that valued customers no longer felt welcome. Within 3 years, he destroyed a business that had thrived for 58 years. What went wrong?

In personal dependency, the individual believes that he or she is the one who is making things happen when another person is actually responsible, at least in part. Curt mistakenly took full credit for the store's record sales when, in fact, his role managing the finances was relatively insignificant. His father had the rapport with the customers and the ability to strategically position the company—his father was in the pivotal position.

When the person in the pivotal position goes away or chooses not to do what is required, the personal dependency illusion surfaces and the individual taking the credit is unable to achieve desired outcomes on his or her own. In Curt's case, his father was actually doing the job; in other instances, the pivotal person provides psychological support needed by the individual who is doing the job. Take for example the athlete who successfully handles the intense pressures of competition and performs extraordinarily well as long as his coach is present, but does not realize that the coach is in the pivotal position until the coach can't show up for an event and the athlete is unable to perform.

Some people put themselves in uncontrollable situations by forfeiting the pivotal position to others. Common examples include parents who center their lives around their children and nurses who measure their self-worth by the successful care of their patients. A term for this type of behavior is *codependent.* Some parents or nurses exhibit a codependent behavior pattern because they think they are "giving" to their children or patients when, in essence, they are satisfying themselves and enhancing their own self-worth. When the doing for others is not appreciated, it's not uncommon to hear the codependent say, "I give and give and give and nobody cares." Besides feeling misunderstood, clinical psychiatrist, Harry Croft, explains, the codependent becomes angry, and then gets depressed. Codependents believe that they are in control, but in fact they are dependent on the reactions of others. Their false sense of control is revealed when the pivotal person (whether child, patient, or someone else) does not appreciate their efforts.

Situational dependency arises when someone is *thrust* into the pivotal position rather than attaining it through his or her own effort. Take Lou, who lost his job as part of a companywide downsizing. As a devoted husband and father of two small children, Lou panicked because he did not have any financial security. His job search went much slower than he had anticipated. Then Lou's father died suddenly, leaving him a large sum of money. Now Lou feels as if he is on top of things and in control. This feeling, though, will last only as long as the inheritance money lasts—his sense of control is illusory. Lou was given the pivotal position. Without the investment of his own energies, he cannot sustain the momentum needed to achieve his desired outcomes.

The chemical aspect of the dependency zone occurs when people artificially manipulate energy through the use of drugs or chemical substances. Here the drug assumes the pivotal position and the person's illusion of control becomes apparent when the drug is not available. The drugs we are considering here are not those used under medical supervision to alleviate a physical, mental, or emotional condition. Rather, they are the drugs that people tend to abuse, such as alcohol, speed, marijuana, heroin, cocaine, and crack. Some of these drugs are associated with the ability to unleash creativity or to feel more comfortable with oneself. For instance, a shy and awkward young man feels that when he uses cocaine he is "transformed" into a Herculean character. When undergoing recovery, he is concerned about his inability to come across as an effective person without the drug. As his doctor explained, the young man did not acknowledge that his actions were really his own; he was dependent on the drug because he *believed* that it enabled him to perform.

That young man's problem is hardly unique. Dr. Croft notes that researchers have identified a "dependency-learning state": The individual can reprise the performance only when in the same state in which it was originally conceived. For instance, rock stars who wrote music while on LSD have found that they can fully appreciate the music only when they have taken LSD again. A student who used amphetamines to get through an all-nighter of cramming and the next morning's exam remembers nothing of what he "learned" once the high has worn off.

In a different league and on a much smaller scale, consider our daily doses of caffeine, alcohol, and nicotine. We all know someone who claims, "I can't get going in the morning until I have my cup of coffee," or someone who can't fall asleep at night without Nytol. Has anyone said to you, "Just let me have a drink and relax and then we can talk about it"? Or perhaps you know someone who can't carry on a conversation without a cigarette. The person's belief that he or she cannot function properly when an external crutch is unavailable suggests that he or she has given up some control. Am I suggesting that you cannot have a cup of coffee in the morning or that cigarette? Absolutely not. Rather, the focus is on making sure you are clearly aware that it is not the coffee, cigarette, or drink that is making things happen; *you* are responsible. Otherwise, the dependency on over-the-counter drugs and "social drugs" communicates an insecurity, both mental and physical. When the drug is not available and the user has difficulty functioning, the false sense of control is exposed.

THE BLIND ZONE

> *The blind zone is an ambush of misinformation.*

The third perception-warping zone of illusory control is called the blind zone, because it ambushes people who close their eyes to certain information or are slow to perceive and understand changing circumstances. People operating in the blind zone reach false conclusions about themselves and their situation, thereby putting the desired outcome at risk. In common parlance, they are "operating with blind spots."

As a customer service manager during prosperous times at a telephone company in Jericho, New York, Jimmy was accustomed to being greeted by people on the streets of his small town. Then Jimmy received an offer for a new job in New York City, where he would be managing a much larger group. Proud of this success, Jimmy confided that he had been at the company long enough and it was time to move on. His acceptance of a promotion and the move into the city were a blast of reality for Jimmy when it became apparent that he was not as successful as he had imagined. He soon realized that his peers at the new job were as good as or better than he was. In this case, Jimmy was operating with the illusion of control because he was blinded by being a "big fish in a little pond." When he became a small fish in a much bigger pond, his self-esteem suffered and his confidence was rattled.

Money can push people into the blind zone when it is linked with intangibles such as friendship, trust, respect, and happiness. The delusional linking of money and happiness is nothing new—we've all heard that you can't buy happiness. People with monetary wealth and those with power over the financial well-being of others can find themselves operating in the blind zone, unable to determine whether others are with them because of who they are or because of their money or power.

THE INTERPLAY OF THE THREE ZONES

The three perception-warping zones are not mutually exclusive; rather, they are complementary. The worker who needs a cup of coffee to start the day is dependent upon the caffeine kick she feels; if she is oblivious to her dependence on caffeine, she is also blinding herself as to what is really happening. Likewise, the boss who strives to empower his people at work, but insists that the tasks be completed not only successfully but also his way, is rigid and is blind to his own inconsistency. He believes that the same pattern must be followed to repeat success, and he has closed his mind to other possible ways to achieve his goals.

The examples are endless. What's important, when seeking control, is to be aware of and be quick to recognize these three perception-warping zones. Complete the questionnaire on pages 18–19 to learn if you are in danger of being sidetracked into a false sense of control.

Just as being in good shape physically can help you avoid injury or illness, so keeping your mental condition sharp can help you avoid slipping into thinking you are in control when you are not. My research and experience suggest that four key elements underlie control. These are:

- Flexibility
- Letting go
- Choice
- Clarity

Understanding and exercising these elements readies you to take control.

A PERSONAL LOOK:
ARE YOU REALLY OPERATING WITH A SENSE OF CONTROL?

DIRECTIONS: Circle the number that most closely represents your likely responses in each situation. Answer each question according to what you typically do, as opposed to what you think you ought to do.

1 = Almost never **3** = Sometimes
2 = Occasionally **4** = Frequently
5 = Almost always

1. When others make mistakes are you quick to make the corrections yourself?	1	2	3	4	5
2. When working on a team effort, are you upset and reluctant to change your thinking when steps are taken contrary to what you think is best?	1	2	3	4	5
3. When your idea is partially accepted by others, do you persist in trying to convince them you are right even to the point of being labeled "stubborn"?	1	2	3	4	5
4. Do your feel uncomfortable or sluggish when you miss your morning coffee or tea?	1	2	3	4	5
5. Do your find it difficult to leave work problems at work each day?	1	2	3	4	5
6. When scheduled meetings start late, do you get upset and sub9sequently have difficulty focusing on the agenda issues?	1	2	3	4	5

7. Do you have a difficult time getting projects done because you can't get yourself in the mood?	1	2	3	4	5
8. After you make a mistake, do thoughts about it linger and negatively affect what you do?	1	2	3	4	5
9. Do friends and loved ones complain that all you talk about is your work?	1	2	3	4	5
10. If a meeting participant brings up a good idea that you had not considered, do you resist giving the person credit?	1	2	3	4	5

SCORING AND INTERPRETATION

Add the numerical value for each response to get your total score.

A score of 21 or more moves you into a position of falsely being in control when engaging in everyday activities and striving for goals. Questions 1, 2, 3, 4, and 10 are centered on the rigid zone. Frequent "frequently" answers suggest that you tend to be set in your ways. It takes a lot of energy on other people's part to get you to do or see things differently. Likewise, if you answered questions 5, 6, 7, 8, and 9 "frequently" or "almost always," it's apparent that you need additional skills to help you rebound more quickly and shift gears more smoothly. In other words, if the skills you are using to help you let go of negative thoughts aren't working, you're in trouble. You have very little to draw upon to help you perform at your best when the need arises.

STAYING FLEXIBLE

Envision a palm tree: Its thick trunk and small crown let it sway with the winds of a hurricane. Since you often don't know when or where that next gust of wind may blow, it's important to incorporate a certain degree of flexibility into your life. Here are some things you can do on a daily basis.

> *Direct your energies toward end results.*

1. ***Direct your energies toward the end result, rather than toward uncovering the best way to do something.*** Be aware that several paths can lead to the same point. Ken Heinze, a senior manager at a major New York bank, notes: "Whether working with other team members or by yourself, it's important to keep in mind that there are many ways of reaching the same goal. Select one and go for it, and when everyone is pursuing the goal in the same manner, then the excitement that already exists is magnified."

2. ***Equip yourself with a tool box loaded with a variety of skills.*** By learning and fine-tuning techniques for dealing with criticism, rebounding from mistakes or disappointments, or relaxing and re-energizing, you are in a better position to rely on yourself when necessary, rather than depending on good fortune. Remember that if one technique isn't giving you the results you need in a given setting, you are in a precarious position if you don't have additional techniques in your tool box. Golf professional Lee Trevino provides a valuable perspective when he talks about the importance of having skills and keeping them fine-tuned. He says, "The more I practice, the luckier I get."

3. ***Stay on top of habitual routines.*** From the moment you wake up in the morning, you engage in routines for dressing, eating, and getting yourself off to work, to school, or wherever. Routines are an efficient way to operate. But to keep yourself flexible, you need to alter your routines occasionally. For instance, instead of always doing your work at your desk, try working in other places. By introducing variety, even slight variety, you are challenging yourself, positioning yourself to better handle a wide range of situations. If you broke your

wrist, could you manage the most mundane tasks? If your job suddenly required you to travel frequently, could you work comfortably and effectively away from your desk?

Another reason to be aware of your habitual routines is that routines suited to one situation may be inappropriate in different circumstances. For example, the habit of directing people on your job can carry over when you go home, but your spouse may not appreciate being told how to prune the hedges.

INCORPORATING THE NOTION OF LETTING GO

Letting go is closely related to flexibility. We are not talking about "hanging loose" and letting whatever happens happen. Consider these common experiences:

- Nothing in your day is going right, and the more you try to improve things, the worse they get.
- You are with your loved ones and you can't get your mind off your work. The more you tell yourself to stop thinking about work, the more you think about it.
- You are tackling a problem and the answer isn't coming to you at the moment. The more you try to force yourself to come up with a solution, the more confused you get.
- You are trying to learn a new skill, but it seems that the harder you try, the worse you get at it.

> *Let go by eliminating "the fight."*

In these situations and similar ones, your energies are being misdirected because you are forcing things to happen, fighting either yourself or what you are trying to achieve. The laws of physics tell us that when positive and negative forces collide, they cancel each other out. Incorporate this principal into the notion of letting go. By eliminating the "fight," you create momentum and allow your energies to flow better. Letting go involves a combination of backing off, going with the flow, trusting yourself, and having faith in a higher power.

OPERATING WITH CHOICES

> *As long as you have choices, you are in control.*

"As long as an individual has choices, he or she is in control," Dr. Harry Croft reminds us. "Rules give us order and direct our choices, but the more rules we follow, the less our control. Sitting around a coffee table with friends talking theoretically about the notion of choice and having control wouldn't generate a lot of differences of opinion. In practice, however, when adults are faced with some challenging situations, this notion gets a little unclear. Take, for example, being approached on the street by a mugger who says, 'Give me your wallet.' At that moment, some people would think they have no choice, but they do! The confusion sets in because we may not recognize that choices exist when the options are not of equal weight."

In other words, the "consequence" may be so great that it blocks us from thinking that choices exist. Occasionally we'll hear a news story about a pedestrian on a street corner who overcame the threats posed by a mugger. While this example may represent an extreme circumstance, we can find examples in our everyday lives where we feel boxed in when in fact we aren't.

Suppose an executive complains that he hates his job, but he can't quit. If we consider this situation carefully, it becomes apparent that the executive does *not* have to keep his present job, he *can* quit. He is choosing to keep his job, even though he hates it. Why? Because the consequences of quitting—not having a steady source of income for his family, the possibility that he won't find another job right away, and so on—are worse than his current situation. Here, the options do not hold equal weight, but a choice does exist.

By creating more choices in your life, you advance your pursuit of control. Here are two suggestions.

1. ***Pose what-if questions and create your own fallback position.*** Many of the people I interviewed for this book commented that they have a fallback position in case their jobs are eliminated. Terri Ditman, head of education and training at Hartford Boiler in Connecticut, would return to waiting tables, something she enjoyed doing earlier in her working life. Clayton Bridges, director of business development at Cultor Food Science Inc., would become a postman. Some people keep their résumés current and make a continuous effort to network so they are always prepared for an unexpected change in their job situation.

Of course, we could ask what-if questions about everything in our lives. To retain perspective, think about what's important to you, and then create your own what-if strategy for it. For example, what would happen if one of your parents were to die or become seriously ill? What if your marriage were to end because of divorce or a sudden death? What if you became disabled?

Besides developing what-if strategies for important things, you should invest some time thinking about how best to handle everyday situations that frustrate you. If your bane is being stuck in traffic, you might equip your car with a selection of educational audiotapes so you can make productive use of the time. One of *my* frustrations is last-minute appointment cancellations; my time is an irreplaceable asset when consulting with clients. My what-if strategy involves having my assistant call a day or two ahead of time to rearrange all my appointments and create new ones.

2. ***Operate more often on a want-to basis.*** Options are often perceived as being limited when you are operating on a "have to," "should," or "must" basis. The easiest way to operate on a want-to basis is to ask yourself questions that get you thinking about whether you *have to* or *must* or *should* do something. For example, you might

ask yourself, "Do I have to move all the furniture when cleaning?" Clearly, you don't *have to*. But if you want to have a clean home and you are going to do it yourself, then you *want* to do it, even if it is only a "little want."

When a peer asked Terri Ditman why she appeared so enthusiastic for work each day, Terri explained, "Every morning before I get out of bed, I make a point of asking myself 'Do I want to go to work today?' I start thinking about what's going on that day and, at the same time that I am answering yes to my question, I also have a sense of direction for the day and a feeling of purpose. If there are too many days in a row where I question whether or not I want to go to work, then I will have a more serious issue to start examining. Very rarely do I go to work feeling as if I 'have to.'"

CLARITY

> *Be clear about what attributes to your success.*

When interviewing outstanding athletes and businesspeople—like baseball greats Johnny Bench and Gaylord Perry and CEOs Victor Friedman and Fred Higgins—I have found that they are all very clear about what their success can be attributed to. When you are expecting repeat performances from yourself, and others are expecting them of you, it is essential to understand clearly the factors that contribute to your success. Without clarity regarding your abilities, your confidence level can vacillate. Clarity is also needed to articulate desired outcomes and to determine what it is going to take to achieve them. You can use the following questions to help you gain clarity:

1. In assessing your relationships with your mate and close friends, ask: "What special qualities bond and strengthen my relationships?"
2. Whether you are working in an office or at home, ask your-

self: "What contributes to my effectiveness and what makes me valuable in my current position?"

3. To gain clarity regarding the attributes that lead to your success, ask yourself after every important event: "What did I do well and what worked? What didn't go well and what didn't work?"

The precision with which you can articulate your answers to all these questions serves to clarify where you need to expend your control to achieve your desired end results.

This chapter has demonstrated that trying to make rules for yourself, manage your time, or reach a level of comfort is too simplistic an approach to pursuing control. Likewise, thinking of yourself as being either *in control* or *out of control* is too narrow a view. The next chapter shows you how to avoid disappointments, and instead use your energies more consistently to reach the outcomes you really want.

Here's how you can take control immediately.

1. **STOP** thinking that control is something bad, and that by seeking control you'll become a "control freak"! You're not going after control over others; rather, you are seeking control over yourself (and your situation) in order to reach a desired outcome. Your goal is to realize desired outcomes, and control is your vehicle for getting there—it's not the end result, as it is for those who are seeking control for its own sake.

2. **STOP** equating control with rigidity.

3. **STOP** allowing yourself to get caught up in routines. Pay attention to whether you have said, "We've never done it like this before" or "We've always done it this way."

4. **STOP** thinking that you have "no control" over your emotions and your thoughts.

1. **START** realizing that control is equated with flexibility. Build flexibility by developing a repertoire of skills so that, depending on the situation, you'll have a skill to draw upon to help you handle it better.

2. **START** building flexibility into your day by introducing new routines. For instance, instead of doing your work at your favorite spot, pick another place. See if you can concentrate in your new place as well as you do normally.

3. **START** asking yourself if you "want to" do certain things. By coupling this question with the achievement of desired outcomes, you'll develop a greater level of enthusiasm, because you are acting out of choice instead of feeling as if you're limited in what you can do.

2 GET ON TOP OF THINGS

*Ability may get you to the top, but it takes
character to keep you there.*
—John Wooden, UCLA Bruins Coach

etting ready for the day, you turn on the television and switch to *Good Morning America*. The cohost is interviewing a senator about a difficult issue being deliberated in Washington. She seems well informed and carries the conversation easily. Even though the topic is highly charged, she's cool and collected. Being a TV host is an easy job, you think to yourself. There are producers, directors, scriptwriters, and research assistants telling you what to say and do—not to mention makeup and wardrobe to make you look good. All you have to do is act natural!

But in reality, a lot of time and effort go into making what you see on TV appear easy. "Acting natural" when you know millions of people are watching you takes practice. Even though there are many people working off camera, the one person on camera is responsible for bringing all their efforts together. Joan Lunden once told me that she puts in about four hours of preparation time for a four-minute interview!

Wouldn't you like to have the ability to operate smoothly and be on top of things regardless of the circumstances? Of course you would—who wouldn't? Many of the people interviewed for this book told me that's what control means to them. They also described control as being comfortable with themselves or being "in a groove." We admire people who seem to push themselves to the edge and perform at consistently high levels, without appearing flustered or pressured. Of course, natural ability plays a part, but a lot of work goes into making something look easy. This chapter goes behind the scenes to take a close-up look at what is involved in taking control.

CONTROL: UP CLOSE AND PERSONAL

In your effort to handle today's hectic environment and still maintain a sense of control, you need to recognize that control is a multidimensional process with four distinct facets. Without understanding all the dimensions of control, you will be prone to neglecting some essential ingredients for achieving your desired outcomes.

That is the case with Kathy Howell, a golfer on the LPGA tour. Her goal is to join the ranks of the top money winners, but that's several years down the road. She also expects to marry sometime in the future, but for now she is comfortable with the balance between her personal and professional lives. In preparing for the upcoming season, Kathy decides that she wants to qualify for 70 percent of the tournaments in which she plays. To maintain the high energy levels she needs throughout the season, Kathy plans to get an adequate amount of sleep each night, to eat properly, and to take time to meditate regularly. During tournaments, she intends to incorporate various reenergizing techniques. When it comes to ensuring that she plays a good round of golf, Kathy is establishing a simple routine that involves selecting her club, focusing on a shot, and having a fluid swing with a good follow-through. It sounds as if Kathy has considered all the variables and devised a thorough program for herself—unless you know her!

One of Kathy's biggest problems is that she gets so upset and angry with herself when she misses a shot that she is unable to use the skills she has practiced. Yet her plan fails to deal with this problem, a key ingredient necessary to ensure her desired outcome—she has completely overlooked one dimension.

Whether or not Kathy meets her goal will be easy to determine. Just check the newspapers or record books. In the world of sports, everything is simplified: There are scores and rankings and all sorts of comparative statistics to measure progress or success; there are manuals on proper form and execution; there are coaches or other experts who offer strategies. But in the everyday experiences of most of us, the results of our efforts are often blurred. Most of the time, we don't win or lose; we just keep playing the game. As the complexity of our lives and of our world continues to intensify, the multidimensional aspect of control is becoming more apparent. There are four dimensions of control. Most of us can easily identify them, but few work with them as an interrelated whole:

- Big-picture dimension
- Daily progress dimension
- Damage control dimension
- Energy allocation dimension

These four dimensions are the ways of thinking that facilitate the process of control—they must all be working for you to reach your desired outcomes consistently and feel good about yourself. If any one dimension is not in balance with the others, you experience a sense of being "out of order" and consequently out of control. On the other hand, if you feel out of control, you can use the four dimensions to help you understand where you are and to help you sort things out.

As its name suggests, the big-picture dimension typically presents a macro view of your situation. The other dimensions move frequently between macro and micro perspectives. All four dimensions are of equal value and are interrelated—all four may come into play at any given instant. Learning to use each dimension easily and effectively enables you to direct your energies so you can create your own momentum for making desired things happen. This chapter illustrates how taking control involves utilizing each of the four dimensions.

THE BIG-PICTURE DIMENSION

Each of us has a picture in our minds of ourselves now and in the future. Dr. Harry Croft calls this picture "a self-concept about our lives." The big-picture dimension encompasses our self-concept and the global aspects of our lives, including the quality of our relationships (with mate, family, and friends), our health, our careers, and our roles in society. Addressing the direction of our lives and the fulfillment that we ultimately seek is what this dimension is all about. Typically, we concentrate on the big-picture dimension when we consider our goals and dreams for our future.

The big picture looks different for each of us. Mark Angelino, general manager for a major computer company in New York State, operates with a broad view of what is important to him. He equates success with finding his place in the world, rather than working to be conventionally "successful." For Mark, the big-picture dimension can be described as following his own inner voice.

Sue Couture, senior vice president at a major pharmaceuticals company in New Jersey, has a more detailed plan for her future, prompted by a former boss who encouraged her to write out five-year projections about where she would like to be in her career and how she planned to get there. The idea worked so well for Sue that she has since gone to 10-year plans. Creating this kind of plan, she explained, gives her a clear idea of how and where she can best direct her energies.

Of course, we can't predict every twist and turn that life has in store for us. Glen, a real estate sales manager for a developer in North Carolina, learned that the hard way when he recently began suffering blinding migraine headaches. In addition to handling all the usual things that need to be done each day, Glen must now work closely with his doctor to determine what is causing these incapacitating headaches. Suddenly, a major change in his "big picture" took precedence over other concerns. Now Glen watches his diet closely and pays special attention to various stress factors that may be contributing to his condition. "We often take our health for granted," Glen told me. "I didn't think anything about eating a candy bar or having a bag of potato chips. But when you realize that all these things can make a difference, it sheds a new perspective on what goes on each day and how your performance can be affected." What Glen said comes as no surprise to me: Since our health comes for free, we often don't realize how precious it is until after we lose it.

Health is not the only aspect of our lives that we may neglect in the big-picture dimension. How many times have you thought to yourself, "If I only knew then what I know now"? For instance, your parents encouraged you to pursue an advanced college degree, but you were eager to get out into the real world. Now, you see the value of their advice: That degree is a leverageable variable for attracting greater opportunities. Similarly, because you now have a greater appreciation of the time value of money, you think that you should have saved and invested your money differently. Looking back, you may think that you should have taken better care of your health, or spent more time with your parents and your children. By spending time on the big-picture dimension—by considering how to prepare yourself in a broad way—you can help prevent feelings of regret down the road.

Most people don't stop long enough to ask themselves questions about what they really want and need in their lives. Not long ago I met with a client to discuss giving a presentation for her company. Grace opened our meeting by looking me square in the eyes and saying, "I've got to talk to you about something unrelated to work." She continued, "I have everything that I want in life. After years of working at a terrific job, I have a lovely home, great friends, and a wonderful family. The only missing piece is a significant other in my life. I have been divorced for 15 years, and since I've been single I have had terribly disappointing relationships with men. But 2 months ago, through some connections with a friend, I met the nicest guy. He's unlike anyone I've ever dated, but I'm afraid and confused." Although I was surprised by this confession, I understood that Grace, like so many other people, was searching for a special relationship. So I asked her, "What are you afraid of?" Grace replied that she was concerned that their good feelings for each other would go away. "We are talking about marriage and I'm frightened about taking that extra step."

As Grace talked, it occurred to me how funny it was that she first said she had everything, even though she clearly did not. It's ironic that this woman is able to make decisions all day long as part of her job, and to take incredible risks, yet when it comes to her personal life, she is unsure of what she wants. How many Graces are out there—people who invest a great deal of time in their work and in being knowledgeable about their customers, their products, and their industry, yet when it comes to their personal lives, they have little knowledge about themselves? People like Grace are smart, but they have not taken the time to understand themselves, which is essential to gaining a true sense of control.

Then again, there are times when we do think about our lives and wonder whether what we do each day is worthwhile. In the elevator of my building a stranger who looked to be in her fifties said to me, "I'm exhausted. I've been working too many hours each day. I'm not supposed to be doing this at my age." Many of us are troubled at times by the inconsistencies that exist between reality and our visions of how our lives would enfold. As part of the big-picture dimension, recognizing those inconsistencies leads us to address honestly what we want, need, or consider important, and to adjust our paths accordingly.

The big-picture dimension is operating with the conscious awareness that, as expressed so eloquently by one yoga expert, "you come into this world with nothing, and you leave with nothing. Everything else you fill in." Consider this dimension your long-range guidance system.

DAILY PROGRESS DIMENSION

Whereas the big picture focuses on large-scale, long-term issues, daily progress deals with gaining a true sense of control in everyday situations involving one's self and others. The daily progress dimension applied to a single situation consists of identifying the desired outcome then isolating and implementing the variables—the specific "things" that you do or need to do to control self and situation in order to secure the desired outcome. You already use this system, although you may not be aware of it. For instance, you want to lose 15 pounds—your desired outcome—so you decide to go on a diet and you strategize those things you need to do to stick to your diet. Your variables in this instance might be brown-bagging your lunch and avoiding the office coffee room so you won't be tempted to have an afternoon snack.

But in real life, situations do not exist in isolation or remain constant. A client calls unexpectedly and asks you to meet with him over lunch; you decide to adjust your diet menu for the day. Or perhaps you are able to stick to your diet but still find you are not losing much weight; you then decide that you need to increase your level of exercise to achieve your desired outcome of losing 15 pounds. That is why the daily progress dimension requires ongoing introspection and reevaluation, both of your desired outcomes and of the things you need to do to reach them.

When you are functioning efficiently, the daily progress dimension, manifests itself as consistency in performance. In business, bosses want their employees to perform consistently; in sports, consistency is the hallmark of the champion. Consistently achieving desired outcomes, however, is not reserved for the seasoned athlete or the pro, or for the veteran at work. Nor is it simply a matter of time or experience. You must decide to take control and figure out what variables you need to work with, in detail, to get the desired outcome. Once you've isolated those variables, you must work with them habitually. As Bob Rotella, author of *Golf Is Not a Game of Perfect*, puts it: "For golfers to score consistently, they need to think consistently. A sound pre-shot routine makes it easier. . . . Doing it consistently is a habit that requires disciplined effort."[1]

The key to operating in the daily progress dimension is not to isolate just any variables, but to selectively isolate those variables that will make the greatest difference for you. An example illustrates clearly what I mean. Real estate agents were asked at a meeting to list their various methods of prospecting for sales. When combined, their lists included a total of 23 different ways to prospect. But when each agent was asked to identify which prospecting approaches led to the most sales, many agents named the same 3. In other words, there are 23 legitimate methods of getting the job done, and an agent could be working extremely hard at any one of them to get new clients. But of all these approaches, 3 seem to be most effective, so it makes most sense to concentrate on perfecting those 3. They are the variables that an agent can use to ensure that his or her sales quota will be reached. The other tactics should be filed away for possible use as conditions change.

In many situations that involve dealing with other people, a more complex strategy is required. Take, for example, the boss you hardly ever get to see. Jack, who works at a major publishing house in Manhattan, likes to confer with his boss about important issues and to keep him informed of events as they unfold. But he found that it was difficult to schedule meetings with his boss, and when they did get together, the meetings were short and full of phone interruptions. Jack tried preparing an agenda to ensure they would cover all the issues he thought were important, and even gave his boss a copy in advance, but still issues were left unresolved. He also tried casually walking into his boss's office instead of setting up a formal meeting; he still didn't get what he needed. One day, Jack sent his boss an e-mail message. To Jack's surprise, his boss responded promptly. After several more e-mails, Jack has learned that this is the best way to get his boss to respond. While he still prefers meeting in person, Jack accepts that e-mail is the next best thing.

At times we must recognize that we can't do everything ourselves. Marilyn, the mother of three children, works at a hospital full time. She is concerned about her middle daughter, nine-year-old Cheryl. From an early age, Cheryl has had a self-esteem problem. Marilyn has tried to help in several ways, including talking to Cheryl's teachers and working with Cheryl on her homework. After exhausting all the possible remedies she could implement herself, Marilyn decided that the best course for achieving her desired outcome was to seek professional help for Cheryl.

In essence, the daily progress dimension steers you through each minute of every day. Whether it's taking steps to work through a problem, to develop a plan for reaching a particular intermediary goal, or to deal better with a situation involving others, this dimension handles it all. In the daily progress dimension, you are continuously thinking about your desired outcomes and variables even as you work with them, so you learn what works best for you. You are fine-tuning your personal navigation system.

DAMAGE CONTROL DIMENSION

The damage control dimension helps you get through negative situations. It also enables you to recover from disappointments, a sudden change in health, losing a job, going through a divorce, or having a brush with the law. We all need a set of skills we can rely on to rebound from mistakes, common everyday disappointments, and setbacks; these skills form the foundation of this dimension. More than any of the other three dimensions, the damage control dimension involves our emotions and getting control of them. It also includes taking time to carefully sort out what caused the mistake or disappointment—using introspection rather than putting blinders on and telling yourself never to do this "thing" again or never to let it happen again. At the same time, operating reactively requires that you find the specific actions needed to correct or improve the situation. These actions then become part of your daily progress strategies.

Getting caught in a whirlpool of negativity is easy when things go wrong; that's when the importance of the damage control dimension becomes most evident. When you recognize that you tend to worry a lot, or that you get angry easily, or that you are being unusually critical of yourself, then you are dealing with damage control, just as you are when you find yourself upset over something you hear or read in the news. These are some of the emotional clues that this dimension uses to help you assess where you stand in relationship to taking control.

The damage control dimension endorses the practice of absorbing the mistake and remembering the lesson. In the damage control dimension (as in the daily progress dimension), energies are being used on the spot to handle an immediate situation, while at the same time energies are being invested to help you better handle future situations. This dimension works like a trusted mechanic: assessing damage, making repairs, and providing preventive maintenance.

ENERGY ALLOCATION DIMENSION

The pursuit of control is fueled by our investment of energies. Among the dimensions of control, the energy allocation dimension is the throttle, regulating the flow of fuel to the other systems so we invest our energies wisely. Energy allocation entails distinguishing what we can control from what we can't, deciding what we *want* to control, and determining *how much control* we need, all so we can choose how to invest our energies.

Too often, energy allocation is overlooked. We are so eager to get on the road, that we forget to fill the fuel tank or fail to consider how far we can travel on the fuel we have. Without intelligent decisions in the energy allocation dimension, we squander our energies and run out of gas before we reach our desired outcome. So, keep an eye on that fuel gauge!

UNDERSTANDING THE PARAMETERS OF CONTROL

Recall from Chapter 1 that total control is unattainable; what we are striving for is a true *sense* of control. How do we determine what we can and cannot control? Let's begin with a short exercise.

1. On a sheet of paper, list the most frustrating and stress-producing situations you encounter on a regular basis, whether at work or at home.
2. Next to each item on your list, indicate yes if you think you can control that situation or no if you think you can't control it.
3. On a second sheet of paper, list the factors you considered in deciding to write yes or no beside each situation.

The factors listed in item 3 are the criteria that you use to distinguish what you can control from what you cannot. This exercise reveals that each of us has such a set of criteria, although we may not be aware of it.

The set of criteria that you work with helps define the parameters, or limits, of control, and thus gives you the guidelines needed to determine where best to direct your energies. The three parameters of control are:

- Can you eliminate or avoid the situation?
- Can you positively influence the situation?
- Can you change your perception of the situation?

Parameter 1: Can you eliminate or avoid the situation?

In some circumstances, one way (or perhaps the only way) to take control is by avoiding or eliminating the situation. When you confront an unpleasant situation, ask yourself first, "Can I eliminate or avoid this situation?"

Many people are afraid or uncomfortable flying on a commercial airline. Samantha feels that way, so she decided to avoid flying altogether; instead, she drives or takes trains when she travels. Likewise, sports commentator John Madden crisscrosses the country for weekly telecasts during the football season—in his own luxury motor coach. In another example, arguments erupt in many families whenever the conversation turns to politics. Mitchell found that his family's get-togethers always degenerated into such disputes, so he started steering the conversation toward other subjects, such as recent vacations and his children's activities.

Note that in deciding to eliminate or avoid a situation, you should focus clearly on where the difficulty lies so that you don't limit your options unduly. Samantha did not stop traveling; she just chose means other than flying. Mitchell did not stop visiting his parents; he merely avoided getting caught up in politically charged conversations.

Eliminating or avoiding a situation does not relieve us of our responsibilities. Every time Kerry bumps into her boss in the hallway, he conducts an "instant meeting." His forceful nature obliges her to attempt to answer his questions, even when she is unprepared. But her answers prompt more probing questions from her boss, until finally Kerry insists that she will have to get back to him at another time. Kerry hates being caught in this awkward situation, so she manages to avoid such chance meetings most of the time by paying closer attention to her boss's schedule and altering her own accordingly. However, she recognizes that it's important to keep her boss informed, so Kerry makes a special effort to arrange meetings with him, despite his busy schedule, so she can keep him up to date.

Parameter 2: Can you positively influence or change the situation?

The second criterion for determining if you can control a given situation is whether or not you can change that situation. This criterion actually involves two questions: First, can you say or do something that will positively affect the situation? Second, how much influence can you have?

To understand more clearly the degree of influence (and thus of control) you can have in any given situation, envision yourself as functioning within spheres. Most people make distinctions between their personal and professional lives—these are two obvious spheres. For most of us, the personal sphere includes our social as well as leisure activities, our family, and our loved ones, while the professional sphere includes the people and things that are related to work. In addition, we view ourselves as members of the community, be it neighborhood, town, or city. When it comes to major holidays or issues of world importance, we naturally consider ourselves to be citizens of our nation.

The degree of impact we can have is related to the size of the sphere and our significance in it. For example, a letter recommending changes to certain policies at work has a much greater chance of being acted upon than a letter written to a senator. Likewise, if war breaks out in some remote country, our ability to change the course of events there is minute in comparison with our ability to deal with a family dispute.

In some instances, the things we do have an effect on more than one sphere, but the impact of that effect lessens as the sphere expands. For example, by running errands on foot rather than by car, we cut down on pollutants being released into the atmosphere, but the impact on local air quality is much greater than the impact on the global greenhouse effect.

Parameter 3: Can you change your perception of the situation?

When you can't eliminate or avoid a situation and you can't alter it in any way, you can still control your perception of that situation.

Sometimes it's just a matter of how you see things. Is the glass half empty or is it half full? You can view each day as a routine, where every action mirrors the previous day. The alarm goes off at the same time each morning and you get yourself ready for the day—the same old breakfast, the same boring clothes to wear, and the same routine at work. Or you can change your perception and view each day as an adventure that is yet to be explored and experienced; with each task you undertake a fresh challenge. Even Kellogg's advertisements ask people to taste cornflakes "again for the first time."

Often, our first impression of a situation is inaccurate, possibly because our information is incomplete or our reaction is colored by our attitude. That was the case with Tony, general manager of a medium-size company in Georgia. For the past four years, his division has shown some hefty profits, but those successes are now threatened by technological changes and new competitors in the field. When Tony's boss removed Tony from his normal routine of running the plant and assigned him to look around the country for new acquisitions, Tony's immediate reaction was that the company was giving him a "send-off" message. He was devastated. But Tony's wife saw the new assignment differently: The company must believe in Tony and trust him, because the board is asking him for recommendations on where to spend large sums of money. Once Tony thought about it, he agreed with his wife. Tony watched carefully in the ensuing weeks for unspoken signs of his value to the company, and all indications were that he was indeed highly regarded. Now Tony is thrilled about his new assignment and sees it as a challenge to help the company grow.

The mutual understanding that makes a relationship work often involves adjusting our perceptions of a situation. Sharon and Keith are both professionals with high-powered, high-pressure jobs. For the eight years they have been married, Keith has yelled a lot at Sharon. If he can't find something right away or if the house is cluttered, he immediately blames Sharon. If Sharon isn't doing her part as they prepare dinner together, Keith jumps all over her for not paying attention. Sharon's sister Sally, who has observed many of Keith's emotional outbursts, finally decided to ask her sister, "How can you put up with Keith always yelling at you the way he does? I couldn't take it. Is your marriage OK?" To Sally's surprise, Sharon smiled and said, "Yes, my marriage is fine. I'm as happy as ever. When we were first dating, I took Keith's yelling personally. There were nights when I would go to bed feeling terrible about what I had done, only to learn the next day that Keith had forgotten about it. I soon realized that Keith wasn't really yelling at me. It's just his way of letting out his frustrations. He knows that he can take it out on me without my personalizing it. The only time it becomes a problem is when I'm not so strong because of all the pressure I experience at work. When that happens, I simply tell Keith to back off—and he usually does."

YOU CAN'T CONTROL EVERYTHING

Every day you face situations, large or small, important or insignificant, that you cannot control. If another car cuts in front of yours, kicking up a piece of debris that hits the underside of your car and damages the air conditioner, that was out of your control. If as an independent consultant, you prepare and submit an excellent proposal that is rejected solely because the client's budget is severely cut, then you can't do anything to secure that client. If you work for someone else, you have no control over whether the owner or president decides to sell off a part of the business or close it down. You can't control the weather, what will happen in the stock market, or whether your favorite team will win the championship title. The energy allocation dimension helps you recognize the things you can't control, so you don't waste your energies.

What about having control over other adults? As we saw in Chapter 1, choice is an element of control: As long as someone has a choice, he or she has ultimate control. But we can use our energies in such a way as to direct the person to *choose* the direction we are seeking; that is the control available to us. All of us have heard the saying, "You can bring a horse to water, but you can't make it drink." To that we can add: "However, you can make the horse thirsty." In sales, this theorem is known as "selling" the customer on the product or service; in management, it's referred to as "influencing others." Rather than controlling others, all we can do is influence the situation in varying degrees.

TO INVEST OR NOT TO INVEST YOUR ENERGIES?

Determining whether you can control a certain situation is just the first consideration in energy allocation. To formulate your strategy for how best to utilize your energies, you must also judge the value—to you—of control in that situation. Two questions, when used on a habitual basis, can help you think through your strategy: "Do I want to take control?" and "If so, how much control is needed?" These two questions are so closely related that they must be considered together. When contemplating these questions, focus on whether it is necessary to invest your energies in order to secure a desired outcome.

It's easy to see how the question "Do I want to take control?" applies in many everyday situations. We are asked to make many choices each day; to many of them, we can honestly respond, "I don't care." There are alternatives about which TV show or movie to watch, what route to take on a walk or a drive, where to eat lunch or dinner, who will do which household chores, and so on. Often, your desired outcome can be achieved regardless of the details. Sometimes you honestly have no preference; at other times your companion's preference is more important to you than your own. For example, if you want to spend a fun afternoon with your son, you can achieve that desired outcome whether he chooses to go to the amusement park or to the zoo.

Here's a familiar situation that illustrates the interaction of the two questions. A group of friends is dining in a restaurant where the service is less than satisfactory. The conversation at the table turns to how poor the service is and someone asks, "Should we say something to the management?" Decisions can go either way. People may agree that since the meal has already been served, their enjoyment of the rest of the evening won't be hampered by the service, but they likely will not return to this restaurant. Here, the diners conclude that they can achieve their desired outcome—a pleasant evening with friends— without exerting control over the situation; they need take control only of their own perceptions. Alternatively, the decision may lean in favor of taking control of the situation, with the diners concluding, "If we don't say anything, how will management know it has a prob- lem?" The latter route requires a greater investment of energies; cir- cumstances can make the investment worthwhile if, for instance, the friends have enjoyed dining in the restaurant on other occasions.

Let's consider another example. The Smiths, Steve and Barbara, and two other couples are making plans for dinner. Barbara suggests that everyone have dinner at the Smiths' home. Steve quickly assesses the situation and realizes he can exert control if he so chooses: He can jump in and insist that everyone meet at a restaurant. But Steve's desired outcome is to have a fun, relaxing evening, and he quickly determines that he can have fun and relax either at their home or at a restaurant. There is no need for Steve to invest his energies, so he supports Barbara's decision. When it comes to dinner preparation, Steve cooks the meat on the grill and Barbara does everything else. Steve basically stays out of Barbara's way, because he knows that Barbara won't put up with him ordering her around the kitchen.

The Smiths' friends, Bob and Judy Parsons, have a different arrangement. For Bob, a project manager at a major communications company, cooking with his wife is like building a technical device at work. He gives Judy strict time lines to follow, and the sequence of events has to be according to Bob's plan. Even though Judy has been cooking on her own for 15 years, once her husband enters the kitchen, she has to obey his every order.

When you look at the dynamics of the relationships between each of these partners, it becomes evident that everyone is jockeying for control. Bob and Steve both like everything to be ready on time and to have a nice-looking dinner table. But Bob has decided to hold on to his control—luckily, Judy doesn't mind—while Steve has decided to share his with Barbara. They all have different answers to the question "How much control is needed?"

If you are used to making decisions and directing the actions of others at work, it is sometimes difficult to make the transition from being the boss to being a member of a family, especially when an important event is involved. That was the case for Frank. As the president of a large retail company, Frank is typically involved in strategizing the direction of the company and thinking about key corporate events. When his oldest daughter announced that she was going to be married and she wanted to hold the reception at home, Frank found himself planning out the wedding in his mind. He interrupted his solitary planning to ask himself if he really wanted to take control of everything—and decided he did not. Frank and his wife agreed on a budget for the wedding; once his financial concerns were put to rest, what Frank wanted most was for everyone to enjoy themselves during the affair. Frank recognized that his wife and daughter were more qualified to make decisions about the number of people to invite, how dinner was to be served, and what the menu would include, so he just provided suggestions and opinions when needed.

"On the surface," explains Dr. Harry Croft, "it may appear that Frank is condescending or that he does not think his daughter's wedding is important. Quite the contrary. Frank hasn't withdrawn from the upcoming event at all. Rather, he has decided to leverage his control so that he contributes to the 'family team.' He is offering his advice and input, but he isn't exerting so much control that his daughter feels that things have to be done his way. Likewise with Steve. He kept his energies focused on having a fun and relaxing evening, with less emphasis on his need to be in control."

There is a common denominator in all these scenes: The people involved were in a position to take control, but they stopped themselves long enough to assess how important exerting control was in terms of the desired outcome. The formula for energy allocation can be summarized in two steps:

1. Know your desired outcome.
2. Stay focused on your desired outcome.

Considering whether you want control helps you gauge how much control you need in a given situation.

PUTTING IT ALL TOGETHER

The vehicle of control relies on four systems to keep it on track. The big-picture dimension maps out our course, the daily progress dimension steers us through each day, the damage control dimension minimizes the cost when we hit the inevitable bumps in the road (and keeps us from hitting the same bumps again), and the energy allocation dimension allots the fuel that keeps all the systems running. Now that you understand each of the dimensions of control, let's look at them in use in two examples. Keep in mind that in any situation, all four dimensions come into play, even when we are concentrating on only one or two.

Roberta, her husband Terry, and their two children, ages 6 and 10, have been living in a cramped apartment for several months while their new house is being built. Roberta has taken primary responsibility for dealing with the builder and coordinating the entire move, scheduled for the end of October. As the move-in date approaches, the electrician informs Roberta that there will be a 3½-week delay. Roberta becomes first irate and then disappointed, although she is not completely surprised: There has been one problem after another during construction. Roberta mentally zooms into the energy allocation dimension, where she uses the parameters of control to determine that she might be able to improve the situation; then she starts thinking about how best to invest her energies. Roberta moves on to damage control. Calming herself down, she assesses the disappointing news, then starts to isolate those variables she can work with to secure her desired outcome—moving her family into the newly constructed home as originally scheduled.

As Roberta puts her strategy together, she shifts mentally to the daily progress mode. The clear option is to contact the builder, and Roberta decides that it's best to talk directly to the president. She considers seeing him in person, but quickly discards that idea because it is not practical; instead she decides to phone. In order to have privacy when on the phone, she will call from her home. So she will have all the facts at hand, Roberta writes out all the difficulties encountered thus far. To feel more confident, she reviews with her husband the conversation she intends to have with the building company president.

Still operating in the daily progress dimension, Roberta implements her plan. The phone conversation with the president goes just as she rehearsed it, with one hitch—the president doesn't give Roberta the answer she was hoping for. He tells her that the most he can do is cut the length of the delay by one week. Roberta knows that she has done the best she could given the circumstances, but still she feels disappointed. At this point, the energy allocation, big-picture, and damage control dimensions are all functioning simultaneously. Roberta knows she can't alter the situation, but she realizes she can change another parameter—how she perceives what is happening. She reasons to herself that even though the delay is unfortunate, at least she and her husband have a roof over their heads, food on the table, good health, and good schools for the kids—things that are most important in the big-picture dimension. "If this is the worst thing we have to put up with as a family," she concludes, "we are lucky." Since there's nothing more they can do but wait, operating reactively leads Roberta to decide that the best strategy is to make the most of the situation. Her thoughts now shift to the daily progress dimension, where she directs her energies to developing ideas about how the family can adjust to the new move-in date.

Several days later, Roberta tells a colleague at work about the situation. The colleague points out that Roberta and her family could have received some remuneration or special accommodations if they had included a provision regarding delays in their original contract. Roberta thinks to herself, "I handled everything well enough, but if I had known what my colleague just told me, I would have handled some things differently." If she had been familiar with that type of contract clause, she could have had greater control over the situation. Roberta has discovered, as we all do at some time, that control is an ongoing pursuit. Through the process of learning, we can articulate more clearly what happens around us and identify more accurately the key factors. This insight is what makes us think, "I could have done better if only I had known that" or "This wouldn't have happened if I had thought of that."

By now it's apparent that even though control is based on action, it starts with thinking. Let's examine another common situation—making a presentation before an audience. As the president of a successful real estate company in the South, George has to make a presentation to Wall Street investors. The marketing and finance departments work hard to put together the final speech. The CFO, who knows George well, advises him to read the speech, because some tricky financial terms in the text need to be presented in a clear and concise manner. He assures George that you can't go around ad-libbing when working with the people on Wall Street. George takes his CFO's advice and reads the speech to the audience of investors.

Operating in the daily progress dimension, George draws upon the controllable variables that he has used over the years to help him consistently deliver an effective presentation. For instance, he has a cup of coffee to give him an extra boost and wears a comfortable, confidence-building suit. He smiles throughout the presentation, reviews each section before moving on to the next, and is conscious of his timing and his use of pauses. But in spite of George's best efforts, he knows the presentation is not going well—the audience is not receptive; something is wrong.

When the meeting is over, George is upset with himself. How could he have stood in front of a group of people like that and not been able to win them over? George's self-concept, formed in the big-picture dimension, includes an image of himself as an engaging and persuasive speaker. But this time there was no energy in the room, as there usually is when he makes a presentation. Concentrating on the damage control dimension, George assesses why the presentation didn't go as well as he had expected. First, he examines the speech itself and concludes the content is not the problem. Then he runs through a litany of things he did before and during the speech, accounting for all the variables that have worked for him in the past—all the leverageable variables but one. George doesn't usually read his speeches; instead he talks to his audience, guided by an outline that he has prepared for himself.

In the energy allocation dimension, George determines that this is a situation where he can take control, then focuses on how best to direct his energies the next time. Operating reactively once again, George concludes that the way for him to deliver high energy, top-quality speeches is to work with an outline rather than a script. He also reaffirms the importance of organizing his own speeches, rather than letting others do it for him. These variables are now shifted in his mind to the daily progress dimension, and are stored as important leverageable variables for George's success. Next time, he'll remember to stay in charge.

In an effort to be and do our best, each of us tries to isolate those things we do that contribute most to achieving the desired outcome. In George's case, he looked to himself and assessed what works for him. At the first go-round, George followed what others told him to do, but after his disappointing speech, he evaluated his presentation. That is when George decided to regard the advice he had been given as "worth considering," rather than as a "directive." He concluded that he needs to try doing it his way the next time; if he doesn't deliver an effective speech using a self-prepared outline, he will reconsider the suggestions of his staff. By staying flexible and open-minded, George avoids stumbling into an illusory zone of control.

Because George operates with a true sense of control—in this instance, a sharp awareness of what factors go into an effective presentation—he readily accepts that he may need to change his tactics in order to achieve his desired outcome consistently. Without this true sense of control, George could just as easily conclude that something is wrong with him. Gaining a true sense of control involves both introspection and careful analysis of a situation. As a matter of fact, thinking is to control what investment is to wealth. The better you invest, the more wealth you accumulate. Likewise, the clearer your thinking, the better you are positioned to consistently achieve desired outcomes and move forward toward the realization of your goals.

TROUBLE-SHOOTING PROBLEM SITUATIONS

When you have plotted a course on your road map and made sure your vehicle is in good working order—and you are a skilled driver—you are operating with a true sense of control. But it's a long trip and many things can go wrong. For instance, you may be moving so fast toward a goal that you miss an important road sign or signal. Then again, you may find yourself so determined to reach a particular goal that you fail to check the rearview mirror.

When we pay too much attention to the end result, we fail to notice how we approach things. When things seem to be going smoothly, it's easy to fall into habitual patterns that can distort or obscure certain information. Both of these paths commonly lead to the illusion of control. In life, when we hit a rapid succession of bumps or one big one, we may decide—consciously or subconsciously—not to take that route again.

SOMETIMES WE ONLY *THINK* WE LACK CONTROL

When control is not easy to see, we may conclude that we do not have any control even though we do. Poor approaches and disappointing outcomes can convince us wrongly that we can't do anything about a situation. Similarly, certain assumptions can lead us to believe that we can't change a situation. Let's look at three common work situations in which employees typically think they have no control.

One common scenario involves the boss who keeps projects sitting on her desk for long periods of time and then delegates them to staff members with extremely tight deadlines. Employees with this kind of boss typically describe their dilemma as one they can do nothing about. Well, there's no need to let assumptions about the chain of command force you into a victimized position! You can do something to improve the situation. For example, you can approach your boss at key times throughout the day and ask if there is anything pending that needs to be done. Besides lowering your stress level, this approach helps ensure that important projects get done on time—something any boss would be in favor of!

Another common complaint involves the boss who fails to give his employees feedback about how they are doing. To deal with this problem, an employee may set up a formal meeting with the boss and begin by complaining about the lack of feedback. Or the employee may confront the boss in a staff meeting and essentially demand a performance review right then and there. If the boss obliges at all, it is to discuss performance-related issues in very general terms, so the conversation has little value. The employee becomes convinced that getting the boss to open up is impossible. But it is not surprising that the boss may be uncomfortable and unwilling to talk when confronted in these ways. Here, the employee's poor approach to the situation clouds the real issue—whether the employee has any control over getting feedback from the boss.

To take control in this situation, you can direct your energies in several ways to get the feedback you need. A casual tack is often effective. Approach your boss in an informal setting and ask some specific questions about how you are doing on certain projects or tasks. If possible, limit your boss's responses to simple yes or no answers. For example, review everything you are doing on a particular project and ask, "Is there anything else you think I should be working on in regard to this project?" Or, if your boss has suggested that you need to take more initiative, provide some examples of what you have done recently, then ask, "Have you seen some improvement in this area?"

A similar problem occurs on the next rung of the corporate ladder. Poor communication from top management is one of the most frustrating and emotionally charged situations that managers confront, according to the managers who participated in a joint study conducted by Bright Enterprises and the American Management Association in 1995. Many managers (and employees) think that they have no control when senior management doesn't keep them adequately informed. But they are mistaken.

Often senior management's failure to clarify the company's direction isn't a deliberate attempt at self-isolation; rather, the lack of communication is a symptom of our times. With everyone bouncing from one challenging project to another, it's easy to get into the habit of thinking that if nothing is said, then everything must be fine. In this case, top management assumes that employees have a clear idea of where the company is going and how it plans to get there. But that assumption is, in essence, an abdication of control. You, as a manager or employee, can take control by approaching your boss about your need to know more.

Sometimes the focus shifts from the issue at hand to who should make the first move. Managers and employees may be intimidated by the organizational chart, which shows them as doers and senior management as leaders. Many employees assume that they should speak only when spoken to. So they keep waiting and complaining while top management goes on thinking that everything is OK because "no news is good news." This situation illustrates the detrimental effect (for everyone involved) of assuming that nothing can be done about a situation. If the message from the top is unclear, the responsibility to say something to senior management falls on managers and employees alike.

Confusion about the boundaries of control is not limited to the workplace. When money is tight, paying bills can create a lot of tension. Recognize that as a customer you do not have to bow to your creditors' every demand just because a bill states a particular due date and amount. If you contact your service provider and explain your situation, in most cases the service provider will be willing to work with you. The worst thing to do is to say nothing at all and not pay. Most of us know this, but we may not act on it out of embarrassment or lethargy. The point is that taking control and staying in control involves thinking things through and taking action.

A visit to the doctor is another occasion when people feel they have no control. First, there's often a long wait beyond the scheduled time of the appointment. Then when you do see the doctor, you may be reluctant to question his or her directions—after all, the doctor knows best! But you can do something to take control of your visit to the doctor.

When you have a doctor's appointment, call the receptionist before heading out. If the receptionist tells you the doctor is running late, you can adjust your plans accordingly and avoid the long wait. If the doctor says something that you don't understand, insist on an explanation. If the doctor orders tests that you feel are unnecessary, say so. Doctors are often unaware that you have recently had tests done elsewhere; in some instances, they are trying to cover all bases, some of which you may feel are already covered. By asking questions and expressing doubts, you can develop a better rapport with your doctor. Focus on determining where your control lies and on exerting yourself to ensure the desired outcome—to get the greatest benefit from your doctor's appointment with the least expenditure of time and money.

What about control over your emotions and thoughts? In his recent book *Feeling Good*, David Burns explains in "user-friendly terms" the work of Aaron T. Beck, professor of psychology at the University of Pennsylvania School of Medicine. Dr. Burns maintains that all thoughts bring about an emotional response, and that "intense negative thinking always accompanies a depressive episode, or any painful emotion, for that matter." In other words, "every bad feeling you have is the result of your distorted negative thinking." So, your feelings are created by your thoughts, and not the actual event. "Likewise, illogical pessimistic attitudes," says Burns, "play the central role in the development and continuation of all your symptoms."[2] In advising his readers about depression, Dr. Burns describes the symptoms: "Your mood slumps, your image crumbles, your body doesn't function properly, and willpower becomes paralyzed." Whether we are talking about depression or handling everyday situations, the message is clear: Besides not having to act the way you feel, as you have commonly been told, *you don't have to feel the way you do*. You control your feelings and thoughts at any given moment. Years ago, Norman Cousins showed in his book *Getting Well Again* that by controlling his emotions and thoughts through laughter, he could cure himself of cancer, a disease which, up until that point, everyone thought was beyond people's control.

HOW MUCH CONTROL IS TOO MUCH?

Some people never take the time to ask themselves how much control is needed in order to determine just how much energy they want to invest. People who do not vary the intensity of their control can be referred to as "control freaks." There is the controlling boss, also known as the "micro manager," who has to make every decision, dot every I and cross every T." Or consider the back-seat driver who gives an ongoing commentary on how the front-seat driver is doing, not once taking into consideration that the driver has an excellent driving record or that the comments are falling on deaf ears. Then there is the person who constantly corrects his or her mate in conversations. A typical dialogue goes something like this:

> "We left Tuesday morning for our vacation in Virginia . . . " (interrupted)
> "No, by the time we got the car loaded up, as you will recall, it was afternoon."
> "Well, OK. As I was saying, we drove to Virginia. I guess it took about seven hours, and when we . . ." (interrupted)
> "That's not right—we drove for over nine hours. We hit a lot of unexpected traffic."
> "Do you want to tell the story?"
> "No, you're doing fine."

For these people, the focus is on exerting control for the sake of control. You've heard about the couple who have been dating or living together very happily, for years, but the whole relationship changes when they decide to get married. "What happens," explains Dr. Harry Croft, "is that some partners bring into the marriage the expectation of dominance and control. The man has been told throughout his life that he needs to take responsibility for his wife and his family, while the woman enters into the relationship with the expectation of 'dressing' and 'shaping up' her mate. For years, I've heard couples in therapy say, 'Everything was so great when we were dating or living together. I can't understand what's happening to us.'

"A similar thing occurs with the couple that has been together for years, and when they reach retirement, rather than enjoying being together as they had anticipated for so long, they find themselves bickering. Typically, if the man has been working, he will bring the control home with him and start ordering his wife around. 'For years everything was fine,' expresses the wife. 'I served him dinner whenever it was ready, and he always ate it and never complained. Now he complains that dinner isn't on time, or that he doesn't like the way it's prepared, and on and on.'

"Many people let their need for control dominate their actions. The state of being in control becomes the goal and the end result. It's almost as if people get into the habit of exerting their control. If they aren't using their energies to direct everything, then things might not turn out 'like they should.' As a result, they often expend their energies on all the little details and don't have enough energy left to see their efforts through to the end result. This is the situation with the couple who finally marry with the dream of building a good life together, then find their dream falling apart as one partner dominates while the other grows resentful and elects to do nothing. It's also the case with the arguments that follow the back-seat driver or the interrupting spouse."

When being in control becomes the goal, you have entered into the illusory zones of control and the underlying desired outcome is at risk. To escape the illusion of control, concentrate on energy allocation to redirect your energies. Examine the big picture to refocus what is truly important to you. Then, as situations arise, you can shift to the daily progress dimension to figure out what your desired outcome is and so identify the leverageable variables you need to help you reach that outcome.

CAN YOU TRY TOO HARD?

When you fail to achieve the results you are seeking, it's not uncommon for onlookers to suggest that one reason could be you are "trying too hard." Can you really try too hard? "If you want something badly enough, then you can't try too hard," says Dr. Croft. "You'll stay in there until you get the job done. The phrase 'trying too hard' implies that you are spending too much energy in an effort to make something happen." Of course, investing *less* energy rarely yields the desired results!

For most of us, the problem is not that we are expending too much or too little or even the right amount of energy. Rather, our system for energy allocation is not operating efficiently, so our energies are being directed in the wrong place and/or at the wrong time. In addition, we may not have focused sufficiently on the daily progress or damage control dimensions: We may have misidentified the key factors or overlooked some of them, or we may not be in the pivotal position for using them.

Typically, when you zero in too intensely on any one aspect of what you are trying to do, your energies get misdirected, your focus shifts, and the desired outcome is put at risk. Take, for example, writing a song. A songwriter can't try too hard to write a good song, but he or she can try too hard to use colorful words. All the energy is then directed at finding the perfect flashy and unusual words. In the end, however, the audience may not be able to relate to the words, or the words may no longer match the style of the music they were originally intended to go with.

When your energies are focused on one particular detail in order to make something happen and it doesn't, your momentum comes grinding to a halt. Impatience, frustration, and fatigue take center stage. Thoughts that were once directed at deciding what needed to be done are replaced by more negative ideas about why "things aren't happening the way they should." As your emotions heighten and the tension builds, your trust and belief in yourself deteriorate. The mixture of thoughts and emotions that flood your mind creates its own momentum. You get so tense that any additional efforts exerted along the same track only further immobilize you, so it seems that "the more you try, the worse it gets." This is the stage where you can't recall the answer to a question or implement what your instructor is telling you to do; it's also the moment of writer's block. At this stage, any further investment of energies is likely to be misdirected, and the best solution is to "let go." Stop what you are doing and return to the task later! In essence, you are using the energy allocation dimension to take control by redirecting your energies elsewhere.

CONTROL BUILDS CONFIDENCE

Understanding the dynamics of control builds personal confidence, as Dr. Croft points out. You look to yourself to make something happen. You set goals and develop a strategy for getting there. Confidence builds because you are moving yourself forward; at the same time, you are clearly aware of what's getting you there. When setbacks arise, as they will, they don't get in the way. There is a stick-to-itiveness that surfaces because you understand and can use the skills needed to rebound. As a result, you can keep the desired outcome or goal clearly in mind. Self-confidence, then, is not something that descends magically upon you. Rather, confidence builds because you have a greater knowledge of yourself and the world around you as you experience successes.

1. **STOP** thinking about who is involved or if others are at fault when figuring out how to solve a problem or overcome a challenge.

2. **STOP** thinking about controlling others.

3. **STOP** long enough to consider how you want to take control, and if so, how much control is needed before taking action.

4. **STOP** long enough to consider the big-picture dimension of control when considering your investment of energy each day.

START

1. **START** taking control by considering the situation at hand and what you want the desired outcome to be.

2. **START** investing your energies to decide where your control lies, and start asking yourself:

   • Can I eliminate the situation?
   • Can I positively influence or change the situation?
   • Can I change my perception of the situation?

   Once you've answered these questions, **START** factoring in what you know about each of the people involved.

3 KEEP PROMISES TO YOURSELF AND OTHERS

Never give up—never, never give up.
—Winston Churchill

WHAT IS PERSONAL RESPONSIBLENESS?

Take a ride with me to the airport. The cab driver successfully fights through Manhattan traffic, then speeds along the interstate until a sudden tie-up slows traffic to a crawl for several miles. Not delayed too long, I can still catch my shuttle flight to Washington, D.C.—but now every minute counts. When I arrive at the airport, there are no skycaps available. My frustration must be obvious—a sympathetic passerby offers to help me get my luggage to the ticket counter. There, the ticket agent is talking to another passenger. I try to interrupt the agent's conversation and ask for help. With an indifferent glance, the agent picks up the phone, pushes a button, and says a few words, then he resumes his conversation.

Minutes pass but no skycap appears. When I interrupt again, the agent replies, "I called for a skycap—he'll be here soon." Then he once again resumes his conversation. I realize that if I don't do something quickly, I will miss my flight, so I ask the passenger who has been talking with the agent if he will help me. He agrees, picks up my heavy bags, and off we go down three long corridors, reaching the gate just as they are closing the door. I have just enough time to thank the helpful passenger and to ask him what made him go out of his way. In between huffs and puffs, with a smile on his face, he replies, "You obviously needed some help, and I was in a position to give it to you, so I chose to do so, and here we are."

Reflecting on the situation as I settle into my seat, I ask myself: "Did the ticket agent do anything wrong?" Not necessarily. He performed the tasks assigned to him, but he failed to satisfy his customer by seeing a task through to the end. On the other hand, the passenger who carried my bags to the gate invested his energies to make a positive difference. What would you have done if you were in either man's shoes?

Let's expand our focus from everyday experiences to broader concerns. Take a few minutes to think back 10, 15, or 20 years, and recall what you wanted your life to be like. How did it turn out? If things didn't turn out the way you envisioned, what reasons or excuses can you come up with? A surprisingly small percentage of us would say that we didn't get what we wanted because of circumstances beyond our control—circumstances like personal injury, serious family matters, or the economy. As our lives unfold, it's interesting to note how certain things meant so much to us years ago, but became less important or less central as time went on.

For the most part, we now know that many of the things that we believed interfered with our life's plans were really in our control. Maybe we just didn't want some things badly enough. Or perhaps we now think, "I should have finished college," "I should have spent more time with my kids," "I should have listened more closely to my father, teacher, or boss," "I should have left my job a long time ago," "I should not have let this relationship drag on." All these are common regrets people grudgingly express when they look back at circumstances that were within their control and that could have turned out differently.

Now think of the things that it's not too late to do something about—those patterns and mind-sets you're practicing now that, if not remedied, will soon take you down another road you don't wish to be on. What is stopping you from taking the kind of action that is necessary? You might be telling yourself, "I don't have the time or the energy," "I'm too old," or "You can't teach an old dog new tricks." Naturally, there's a long list of excuses. But when things that may negatively impact our lives start to gnaw at us, eventually we decide to do something about the situation. When we reach this point, we are exercising the most powerful personal attribute available to all of us—personal responsibleness.

What is personal responsibleness, and can you learn to operate with it? Can a manager instill personal responsibleness in those who don't display it? The detailed explanations, exercises, and activities explored in this chapter will provide answers to these questions and more. For instance, you will gain a clearer understanding of what your boss really means when he or she talks about empowerment, commitment, accountability, ownership, and taking personal responsibility. Although you may think personal responsibleness may seem similar to all these terms, you'll learn that it encompasses much more. Take a moment to practice saying it out loud . . . personal responsibleness . . . personal responsibleness . . . *personal responsibleness*. It takes a bit of effort to enunciate the words properly, and many people discover that this effort makes them pay closer attention to what the words mean. We are all much more accustomed to hearing and saying personal responsibility. Personal reponsibility is something that we take or that is given to us. Personal responsibleness, in contrast, is a state of being. It describes a characteristic that engenders an inherent competence and trustworthiness to the maximum fulfillment of responsibilities. But let's look further at how personal responsibleness differs from personal responsibility.

RESPONSIBILITIES VS. RESPONSIBLENESS: A SOCIAL PERSPECTIVE

> *William Ernest Henley said it best: "I am the master of my fate, I am the captain of my soul."*

In the thirteenth century, St. Thomas Aquinas wrote that man has reason, and does not have to be steered by the hand of God. While Aquinas' expressed notion of free will may have been a relief to many in the world, it forever eliminated a very convenient excuse we use to justify our fate.

> *Individualism is not "every man for himself." Rather, it's elevating the individual to the global level.*

Many of us allow ourselves to be swept along by external forces. An "it's not my fault, don't blame me" mentality prevails. But a shift in attitude is spreading. In their book *Megatrends 2000*, John Naisbitt and Patricia Aburdene refer to it as individual responsibility. Individual responsibility, they write, "stresses the present; each individual is responsible for everything he or she does. This is not an "every man for himself" type of individualism, gratifying one's desires for their own sake, and to hell with everyone else. It is an ethical philosophy that elevates the individual to the global level. . . ."[1]

Through law and ritual, society can impose responsibilities on its citizens, but ultimately those citizens must discipline themselves to have personal responsibleness. Personal responsibleness encompasses individual responsibility, and goes much further. Responsibilities are "given" to you by others—your boss, peers, mate, parents, or society in general; fulfilling your responsibilities entails doing specific things for others. When people with personal responsibleness are given or assume a task, they look not only at how they can fulfill the responsibility but also at how they can best use their energies to make a valuable difference. In essence, they are taking control.

PERSONAL RESPONSIBLENESS AND CONTROL

> *A motto for personal responsibleness: "It's up to me to make things happen . . . unless that is made impossible by circumstances beyond my control."*

Being introduced to control is not unlike being told as a child what is right and what is wrong. Once you have been exposed to this information, there's no denying it. You can no longer claim ignorance on the subject—the choice now is whether or not to use your newly acquired knowledge. When you understand the dynamics of control and choose to take control, you have accepted personal responsibleness. With this acceptance comes the motto: *It's up to me to make things happen . . . unless that is made impossible by circumstances beyond my control.*

When you have internalized an understanding of your control in any given situation, and the consequences that can result if that control is ignored or misused, personal responsibleness becomes a characteristic that defines your being. When you have personal responsibleness, you develop it at work, at home, and within your community. Personal responsibleness is not a situational mode of thinking, which can be turned on and off like a faucet; rather, it is the way you are—because you choose to be that way.

RECOGNIZING PERSONAL RESPONSIBLENESS

Here's a quick and fun exercise that illustrates personal responsibleness. Imagine that you have just completed a series of scuba diving lessons. You are ready to make your first dive into the ocean, and will swim to depths you've never seen before. To prepare for your first major dive, you have to select someone else to check your equipment for defects and fill your air tank—it's a common practice at the school from which you are graduating. You happen to be in a class full of celebrities. From the list of celebrities below, choose the one you would want to fill your tank:

- John Gotti, Mafia leader
- Howard Stern, radio personality known for his blunt viewpoints
- Mario Andretti, racing legend and holder of numerous Indianapolis 500 titles
- Tony Randall, actor who, like his character Felix on *The Odd Couple*, is known as a stickler for doing everything properly
- Bill Murray, actor and comic director who got his start on *Saturday Night Live*

Which of the celebrities did you pick? Imagining how each of them might behave in this situation is amusing. But when it comes down to making a choice, there is no right answer. As you might have surmised, what's important is the reasoning behind your selection. If you were thinking "because he will do it right," "because he understands danger and would take the necessary steps to ensure my safety," or "because his work is of the highest quality, and I can depend on him to come through for me," then you have isolated some of the key traits that characterize people with personal responsibleness.

WE ADMIRE THOSE WHO HAVE PERSONAL RESPONSIBLENESS

When Mickey Mantle, in his final years, confessed to the public that he had ruined his health with his reckless behavior and urged youngsters not to repeat his mistakes, America treated him as a hero once again. When public figures like Mantle, Darryl Strawberry, and Steven Tyler of Aerosmith admit their mistakes and show us they have learned from them, we admire their convictions and the strength it takes to own up to their actions. Although we commend people for admitting their mistakes, we also know deep down inside that acknowledgement is not enough. Thinking about doing something and talking about it are both aspects of personal responsibleness, but taking action by taking control is what moves a person into the center stage of personal responsibleness.

We can truly *admire* people who have personal responsibleness. Let's listen to some of their stories.

When I first met Bob Annunziata, CEO at Teleport Communications Group, I felt as if the room was charged with a bolt of energy that streamed out from him as he laughed and smiled at a comment I had made. Perhaps it is easy for Bob to be upbeat, since Teleport Communications Group, his pioneering local phone service company which is growing by leaps and bounds was reported to be the telecommunication industry's most desirable takeover candidate. On January 8, 1998, AT&T agreed to buy Teleport for approximately $11.2 billion. But Bob's energy and enthusiasm go beyond the gratification one gets from starting up a company and watching it grow into a giant; this is just the way Bob is.

At an early age, Bob learned about responsibilities and the need to look to himself as a valuable resource. When he graduated from high school, many of his classmates were debating which college to choose, but Bob was concerned about how he would support his wife and the child they were expecting. Bob dropped any thoughts about college and instead set his sights on becoming an electrician. Later, as a technician with AT&T, Bob kept taking on more and more responsibilities; by the time he turned 21, he was managing over 100 technicians.

(*Continued*)

After eight years in Operations with AT&T, Bob moved into sales. Nine years later, Merrill Lynch, one of his customers, came to Bob with a proposal. The local phone company was slow in upgrading its service, so Merrill Lynch planned to install its own high-capacity fiber optic link from its New York City headquarters to a satellite dish, which would give the firm access to its offices and customers worldwide. Merrill Lynch wanted Bob to run this new operation. Bob agreed, since he realized that without a college degree, his chances for advancement at AT&T were limited. Then Bob turned around and offered Merrill Lynch a better idea: He proposed offering private line services to other large, New York City-based companies, bypassing New York Telephone. Merrill Lynch liked the idea and, together with Western Union, gave Bob the $18 million he needed to develop Teleport—and a new industry was born.

Bob is known for telling his people that he will take care of the future if they take care of the day-to-day. At Teleport, employees are told, you can have as many responsibilities in the company as you want, and you can do whatever you want, as long as you are willing to be accountable for making your efforts succeed. But if Bob Annunziata asks, be prepared to explain in 30 seconds why you want to do something. If you can't, you need to rethink it. This is Bob's way of making sure that people have thought through their ideas completely.

Bob believes in responsibility. At a meeting, an issue came up concerning what to do about a long-distance customer that was making what seemed to be unreasonable demands. Bob asked the managers who reported to him if they believed in the system they had created. When they said yes, Bob suggested that they go *beyond* what the customer was asking for: "We'll say that for every second of outage or any interruption in service, they'll receive one month of service for free."

My observations of the people at Teleport added credibility to Bob's words. For instance, as I left Bob's office, I noticed that employees seemed unaffected by running into the CEO; as they walked by, they said hello and Bob returned their warm greetings. In the hallways, people were smiling and carrying on conversations about work-related issues— not their plans for the upcoming weekend or which football team had the best shot at making the playoffs. As I passed by, people stopped what they were doing to offer to help me find my way. The atmosphere was friendly, comfortable, and energized all at the same time. It seemed as if all employees felt they had a part to play, and Bob Annunziata was leading from right among them.

> *Personal responsibleness takes into account not only words, but also what people do.*

"Education was always stressed in our house," Marlene Cintron told me. "I couldn't imagine myself not going to college, even though my father had only a third-grade education and my mother got her GED." Although Marlene always envisioned herself getting a college education, pursuing her dream wasn't without challenges. In the New York City of her youth, only 3 percent of graduating Hispanic seniors went on to college and only 1 percent graduated from college. Those statistics became a personal challenge to Marlene in her senior year. She had been preparing applications to several major colleges and universities when she went for the required interview with a high school counselor. The first thing the counselor said to Marlene was, "*You* want to go to college? You'll be lucky if you get into a junior college. That's where people with your background need to go." Marlene was stunned.

(Continued)

Marlene didn't know what to make of the counselor's comments. Her parents had always taught Marlene to respect adults and authority figures, and this counselor was both. Teachers were the law. Still in a state of shock, Marlene took her troubles to ASPIRA, an educational youth organization organized by a Puerto Rican woman. Besides being a place where kids could go after school each day and an invaluable support group, ASPIRA taught students like Marlene to take responsibility, develop leadership skills, and appreciate their cultural heritage. There, Marlene met with one of the coordinators, who wisely told her, "Not everyone you meet in your life will have your best interests in mind." She advised Marlene to go ahead and apply to the colleges she wanted to attend. Marlene did, and was accepted, and in three years she graduated from the State University of New York.

Marlene went to work for the government, where she focused on the ills of urban life. Realizing that she needed the proper credentials to effect change in the capacity she wanted, Marlene continued her education, earning a law degree from Georgetown University and a master's in education from Fordham University. Marlene acknowledges the help she received. She told me, "It was through the help of programs that corporations and the United States government formed that I had the opportunity to help myself and move ahead." In a stint as director of the Puerto Rican Federal Affairs Administration in New York City, she tried to ensure that government and corporations upheld their responsibility to humanity and provided opportunities to the youth of this country. But she also wanted today's youth to understand the lesson she learned: "When you're told early on that you can't do something, instead of giving up, what you do is look inward and rely on yourself to move forward. Just because I am a minority, doesn't mean that I couldn't get what I wanted." After working for years on economic empowerment of minorities, Marlene was ready for a new adventure. Now, as a financial adviser for Merrill Lynch, she is working on financial empowerment of individuals.

> *With personal responsibleness, people look to themselves to make a valuable difference.*

Regardless of their past, people like Bob and Marlene have chosen to look to themselves to make a difference in their own lives and in the lives of the people they touch. Making a difference goes beyond simple rhetoric. These people understand the link between control and personal responsibleness. By determining the limits of their control and how best to use their energies, they can create a momentum that propels them forward, leading them toward the achievement of desired outcomes and ultimately life's goals. People with personal responsibleness recognize the importance of understanding control and how it partners with commitment.

FALLING SHORT

> *With personal responsibleness, people recognize and accept control.*

Employees in all sectors share a well-known refrain, "Sorry, it's not my job." In a restaurant, you ask for something and the employee says "Sorry, it's not my table," and goes about his or her business, disregarding whatever you said. Or you call customer service for help, only what you're asking for doesn't fall within the range of customer service, so the employee tells you, "You need to call another department," instead of connecting you with that department. Or you ask for some help storing your luggage, and the flight attendant says curtly, "I don't lift bags." Or the employee to whom you assigned a time-sensitive project explains that the job is late because "someone else" failed to deliver. When you ask what the employee did to ensure that the necessary preliminary work would be completed on time, he says, "Well

I called with a reminder—what more can I do?" Probing further, you learn that the employee called the "someone else" once, and that person wasn't in, so he left a voice mail message. Sound familiar?

In the early 1990s when U.S. organizations began to "reengineer" themselves, many employees at first resisted their companies' decision to flatten and reorganize into teams. This was the situation at a major bank in New York, where Rhonda was a quality manager. She told me that employees justified their refusal to support teams by saying, "Upper management fails to work cooperatively, so why should we?" Rhonda challenged their thinking by replying: "So, you are telling me that if these same managers are going to jump out of a plane without the proper equipment, you will too." People quickly got the point, Rhonda said, but not all were willing to examine themselves more closely.

Outside the professional sphere as well, making excuses is rampant. A driver drops her gum wrapper out the car window, because there's already litter along the roadside. A homeowner doesn't rake the fallen leaves from his front lawn, because his neighbors haven't done so and more leaves will just blow over. Parents don't take the time to meet their children's teachers, but if the children don't do well in classes, the parents blame the school system. Teachers do less than their best, because they feel they don't get paid enough to do more.

These people—the "don't blame me" crowd—all give in too easily. For them, obstacles are too great to overcome; temptations are too strong to resist. They may say they have a lousy manager or boss to explain why they are unproductive and demoralized. Or they may blame their lack of drive and low self-esteem on their parents and *their* failure to provide the kind of support and childhood experiences that would have fostered a desire to excel. The media fuels this way of thinking, and our legal system tries to justify it.

In his San Antonio-based psychiatric practice, Dr. Harry Croft sees many patients who want to unravel and talk about their past experiences—not so they can understand why they feel the way they do and then move on, but simply to justify why they are the way they are. They tell him, "No wonder I am the way I am. What more can you expect when you grow up under these conditions?" Yes, they are the *victims*—the ones who have decided to give up their control and let past and present circumstances determine their future and explain away their failures. But a victimized mentality has no footing in the domain of those with personal responsibleness. For such people, unraveling the past would be a means to understand their behavior better in order to achieve greater control and move in a more desirable direction.

FROM SELF-EXAMINATION TO SELF-RELIANCE

> *Accepting personal responsibleness begins with going from self-examination to self-reliance.*

The first step in accepting personal responsibleness is going from self-examination to self-reliance. When you start by examining your day, it's easy to see how you can get caught up in the hectic routine of handling all your responsibilities. All of us jump from one task to another as if our responsibilities develop a momentum of their own that grabs control of us. Along the way, we never really think about what we are doing and what difference, if any, it will make; we also lose sight of the promises we have made and the things we value and enjoy. With the rapid pace of our lives, we need to incorporate our own instant "checkpoints." Periodically, we need to *stop* and determine what our parameters of control are in a given situation and whether we are living up to the motto of personal responsibleness: "We must look to ourselves to make things happen—unless that is made impossible by circumstances that are beyond our control."

As an adolescent, you no doubt said to yourself, "I can't wait until I grow up, because then I'll do my own thing." If you felt this way, then in essence you made a commitment to yourself to take control. How are you doing? Are you keeping your promise and taking the control you always wanted?

Here is a quick way to determine whether you are moving from self-examination to self-reliance: When other people tell you what to do, do you tend to do as they say? Conversely, do you think about what they are saying, find the elements of their instructions or advice that have relevance and meaning for you, and then take action? When you do what other people tell you to do without thinking for yourself, either because you value their opinions more than your own or because you want to please them, you run the risk of capturing the illusion of control. That is, you think you are moving forward smoothly toward achieving what you want, but in reality you are headed for some bumpy roads and disappointments. Do any of the following examples remind you of someone you know.

> Larry, who is the father of two children and has been married for more than 10 years, recently lost his job. Because his family and friends love and care about Larry, they are all offering help. Larry listens to everyone's advice and tries to do what everyone tells him. But when several weeks pass without any job prospects, Larry begins to feel frustrated and confused, as if he is a Ping-Pong ball bouncing from one suggestion to another. Although he professes to be very busy, inside he feels as if he is floundering.

> Carol has survived three downsizings in her company. Her boss of nine months asks Carol to put together a report that incorporates his ideas and those of his peers. As she prepares the report, Carol has a few ideas of her own that she thinks could be of value. She is hesitant to say anything to her boss because she is fearful of what he might

think of her, so she mentions her ideas to a couple of peers at work. One says that the ideas are "OK," and another says that they simply wouldn't work. On the basis of their reactions, Carol decides to let the whole thing drop and just do what her boss told her to do in the first place. Three weeks later, somebody else in the department presents an idea similar to Carol's and the boss likes it. When Carol finds out, she is surprised and disappointed with herself. Although she recognizes that she was in a position to take control, she didn't invest her energies to think on her own—sorting out what her peers thought from what she believed in—and to weigh the possible consequences of telling her boss.

Jasmine is a single parent with two young daughters. After her divorce three years ago, she moved from Massachusetts, where she and her husband had their home, to San Diego, where Jasmine's family lives. Jasmine's mother has offered to watch the girls so she can go out. Her father is a little more up front, and keeps singing the same song, which goes something like, "When are you going to remarry?" On occasion, her married sister sets Jasmine up on a blind date. Jasmine is dating more to please her family than to satisfy herself; she would prefer to devote her time to her children, her work, and her hobbies. For now, she is "very comfortable—everything fits, and I don't have the energy to invest in a man." Why doesn't she just tell her family how she feels? Jasmine says, "They would probably think I'm afraid of getting hurt. Who knows? Maybe they're right."

You might say that Larry, Carol, and Jasmine don't trust themselves and lack confidence, and you're probably right. You too may doubt yourself from time to time, and as a result seek out the opinions of others. When you have accepted personal responsibleness, you take the time to examine those opinions and determine for yourself what actions are needed. You are willing to accept the consequences of your decisions because, at the same time that you are fulfilling what others ask of you, you are upholding your obligations to yourself.

Now is the time for all of us to stop and reflect on personal responsibleness. Since many of us find it easier to be objective when considering the professional sphere, let's start with a questionnaire on personal responsibleness at work.

INVENTORY OF PERSONAL RESPONSIBLENESS AT WORK

DIRECTIONS: Circle the response that most accurately reflects what you actually do, not what you think you should do.

1 = Almost never	3 = Sometimes
2 = Occasionally	4 = Frequently
	5 = Almost always

1. When your boss tells you to do something with which you totally disagree, do you do it without question?

    1   2   3   4   5

2. As events unfold at work, you think you are the last to know. Do you feel resentful and complain to others that management is not keeping you informed as it should?

    1   2   3   4   5

3. Someone from another department approaches you in an aggressive and tactless way. Do you let his or her manner determine whether you will cooperate?

    1   2   3   4   5

4. Someone from another department comes to you with a problem. Do you discuss the situation as if the problem is still solely the other person's?

    1   2   3   4   5

---

5. You are working on a report or project for a peer. Do you submit it even though you know that you could do a better job (and still meet the deadline)?

1   2   3   4   5

6. As a deadline approaches, you are still waiting for information that was promised to you from another department. Do you feel that the failure to deliver the information is a justifiable explanation to give to your boss when he or she questions your progress?

1   2   3   4   5

7. A peer is not performing up to standard. Do you avoid saying anything to him or her for fear of facing a potential confrontation?

1   2   3   4   5

8. Do you have difficulty getting tasks assigned to you done on time because of a lack of cooperation from others?

1   2   3   4   5

9. If no one knew what time you started work, would you sleep later in the morning?

1   2   3   4   5

10. If your boss sets goals that you believe are unrealistic, do you complain to others?

1   2   3   4   5

SCORING AND INTERPRETATION

Add the numerical value for each response to get your total score. Refer to the following scale for interpretation.

15 and under	High degree of personal responsibleness
16-21	Moderate degree of personal responsibleness
22-27	Low degree of personal responsibleness
28 and above	Needs improvement

These questions are intended to bring out the distinction between responsibilities and personal responsibleness—to determine whether you work to satisfy responsibilities or whether your work is driven by personal responsibleness. When you accept personal responsibleness, you are not looking simply at whether a responsibility is yours; rather, you are thinking about what it is going to take to move the ball forward, regardless of the extent of your involvement in the entire process. The focus is on doing whatever is in your control to ensure that something gets done and that a valuable difference results.

Personal responsibleness is an invisible part of you that affects your actions and the actions of others every day. It is rooted in the belief that it is up to you to make things happen, to set and uphold high standards, and to invest energy to ensure a smooth work flow. Personal responsibleness begins with how you think and feel about things and encompasses sensitivity to the personal and managerial impact you have on others.

At work, personal responsibleness manifests itself in three essential behavior patterns:

- Making sure to facilitate the completion of work
- Setting your own internal standards for ensuring quality
- Paying attention to personal and managerial wake (how you affect others by your actions)

> *You don't have personal responsibleness because of what you do; you do what you do because you have personal responsibleness.*

But personal responsibleness is not a set of behaviors or a system of rules; rather, it is the driving force behind your behaviors and self-imposed standards. In other words, you don't have personal responsibleness because of what you do—you do what you do because you have personal responsibleness.

Your score on the Inventory of Personal Responsibleness at Work may depend on the distinction you made between "occasionally," "sometimes," and "frequently." However, the litmus test of personal responsibleness is looking into the mirror and asking, "If I interviewed a prospective employee who thought and felt the way I do about my work and how I approach it, would I hire him or her?"

Reexamine each of the questions in the inventory and ask yourself, "What are the parameters of control in this situation?" None of these situations requires the introduction of any new policies or procedures. Rather, effectively handling situations is simply a matter looking to yourself to take the control that is available to you and to live up to the standards that you set for yourself.

Self-examination begins with understanding control and its dimensions. You need to examine what you want (big-picture dimension), recognize your abilities and limitations (daily progress and damage control dimensions), and determine how best to utilize your energies (energy allocation dimension). By recognizing that you are the gateway for formulating what is happening around you and that you can pull the available levers of control, you are grounding yourself and forming the basis for the habit of achieving desired outcomes—you are developing self-reliance. When you get in the habit of thinking for yourself, and when you reach desired outcomes, confidence levels rise. Self-reliance is fostered as trust in self is heightened, and a new sense of control is realized.

PERSONAL RESPONSIBLENESS FOR WHAT YOU DO

Reaching desired outcomes involves taking control of the standards that you set for yourself. These standards are evidenced in what you do. Some of my own experiences provide terrific examples of people who exemplify personal responsibleness.

A few years ago, I traveled to Virginia to meet a prospective client. Working in my hotel room the night before the meeting, I ordered room service. As the valet placed the tray with my dinner on a table, he noticed the paperwork strewn around the room and commented to me that the lighting was inadequate for reading. I agreed with him, so before he left, he called the hotel engineer to request higher-wattage light bulbs. When I was about halfway through my dinner, the phone rang—it was the valet calling to ask if my lighting situation had improved. I regretfully told him no. Within five minutes, an electrician showed up, explained about fire hazard laws and why I couldn't have brighter light bulbs, then left! The room service valet called my room again to see how things were going and I explained that it was not possible to get higher-wattage bulbs. In less than 10 minutes, an electrician was at my door with a lamp that he set up for me. When the valet came to pick up my empty plates, I couldn't stop myself from saying, "You really helped me out tonight. Was this effort the result of some hotel training program or campaign?" His face lit up as he replied, "No, it's just the way I am. I set my own standards. It looked to me as if the lighting in the room was really poor, and it's hard to work when you don't have adequate lighting. So I did what I had to do."

Like many two-career couples, my husband and I eat out often. After a long day at work, there's nothing more refreshing than to have good company and a friendly waiter who truly wants to help make the evening enjoyable. Recently, at one of our favorite neighborhood restaurants, the waiter greeted my husband and me with a warm smile and a robust hello as he welcomed us back. He helped us make selections that would please us and was attentive throughout the meal. When dessert time came around, we hesitated, but turned down the offer.

Much to our surprise, he said, "I'm going to give you folks a treat. It's on the house, and I think you'll enjoy it." The cappuccinos that we previously refused were ordered as we awaited our dessert. Indeed, it was special. Besides enjoying a great dessert, we were glad to know that someone appreciated our patronage. For us, the waiter was the evening's real treat!

In these examples, both men were giving of themselves. There were no companywide campaigns, no posters or pictures on the wall telling them what to do, no buttons with slogans printed on them. Rather, these people had personal responsibleness: They understood the dynamics of control and how to use it to set their own standards. The way that people with personal responsibleness carry out their jobs not only delights the recipients; it also is gratifying to the doers because they are setting their own standards and fulfilling obligations to themselves.

> *With personal responsibleness, you set your own standards, including the ethics that govern your conduct.*

An integral part of the standards you set for yourself (and thus of personal responsibleness) are the ethics that govern your conduct when engaging in the completion of tasks. Think about your workday. How much time do you allow yourself to handle personal matters? How much time do you spend talking about issues unrelated to work? How much time do you spend surfing the Internet? Ethics include taking responsibility for how you use time; they also apply to your use of resources. Should you use the company's computer for your personal needs? Should you photocopy those flyers for your son's Boy Scout troop on the company's copier without permission? Should you fudge your expense report?

Employees are given a lot of independence from their employers. The companies thus expect the employees to act professionally. In essence, the company is giving the employee the control handles to operate ethically. A person with personal responsibleness recognizes that his or her conduct is not only a matter of making sure that he or she doesn't shortchange the company; his or her reputation is at stake as well. If you cut corners or do something borderline in one area, onlookers think to themselves, "Well, you probably do the same in other areas—maybe in my area, too." Although nothing may be said, the intangible ingredients of trust, respect, and credibility are tarnished, and peer relationships are never solidified.

If you are like many people interviewed for this book, you feel like bad manners are more common than good ones these days. Making your way onto a busy highway from one of the on-ramps can be a trying experience. Rather than yielding their lane or slowing down long enough for you to enter safely, many drivers seem to accelerate their cars, as if they would like to smash into you. And this rudeness is not limited to roadways. When entering buildings, the person in front of you acts as if he or she is unaware of your presence, and lets the door slam closed in your face. Or someone darts to the front of a long line, ignoring all those who are waiting their turn. Gifts are not acknowledged and loaned objects are not returned unless you request them. At work, people fail to turn in reports on time without apologizing. They arrive late for meetings or leave early without any explanation or comment. People no longer pick up their trash at the end of meetings. They fail to return phone calls and cancel appointments at the last minute. The examples are endless, but I think I've made my point.

With personal responsibleness, you pay attention to what is going on around you, while at the same time considering how your actions impact the situation. Personal responsibleness involves a continuing awareness of the importance of taking control of what you do, including the manners you display.

KEEPING PROMISES TO YOURSELF AND TO OTHERS

> *Personal responsibleness involves taking
> action—and keeping promises to yourself
> and to others.*

We all know that saying you'll do something is not the same as actually doing it. At work, employees keep an eye out for whether management is "walking the talk." Personal responsibleness, like control, is characterized by action. Central to that action is the ability to keep promises—the root of dependability and reliability. Not only do people with personal responsibleness set standards that match or exceed the expectations of others; they can be looked upon as people who always come through. A simple test of personal responsibleness involves waiting to meet up with someone. If this person has personal responsibleness, you will wait even if your companion is late. Because you *know* the person will show up, your energies are directed more at concern about whether something serious has happened than at whether the person will keep your appointment.

The trust that personal responsibleness engenders in others is rooted in the standards that you set for yourself. The standard goes beyond the word *committed*—that's not enough. A task that is given to you becomes more than a task to complete for somebody else. Rather, completing the task has greater personal meaning because it also reflects on you and how you use control to live up to your own personal standards. Because you are operating with an understanding of the dynamics of control, you know that you can look to yourself to have the energy needed to see something through to its completion.

Many of us would never break promises to others—because we don't want to let them down. But at times we do let ourselves down. Is it possible to have personal responsibleness with others and not with yourself? The answer is no. Personal responsibleness is a state of being. The keeping of promises is an indispensable component of the way you operate, so the focus is on living up to your promises—regardless of to whom they are made. Exercising, eating properly, calling people back, or going to the doctor are all things you just do because you are going to do them. Why? Because not only are you driven "not to want to disappoint others or yourself"; you also have the ability to use control in such a way as to get desired outcomes. What's being said here might be likened to what a professional golfer goes through when playing in a tournament. The golfer has a strategy in mind, along with a clear vision of her goals. Playing in the tournament is not only a matter of winning; it's doing her best. Doing her best is a matter of keeping all promises to herself: She must stay in control, stick to the strategy, and live up to the performance standards that were set prior to the tournament. Winning is nice, but winning consistently comes from having faced the realities, knowing what control levers to draw upon, and realizing that you have the ability to keep your promises to yourself, regardless of the obstacles encountered along the way.

> *Keeping agreements is simply an expression of taking control for yourself.*

Living up to your promises is an integral aspect of self-reliance. It is also a good checkpoint for you to use to determine if you have internalized a clear understanding of the dynamics of control. If you understand and accept taking control for yourself, then keeping agreements is simply an expression of that control.

OPERATING WITH PURE WINS AND FAILURES

The standard of working with pure wins and failures is powerful, and an essential element of personal responsibleness. But what does it mean? Consider an athlete who trains 3 to 4 hours per day for an upcoming competition. The night before the event, the athlete goes to a party, drinks, stays up late, and goes to bed exhausted. At the competition the next day, the athlete loses. When reviewing what happened, can the athlete determine if he had the ability to win? Can the athlete figure out what he needs to do better or differently in order to win in the future? These questions are difficult to answer, because the athlete might say or think, "If only I hadn't had so much to drink last night, I could have done better," or "I could have performed better if only I wasn't so tired." In other words, the *ifs* and *buts* blur the athlete's ability to see clearly what contributes to his winning or losing. When an athlete operates with pure wins and failures, he is saying, "I did everything within my control. If I didn't win, it wasn't because I didn't try or do whatever I could; I didn't win because I wasn't meant to, that's all."

> **With personal responsibleness, you work with pure failures and successes.**

This perspective is very much what Vince Lombardi, legendary Green Bay Packers coach, meant when he said, "Winning isn't everything; it's the only thing." For years, people have interpreted Lombardi's famous line to mean that you win at all costs. Football players who were coached by Lombardi, however, have said that what he really meant was that when a football player goes into a game, he goes in prepared to win; and if by chance the team should lose, it is only because the other players were better! The "purity" in the failure is important because the athlete or the coach can more accurately determine the weak points and how to improve. By purity, I am referring to the fact that the "failure" is clearly not due to the player's using every control factor he knows to the best of his ability. Rather, the failure occurs because of factors that are outside the player's control or knowledge base.

At work, as in sports, being successful and moving ahead require an understanding of "pure failures." When you operate this way, you can easily pinpoint what led to your not getting a desired outcome and what you need to do differently or even better next time. Only then do you get "good information"—information that isn't clouded by *buts* and *ifs*—thus enabling you as a leader, manager, or employee to reason out what strategy and action steps are needed to start and sustain a positive momentum. Every time you introduce into your thinking or your conversation the infamous *but* or *if*, you are giving up some control. You are saying, "I could have been successful in this particular endeavor, but I'm not because of some things that existed that were out of my control."

Failures and setbacks are unfortunate, and things we rarely set out to do. However, they are a part of life. What we really should concern ourselves with is the repetition of the same failures and setbacks. By understanding control and operating reactively, we can avoid repeating our mistakes. Although people with personal responsibleness dislike failures and disappointments just as much as the rest of us, they know that they have used whatever control they had to make a positive difference. Realistically, what more can people ask of themselves?

PERSONAL RESPONSIBLENESS FOR WHAT YOU SAY

Personal responsibleness extends beyond what you do; it is reflected in what you say. As news commentator and writer George Will says, "Words have punch." The argument that words are cheap might be contested by people in the spotlight. Here's a good example. Many sports enthusiasts can recall the sad saga of golf analyst Ben Wright, whose 23-year tenure at CBS ended because of his admitted "insensitivity." Disparaging remarks about lesbians in the Ladies Professional Golfers Association were the sparks that ultimately burned his career. A newspaper quoted Wright as saying that "lesbians in the sport hurt golf" and that women golfers can never keep a straight left arm, one of the basic tenets of the game. Although Wright maintains that he was misquoted and misunderstood, CBS dismissed him amid the uproar surrounding his reported statements. As Wright found out, words can be costly.

> *With personal responsibleness, you accept control for what you say.*

Even if you are not in the public eye, you need to be careful of your words. Often we are lax and say whatever we feel, especially at home. Piercing words come flying out at emotional moments. We say things like "Even a moron could have figured that out" and "You're so fat why would anyone want to be seen with you?" Such demeaning remarks serve only to express anger or frustration. They cannot possibly benefit the relationship; they just hurt the ones we love. This sign next to a Manhattan church expressed it well: "Stick and stones may break my bones, but words can break my heart."

> *Words can't break bones, but they can break hearts.*

With personal responsibleness, you take time to think about what you are saying, and to assess to the best of your ability what impact your words will have. If you fail to invest your energies wisely, your real message can get deflected when you choose your words poorly. Consider two examples from the workplace, where many of us get into the habit of focusing on what we do, overlooking the importance of what we say. Someone says to a group, "Men, I know fulfilling your dreams hasn't been easy, and I realize the same holds true for you girls." Even if nothing negative is intended by calling women "girls," many women quickly jump into another track of thinking. Another comment that can elicit unintended negative reactions is "When I was working at my last job, I did it this way."

Hearing this, many people think, "We don't care about the way you did it at your last job; we need to take a look at what's going on in this company, right now."

> *With personal responsibleness, you understand the difference between venting and bad-mouthing.*

What about when you are angry or upset at a situation? With personal responsibleness, you understand the difference between venting and bad-mouthing. When you are venting, your purpose is to express anger or frustration over a situation or over your inability to perform at a certain level. The ventee is selected carefully. Once you've gotten it "off your chest," you're ready to get back into action.

Bad-mouthing, on the other hand, involves personal attacks on others and how they are failing to live up to your expectations. The purpose of bad-mouthing is to "tear down" others and the situations they are involved in, as opposed to expressing *your* feelings. Typically, bad-mouthers direct their attacks to anyone who will listen. Rarely do they have any intention of doing something about what's bothering them.

> *With personal responsibleness, you don't have to act the way you feel—you understand and accept control.*

With personal responsibleness, you understand control and the ability to manage your emotions. You don't have to express the way you feel to just anyone or all the time. You are able to assess a situation quickly. You take into consideration that what you say, how you say it, and to whom you say it is more important, because of its long-term impact, than just releasing your emotions to make yourself feel better right now. Likewise, with personal responsibleness, you recognize that words can hurt others, whether at work or at home.

PERSONAL RESPONSIBLENESS WITH YOUR MATE

"We're both adults here—we should be able to figure this out." This common statement is an acknowledgment that, as adults, two people confronting a problem have the control to build a meaningful, loving relationship. The question is: Are you using your control and investing your energies to enrich the quality of your relationship? The accompanying short questionnaire is intended to get your attention and to help you to recognize how all the "little things" nurture a relationship.

INVENTORY OF PERSONAL RESPONSIBLENESS WITH YOUR MATE

DIRECTIONS: Circle the response that most accurately reflects what you do, not what you think you should do.

1 = Almost never	**3** = Sometimes
2 = Occasionally	**4** = Frequently
	5 = Almost always

	1	2	3	4	5
1. When having a disagreement with your mate, do you stand firm on your position even though you realize that you may be wrong?	1	2	3	4	5
2. When you mate is talking to you, do you wish he or she would hurry up and finish so that you can get on with other things?	1	2	3	4	5
3. When your mate fails to pick up on and acknowledge that you are upset, do you take it personally and then hold a grudge?	1	2	3	4	5
4. When your mate hurts your feelings, do you think to yourself about how you will pay him or her back?	1	2	3	4	5
5. When your mate goes over budget by spending a lot of money on clothes or other personal items, do you think to yourself that he or she is being unfair, so now you can do the same?	1	2	3	4	5

6. When working on something that involves your mate, do you avoid trying special things because you think your effort won't be appreciated?   1   2   3   4   5

7. Your mate wants to do one thing and you want to do another; you give in, thinking, "Next time it's my turn." But when the next time comes along, your mate forgets. Do you say nothing and sulk?   1   2   3   4   5

8. When your mate is explaining something, are you far less patient with him or her than you are with coworkers?   1   2   3   4   5

9. When you and your mate are discussing something, do you listen to the first few words, then tune out because you assume you already know the rest of his or her point?   1   2   3   4   5

10. After you and your mate have an argument and things don't go your way, do you seek to "punish" your mate in some way?   1   2   3   4   5

SCORING AND INTERPRETATION

Add the numerical value for each response to get your total score. Refer to the following scale for interpretation.

15 and under	High degree of personal responsibleness
16–21	Moderate degree of personal responsibleness
22–27	Low degree of personal responsibleness
28 and over	Needs improvement

Since we are complex beings and fallible, getting a "perfect" score of 10 is difficult to attain. The important thing is not your score, but looking at the questions themselves and asking yourself whether you know these things. Naturally, you do. Then why don't you act upon what you know consistently?

Try to develop your understanding of how your moods affect your actions and blemish your best intentions. Invest your energies to assess the impact your actions are having on your mate and then take control to change those actions that do not result in desired outcomes. Understand that personal responsibleness is a state of being. It's not something that you exhibit at work only; rather, it's the way you are, even with your mate who loves you.

If your inventory score is above 21, you need to examine carefully your attitudes toward your mate and the expectations you have of your relationship. Also consider whether, over time, your actions have slipped out of alignment with your attitudes and expectations. Too often we let ourselves fall into "habits." Although some of these habits may get us what we want, they may also result in an insensitivity to others.

A high score on the questionnaire may mean you are hard on yourself. You need to examine whether your highly critical self-view is serving as a motivator or is functioning in a way that chips away at your self-esteem and diminishes your energy to act on what you know. Reviewing Chapters 1 and 2 can help you to determine whether you are taking control of your life or just operating with the illusion of control.

Ironically, although we boast to others that our family is our number-one priority in life, when we examine our actions, they don't always match our words. With personal responsibleness, you are aware of what you say and do, and you help ensure that your actions result in desirable outcomes that ultimately nourish the relationship—a relationship that you have chosen to pursue.

All relationships require compromise; the key is how we view compromise. Here's a typical dilemma many couples face: "Which movie do we go to—the action-packed thriller that I want to see or the comedy that you want to see?" If either person feels like the "loser" too often, he or she may sulk throughout the movie, and the evening's original intent—having a good time together—is dampened. That person may say, or think, "I do everything for you" or "We always do what you want" or "I always give up what I want to do for you."

> *With personal responsibleness, individuals*
> *don't give up or give in.*

A person with personal responsibleness doesn't make compromises with the belief that one partner is winning over the other and that the loser is giving up something. When you are facing a choice of movies (or a similar situation), consider that if you want to see this particular movie badly enough, you know how to operate the control handles so you can see it—if not today, then another time. So, it's your free choice to go to the movie your mate prefers. Thus, you are not "giving up" what you want to do; rather, you are shifting the focus from immediate self-gratification to a long-term desired outcome: nurturing the relationship. When you have personal responsibleness, you understand control and you realize that at a particular moment you may choose to invest your energies in strengthening the relationship.

Making this free choice to contribute to the relationship is personally satisfying. It compares to the exhilaration we felt at the onset of a relationship, when we were first dating. As Victor Frankel, developer of logotherapy, points out in *Man's Search for Meaning*: "The more one forgets himself by giving himself to a cause to serve or a person to love, the more human he is and the more he actualizes himself. It's part of the process of discovering the meaning in life; an inescapable primary motivation in life."

If love forms the foundation of a relationship, personal responsibleness is the cement that holds it together. Traditional wedding vows can be likened to a statement of personal responsibleness, and when you accept those vows willingly, you pledge yourself to operate with personal responsibleness. During a traditional Jewish wedding, the rabbi summed up personal responsibleness when he told the new couple after the breaking of the glass ceremony, "Let this be the last broken thing that you walk away from that you don't try your best to put back together." When the partners accept personal responsibleness, they understand that each one is in control of the quality of the relationship.

PERSONAL RESPONSIBLENESS AS A PARENT

Today, we have control over whether we bring children into the world. Perhaps the choice to do so should be accompanied by a pledge similar to our wedding vows—a solemn promise to uphold personal responsibleness when we are at the center of this little person's life, offering direction, values, religion, and love. For a parent, the motto of looking to self to make things happen, unless it is made impossible by circumstances beyond one's control, has a sharp obligatory edge.

Currently, two-career couples are a subject of social debate. Whether both parents should work is not the focus here. Rather, as a parent, you should look inside yourself and honestly assess your reasons for being absent from your child's world for much of the day. You alone are in control of finding the answer to this question and responding with appropriate action. Many parents determine that it is financially necessary for both partners to work. Earning income *is* demonstrating support for the family. As our fathers liked to remind us, "I work hard to put a roof over your head and food on the table, and so that you can have nice clothes and things you want, just like the other kids."

"Many parents who work, but in their hearts would rather stay home, feel that contributing to the family's economic wealth is more important," comments psychiatrist Dr. Harry Croft. "It's not uncommon for parents to come home from work tired and prefer not to be bothered by their kids. So the computer and TV serve as instant and convenient substitutes to occupy children's attention— they are today's baby-sitters." But parents with personal responsibleness understand that even though supporting the family economically is vital, there is more that they can and even need to do.

Teaching Personal Responsibleness to Your Kids

"Parents need to spend time talking with their children," says Dr. Croft. "The talking goes beyond telling children what to do. More than ever before, parents need to teach values, show warmth, and provide direction to their children, whether the issue is AIDS, drugs, sex, or the hurtful things that children say to each other. Nurturance and giving of yourself create the foundation for your child to stand on. Then when tougher times arrive, parents can *really* talk with their kids. Too often I've seen parents who don't know how to have a conversation with their kids. When a serious issue arises, these parents are ill-equipped to help their children."

Parents with personal responsibleness try to teach it to their kids. Typically, early lessons center around helping children learn to think for themselves. For instance, when your son wants to stay up late and you say no, he gives you the classic retort, "My friend Jamie gets to stay up late, why can't I?" Resist the temptation to point out that it is important to live within the family and that "the way we do things around here" is what matters, not what goes on in someone else's family. Instead, use the incident as an opportunity to help your child learn to take personal responsibleness. By anticipating that your son may want to stay up late, you can discuss with him, earlier that day, an agreed-upon time for going to bed. Now your child has an opportunity to learn how to operate with personal responsibleness. When the agreed-upon time comes around, say, "Didn't we agree you were going to go to bed now? And isn't keeping agreements important?" By helping children think for themselves and not just be followers, parents with personal responsibleness are telling kids, "You are in control, and you need to use that control responsibly."

Another important lesson for children is that they must bear the consequences of their actions. For example, your daughter is doing poorly in a subject at school. You recognize that if your first action is to complain about the teacher to the school's principal, you will be sending a message to your child that she had nothing to do with the bad grade, and that the fault lies with the teacher. The better course is to sit down with your daughter and talk about what she can do to improve the situation. Although your child may have a rough time working through it, you are there for support. At the same time, you are teaching your child that such is the way of the world and that through understanding control, she can do something to improve the situation.

Many parents give their children household responsibilities. But if the children fail to do their chores, it's not uncommon for parents to finish the tasks themselves rather than get into hassles. As a parent with personal responsibleness, however, you take the extra time and energy necessary to help your children understand that their words and their agreements are important and need to be upheld. By teaching children to be trustworthy and dependable today, you help them become better adults.

Instilling personal responsibleness in children begins with setting a good example for them to follow. Parents must also communicate openly and clearly with their children. With these two fundamentals in place, there will be many opportunities to demonstrate the basics of personal responsibleness: Think for yourself; recognize control; take action; and keep your promises. When children learn early on to understand and accept personal responsibleness, they will be better equipped, if not to make the road ahead smoother, then at least to withstand life's potholes.

PERSONAL RESPONSIBLENESS OUTLOOK—AS MANAGERS AND EMPLOYEES

Empowerment continues to be a buzzword in many organizations. Even though managers are more comfortable today talking about the term, they face the major issue of implementation. Arguments still prevail about who is actually doing the empowering. Some managers believe that you can't "give" the assignment to others—they must "take" it. To support this belief, it's not uncommon to hear managers talk about the importance of "taking ownership."

Convincing employees of this message has been difficult, because employees know they really don't "own" the particular project or job function. Reality quickly sets in to verify the lack of ownership when management changes direction or cuts the budget. Other managers have tried to convey the importance of "taking personal responsibility." Every time managers explain to employees the need to take personal responsibility and ask them to do so, the employees typically say that they will. The trouble is that, as many managers readily confess, the employees haven't got a clear idea of what they are saying yes to. Personal responsibility may be too closely related to "responsibilities," and we all have responsibilities that are given to us. So it's as if there's an external pressure being applied by someone else, be it a parent, boss, mate, friend, or representative from the company itself.

Although personal responsibility is closer to the real message, the term still has an external connotation. There seems to be no linkage to "self." What makes personal responsibleness meaningful is that the person saying yes is accepting control and is internalizing the importance of the task or project at hand. That person will do everything possible to ensure its successful completion. "Commitment" is often uttered in the same breath as "ownership," "personal responsibility," "accountability," and "empowerment." Once again, employees nod their heads in agreement, but in actuality they are unclear about the practical usage of the term.

Commitment helps describe personal responsibleness, but it's still too narrow a term. As you have seen in this chapter, people with personal responsibleness are not only keeping promises to others; they are fulfilling obligations to themselves. "Taking control," "performing at high standards," "following through," and "making a valuable difference" describe someone with personal responsibleness. Ironically, people function with personal responsibleness not only because it's valued by their bosses, but because it is very personally satisfying. The personal satisfaction derived is one part of the workplace performance formula that has often been overlooked. There's always a good feeling associated with knowing that you've kept your promises to yourself.

How does a manager encourage employees to operate with personal responsibleness? Take, for example, a technical employee who is very talented but consistently misses deadlines. It's not uncommon for a manager to send a message that to meet these deadlines, the employee will need to "work harder and smarter." The employee typically translates this message to mean "work longer hours." The thought can be threatening, especially if the employee values time spent with his or her family. Rather than tackle the disparities that may exist between two opposing value systems, the boss can direct time and energy to helping the employee understand and accept control. By operating with personal responsibleness, the boss can pave the way to show the employee that what once may have been barriers blocking progress may now be within his or her control to change. No longer will the boss hear excuses like "My project leader failed to get back with me with the information," or "I couldn't move forward because the person making that decision didn't call me," or

"It was impossible to get it done, given all the problems I encountered, plus the tight deadlines I had to work under."

In essence, the manager is teaching the employee better ways to go about getting results. What's being recommended may sound pretty familiar to an experienced manager. What's different, however, are the "tools" that the manager is introducing. Although they may not guarantee a 100 percent completion rate on all deadlines, they will result in an improvement. Interestingly, that's all that may be needed—some improvement.

Personal responsibleness is action-oriented, and it is predicated on the understanding and acceptance of control. Unlike personal responsibility, empowerment, and ownership, personal responsibleness encompasses taking control of one's attitude and making sure that it is properly aligned with today's fiercely competitive work environment. Think for a moment about your own attitude set.

1. What have you been taught over the years about the proper attitude set to adopt?
2. How old is this general attitude set of yours? What opinion is it based on? What facts is it based on?
3. Can you rely on this overall attitude set to help you get the results you desire from one situation to the next or from day to day?

With personal responsibleness comes a special outlook, or way of perceiving what is going on around you. Over the years, many authors, educators, and others have promoted the benefits of a "positive attitude." However, that type of outlook is poorly suited for the next millennium, because it fails to encompass all the realities that we face daily. There is a better alternative: the *achieving attitude* that is a natural outgrowth of personal responsibleness, as described in Chapter 4.

1. **STOP** and think about what others tell you to do and what they are saying. Then make up your own mind about what to do before taking any action.

2. **STOP** and ask yourself, "Have I considered what my parameters of control are?" whenever you tell yourself, "There's nothing I can do," or whenever you feel stuck.

3. **STOP** long enough to think before you speak and be personally responsible for what you say.

4. **STOP** periodically to assess whether the actions you are taking will ultimately contribute to making a valuable difference. If not, *stop* what you are doing and take a realistic look at what else you could do that would equate to making a valuable difference.

START

1. **START** the process over again when you get stuck and want to seek help from others. Try to think it through on your own. That way, you'll build confidence.

2. **START** to deliver your message if what you are about to say will make a valuable difference. If not, remain silent.

3. **START** immediately to implement one area to work on if you have accepted control and have incorporated personal responsibleness.

4 BECOME A PRO-ACHIEVER

*Any fact facing us is not as important as our
attitude toward it, for that determines our
success or failure.*

—Norman Vincent Peale

Two young men are among the final candidates interviewing for an entry-level position with a telecommunications company. The résumé of candidate 1 describes his education and the position he has held for the six months he has been out of college. The résumé of candidate 2 indicates that he has an equal level of education; it also lists several unskilled jobs that he held while he was in college. During the interview, candidate 2 leans forward on the interviewer's desk with his shirtsleeves rolled up, looks her squarely in the eye, and says that he will do whatever is necessary to make the department succeed. Candidate 1 also professes to really want this job, but he sits stiffly in his chair, rarely makes eye contact, and seems aloof. The interviewer feels as if she is pulling information from him, as he answers her questions deliberately and with little enthusiasm.

Anyone who has been in a hiring position can relate to the scenario just described. From the perspective of educational preparation, there is virtually no difference between the candidates (as is often the case). Still, from his mannerisms, enthusiasm, and what he had to say, the interviewer leans toward candidate 2 as the kind of person she wants to have in her organization. She assumes that he is a go-getter, since he spoke with pride about working his way through college. She thinks he has a "can do" attitude that is consistent with the job's requirements.

This interviewer made her hiring selection on the basis of candidate 2's attitude. Managers too place high importance on attitude. In fact, according to a national study by the American Management Association and Bright Enterprises, Inc., attitude is one of the three most important attributes that managers identify as contributing to their own success.[1]

The importance of attitude goes beyond job interviews and career success. We engage continuously in forming first impressions of the people we meet, whether in social settings or at work. To do so, we consider a number of things, including the attitudes of those people. Experience teaches us that first impressions are often inaccurate. Still, first impressions often help determine whom we date, befriend, hire, or do business with. Attitude is an important criterion in forming initial impressions—both our own attitude and the perceived attitude of the other person. Attitude is also our "compass setting" for how we approach performance, whether it's making decisions, tackling problems, or simply completing everyday work assignments.

Our attitude is made up of two parts: the internal, which encompasses how we view the world and ourselves in it, and the external, which encompasses how others perceive our mannerisms. Let's look at both parts to clarify a few common misconceptions about attitude.

FROM THE INSIDE

Like a single facet of a cut diamond, attitude is but one side of an individual that helps to explain his or her behavior. Other aspects of an individual's makeup include values, beliefs, motivations, assumptions, premises, principles, motives, will power, and drive—and all are intertwined. We form attitudes internally to develop our ability to interact with others and our environment in ways that allow us not only to survive but also to flourish.

> *Attitude is more than a simple "mind-set."*

Equating attitude and mind-set is too narrow a view. Attitude goes beyond thinking and beliefs to incorporate feelings—this is its important evaluative or judgmental component. Here's an example that illustrates the distinction between beliefs and attitudes. A man with rippling muscles is working out in the center of a track. You watch him throw a javelin incredibly far. You think to yourself, "This man is strong" (observed trait). His next throw travels even further. Again you think to yourself, "I believe this man is really strong" (belief). Then you say to yourself, "I like strong men" (attitude).

Thus your attitude encompasses how you think *and* how you feel about things. The judgmental component of attitude determines whether you like or dislike something, whether you think it's good or bad. Keep in mind that the feelings you have about things, people, and events can be strong or weak. The more you are around people who share the same attitude, the more that attitude becomes acceptable, stable, and enduring.[2]

> *You can change your attitude.*

Attitudes are made up of preferences that allow us to make choices in what we like and dislike. Our attitudes are always vulnerable and subject to revision. The advertising industry is built around the premise that attitudes can and do change; political candidates use sound bites to try to sway our thinking about important social issues. Naturally, we filter how we see our world to shape and support our preferences.

Attitudes tend to be closer to the surface and more conscious than beliefs. Often we are not as aware of our beliefs as we are of our attitudes, or our likes and dislikes. For instance, why do we take a liking to some people right away? Appearance has something to do with it, but our reaction goes much deeper. There are certain unconscious beliefs driving us toward that person. We may extend a level of trust to that person because we *believe* that anybody who looks us in the eye is trustworthy. Also, the person may take an interest in us and what we do, so the conversation isn't focused on the other person. Our underlying belief is that selfless people are nice to be around. Many of us don't check out the validity of our beliefs because we rely on our own "gut feel." But sometimes those gut instincts can be wrong.[3] Our beliefs evolve through experiences. We have only a vague sense of where these personal conclusions came from. Our attitudes, on the other hand, are often clear and easily defensible. They seem to take shape more immediately than our beliefs. We know what we feel.

As we begin to understand and accept control, we take notice of our attitudes at any given moment and determine if they are serving us well. If not, we can change attitudes—not only everyday attitudes, but also overall attitudes toward life. Here are two stories to illustrate what I mean. Although the names are probably familiar to you, the ways in which their attitudes affected their lives may not be.

> At age 16, Billie Jean King was a hefty 140 pounds on a 5′6″ frame. Besides her awkward build, she had vision that tested out at 20/400—her body was not an asset and neither was her attitude. At the time, she was frustrated by being stuck at nineteenth place in the rankings of women tennis players in the United States. With the help of 1930s tennis champion Alice Marble, Billie Jean made a pivotal change in her career—she learned to look at her attitude as an asset and to think like a champion. Her eventual success tells the rest of the story.[4]

While participating in an equestrian event in 1995, actor Christopher Reeve was almost totally paralyzed after falling from his horse. At one time shortly after the accident, Reeve's attitude was such that he was willing to have his family "pull the plug" and end his life. In a televised interview with Barbara Walters, Reeve explained that when he saw the smile on his son's face, he realized that he was needed. At that point he changed his attitude completely. Since then, his recovery effort has been heroic; he has even made plans to resume his movie career as the voice of King Arthur in the animated feature *The Quest for Camelot.*

Changes in attitude occur all the time. Sometimes the changes are dramatic, as in the cases of Billie Jean King and Christopher Reeve. The important thing to remember is that you are in control of your attitudes and you are the one who ultimately changes them. You need to pay attention to your attitudes and what they are doing for you.

> *Attitude can override a bad mood.*

Mood and attitude should not be confused. A mood is an emotional state. It is situational and even closer to the surface than attitude. Consider the following scenario to help differentiate mood and attitude: You are eating your favorite ice cream cone while driving your car. The ice cream melts faster than you can eat it, so it drips all over your clothes and your car seat. What is your mood? (Likely, bad.) Will your attitude toward ice cream change? (Likely not.) As you can see, your mood encompasses your feelings at a given moment, whereas your attitude is more enduring.

As Dr. David Burns points out in *Feeling Good,* your mood results from your thinking. But knowing that you can change your mood is not enough. You can't just "put on a smile" and wait to see a cheery self emerge. You need to understand how to take control and work with yourself to use your thinking and your mannerisms to counteract an emotional state.

Since moods are surface feelings, it's logical to conclude that an attitude can override a bad mood. When Jim Davidson, a senior manager at MCI, wakes up in a bad mood, he says that he is able to "shake it off." Jim has the attitude that he can and should exert a positive influence on the many people he interacts with daily in his job. So, before he leaves his house, he tells himself, "I can't come to work in a toxic mood, and if I don't change it, no one else is going to, so get a grip." And it works.

Changing your mood involves looking below the surface, being willing to adjust how you are thinking and feeling at a given moment, and then reinforcing what you are thinking with actions. As Dr. Harry Croft explains to his patients, "An airline pilot has to have an attitude of safety first and total concentration on what he is doing, regardless of whether he had a serious argument with his wife before leaving home. Just like the pilot, you need to be able to draw upon something bigger than your mood . . . and that's your attitude."

Perhaps we shift gears without our own awareness. Here's an everyday example that illustrates how quickly attitudes change. You are talking to someone on the phone at work. Your attitude toward the person is very negative, and the subject being discussed is controversial—so much so that you lose your patience. In the middle of letting the other person have it, the other telephone line rings. You pick it up, and suddenly say in a very pleasant tone of voice, "Hello." What happened to your negative attitude?

> *Your behavior doesn't always match your attitude.*

Sometimes we behave contrary to our attitudes. All of us have one family relative of whom we aren't particularly fond. But in dealing with that person, we often try to be pleasant. We smile when we need to smile, and we strike up casual conversation to keep harmony. The situation is much more challenging when we don't like a boss whom we need to interact with on a regular basis. We have to keep our jobs because we need the money. So we invest a lot of energy to get along with the boss, even though deep down we still view that boss negatively.

Masking attitude is possible, although it's hard to do for long. But we know we can do it, so the next person can too. So how can we know for sure what another person's attitude is? We can't, which brings us to the external meaning of attitude.

FROM THE OUTSIDE

When it comes to other people, we are quick to describe them as having a negative attitude, a wait-and-see attitude, a lazy attitude, a winning attitude, a selfish attitude, an obnoxious attitude, and so on. Like the interviewer at the beginning of this chapter, we take into consideration what we know about a person's past, what that person says, and what we have observed about that person's behavior and mannerisms. Then we use that information to categorize the person's attitude. Meanwhile, our attitude toward that person develops. But our labeling of other people's attitudes may be wrong.

Here's a familiar situation in regard to our inability to assess other people's attitudes accurately. It's apparent to everyone in the office that Sherry is having difficulties performing her job, even though she seems to have the required skills. After being transferred to another department, Sherry blossoms. Around the coffee machine, coworkers speculate about what made the difference: Was the problem the dynamics between Sherry and her boss? Is the new boss responsible for the improvement? Or did the employee change her attitude? In those situations, we as onlookers never know for sure.

The impossibility of knowing for sure is the very reason some human resources professionals are reluctant to use attitude as an important criterion for measuring performance or for hiring. One human resources executive put it this way: "When hiring, the HR professional's primary concern has been and still is that the candidate meets the appropriate job requirements, such as degrees, credentials, and necessary skill sets. The manager, on the other hand, is concerned that the candidate has the needed skills, but also looks at whether he or she can work with the potential employee. This distinction brings to the forefront that the role of the HR professional is quite different from that of the manager. In a broad sense, the HR professional works to keep the company out of court. Dealing with attitude is too subjective, whether it concerns hiring or performance measurement. HR professionals are uncomfortable working with attitude because they typically work with empirical data."[5]

> *Whom would you rather work with: someone with a good attitude but weaknesses in certain skill areas, or the opposite?*

Other human resources professionals differ with this view and are beginning to recognize that attitudes in the workplace are important for the very reason that people are in control of their attitudes and can change them. "Whether we want to admit it or not," one HR director noted, "attitudes can be the determining factor in deciding who gets promoted. The attitude factor is typically part of the informal company system. While we are reluctant to put attitude in the performance appraisal process because it is so hard to measure, that doesn't mean that we believe attitude is not important. Quite the contrary. I would much rather work with someone who has a good attitude but is weak in certain skill areas than the reverse. It's easier to strengthen someone's skills."[6]

Many managers are of the same opinion. Developing good working relationships with peers and employees is of heightened importance. Still, very few managers feel comfortable talking about what they expect when it comes to employees' attitudes. So few managers coach employees on attitudes and their effect on performance.

> *Other people surmise what your attitude is, but they really don't know for sure.*

INTENTIONS AND ATTITUDE

Perhaps you have encountered a situation where you decided to change your attitude and "look at the bright side." So you took steps to "make peace" with someone and apologize for your behavior. But as you approached the person, something unexpected happened and you found yourself arguing and getting upset all over again. When things calmed down, you might have said to the person, "You know, I came here with the intention of trying to make peace and work things out, but . . ."

Or let's assume that you have a positive attitude toward weekly staff meetings. You believe that the meetings are highly informative and productive, so you intend to be there on time. Just before you leave for the meeting, one of your biggest customers calls you with a problem that needs to be resolved right away. Since he is your customer and you can solve his problem, you take care of the situation. By the time you're done, you are behind schedule. You rush to the meeting and arrive 15 minutes late. At the end of the meeting, while everyone is talking casually, your boss walks up to you and says, "You were late. Don't you care about these meetings?" Naturally, you respond by saying, "Yes, of course I do, but . . ." Then your boss interrupts you and says, "Well, you had better show it."

In both examples, unanticipated occurrences prevented you from carrying out your intentions. The failure to "make peace" in the first example resulted from the quick resurrection of your old attitude toward the other person; your intentions were good, but your old attitude prevailed in the end. In the second example, your boss used your lateness to infer that you don't value the meetings—the boss has mistakenly surmised your attitude.

We are always observing the actions, tone of voice, and facial and bodily movements of the people we encounter, as well as what they say and do. Categorizing people as having a certain attitude enables us to try to anticipate their actions so that we can be better prepared and feel more in control as new situations arise. When we make that leap in determining a person's future actions, we assume, in essence, that a person's attitude can be likened to a car's transmission—that is, attitude ultimately drives a person's behavior. But we can just surmise what a person's attitude is; only the individual knows for sure.

COMMON ATTITUDE TYPES

In our ongoing attempt to understand the people we interact with regularly, let's look more closely at some of the common attitude types.

> *The Negativist is characterized by a negative attitude*

Most of us know people whom we consider difficult to get along with. In my experience, these people often seem to relish reading or hearing bad news—after all, they knew *already* that things were bad. At work, they huddle with their buddies to complain about management's latest decision or to question why management is opting for a particular course of action. If the action fails, they are the first to say, "I told you so." In general, these people seem to converse exclusively with others who think alike and who can do nothing about the situation. When given a chance to express their opinions to someone who has the power to change things, they typically get weak-kneed, and any ideas that they put forth are usually poorly thought-out or unworkable. To explain their reluctance to make an effort to improve things, these people say, "It's no use," or "No one will listen," or "It won't make any difference in the long run."

These expressions and behaviors are indicators of a negative attitude; the person in whom these traits predominate is perceived as a Negativist. Whether at work or in a social setting, the Negativist saps the energy of everyone in the group by continuously criticizing and raising doubts. Questioning and introducing valid criticisms can be helpful, especially when they are coupled with a willingness to consider what can be done to remedy the situation. But the Negativist's constant criticisms are not designed to reveal problems or to produce change; rather, they are intended to disrupt things and to tear at the fabric of morale. The Negativist also promotes a wait-and-see approach—but when an organization is changing processes and structures in an effort to keep pace with competition, watching from the sidelines is a dangerous stance to take.

> *The Entitlist is characterized by a "What's in it for me?" attitude.*

Closely associated with the Negativists are the Entitlists. These people always look out for "number one." Projects or tasks are engaged in first and foremost for personal benefit. Often, Entitlists approach the boss for a raise after being on the job for a short while. When the boss asks what they have done to deserve a raise, Entitlists have little to point to except for the fact that they have been showing up. Sometimes Entitlists reveal themselves when they cry out that they want to raise a family and continue working and that the company should be doing something to make it "easier" for them. From a societal perspective, we recognize Entitlists when they complain that they haven't been given the house or the medical coverage they were "supposed" to have because it is their "right." Since Entitlists see themselves as being "owed" these things, they discount anyone's effort to help them and they rarely thank others. Their failure to show appreciation is not a matter of poor manners. Rather, is is a reflection of their attitude, which focuses entirely on themselves and what they want or need.

> *The Superficial Optimist is characterized by a positive attitude gone too far.*

At the opposite end of the attitudinal spectrum are those people commonly identified as easy to get along with. These people are typically cheerful and enthusiastic. Because they want everyone to be upbeat, they try to stitch together the fabric of morale. Even though their intentions are good, they operate with the undying belief that you can have whatever you want in life as long as you want it badly enough. After all, how many of us have heard people say, "Success comes to those who believe in themselves strongly enough and have an upbeat, positive attitude." These are the Superficial Optimists.

The Superficial Optimist goes beyond the positive thinker in the belief that fate plays a part in the outcome of events. If something doesn't turn out the way the Optimist had hoped, then it wasn't meant to be. Just as love can be blinding, the fatalist attitude seems to lull the Optimist into always seeing things as positive. Because Superficial Optimists are afraid that too much negativity will bring them down, they listen to the news or read today's paper cautiously. Similarly, they do not examine critically their own circumstances. The Superficial Optimist is the one still cheering for the home team when the score is 9 to 2 with two outs in the bottom of the ninth.

In the workplace, the Superficial Optimist rarely, if ever, points to anything that the department, team, or company could do better. Since peers see the Superficial Optimist as operating without depth, this type of individual usually suffers from low credibility. Often called the "company cheerleader," the Superficial Optimist is viewed as standing on the sidelines (along with the Negativist) rather than getting in the game.

> *The Pro-Achiever is characterized by an achieving attitude.*

In these fiercely competitive times, to get in the game and stay there we need to continually seek out opportunities where we can make a valuable difference. Positioning ourselves to do that requires a different attitude set—one that is not easy to categorize. At first glance, some people might label it a "can do" attitude, because it is characterized by an eagerness to get things done. Others might see it as an optimistic or "positive" attitude, because it is shaped by enthusiasm. It even includes elements of a negative attitude, because there is a willingness to see all sides of an issue, even the bad. This different attitude set, which incorporates all these varied characteristics, is what I refer to as the achieving attitude.

To give you a better picture of what comprises Pro-Achievers, consider this question: If you were facing a difficult situation or working on an important project in which you were dependent on others, who would you want those others to be? Of course, you and I don't know the same people. Still I'll wager that I can give you a pretty accurate description of your choices. Your key people show the enthusiasm and energy of Superficial Optimists, but also look at things critically, for the purpose of uncovering problems and making improvements. They go beyond the "good" and "bad," and seek to uncover the root issues. They consistently make things happen; they are persistent, determined, disciplined. These are the people you feel you can always count on.

The people I've just described also have some attributes that you cannot see. Besides being able to get things done, they always keep in mind the interests of everyone else, not merely their own. When asked to do something, they try to understand what is being asked of them, then deliver at a level that matches or exceeds what had been expected. They are always looking to make a valuable difference and distinguish themselves by willpower mixed with all the resources they possess. They operate with an achieving attitude.

> *Pro-Achievers operate with duality of purpose.*

Three essential characteristics differentiate people with achieving attitudes:

1. They are rooted in realism.
2. They view problems not as obstacles, but as challenges.
3. They consistently operate with a dual purpose: achieving exceptional performance and making a valuable difference.

> *You don't "get" an achieving attitude.*

How does someone "get" an achieving attitude? Actually, an achieving attitude comes effortlessly, much the way a well-hit ball takes flight. The similarity was revealed to me by David Glenz, who played on the PGA tour for several years and is now one of golf's outstanding teaching professionals. In Glenz's experience, when beginners first try to play the game, they focus only on hitting the ball. Out on that driving range getting their initial lesson, they put all their efforts into making contact so the ball will go up in the air. The result is generally that the ball goes only a short distance. A professional golfer, on the other hand, puts the entire effort into executing the swing, with little energy devoted to thinking about the ball or hitting it.

Likewise when people try to "get" an achieving attitude, their energies are being misdirected. This approach only touches the surface, so it is unlikely that they will be able to integrate this type of attitude into their way of being. Instead, their energies should be invested in understanding and accepting control. When people accept control and internalize personal responsibleness, they have created the foundation for achieving whatever they set out to do, and an achieving attitude is a natural outgrowth. Control, personal responsibleness, and an achieving attitude bundled together provide the distinguishing elements of the Pro-Achiever.

RECOGNIZING THE PRO-ACHIEVER

How can you spot Pro-Achievers? They are unmistakable, once you know what to look for. You can tell by the way they speak, how they translate their words into action, their level of enthusiasm in pursuing tasks, and their ability to consistently make things happen. Although things seem easy and natural for them, Pro-Achievers are not born that way; they are ordinary people who have made a conscious choice to accept personal responsibleness and have carried through on their promise to themselves. The decision to become a Pro-Achiever can be made at any age. Consider the story of our twenty-sixth President.

At an early age, Theodore Roosevelt was described as a child who was "sinking into what seemed like a chronic invalidism."[7] All through his childhood, Theodore Roosevelt was ill; at times he suffered from severe asthma attacks as often as every three days. Although he enjoyed exercising his mind, his body was so frail that he was often unable to stand on his own. At age 12, after being

(*Continued*)

confronted with the reality of his weak body by his father, Theodore vowed that he would view himself as a person with a strong mind and body. For 2 years, he went through the drudgery of bodybuilding exercises and he thought he was making progress. But at age 14, some youngsters abused and humiliated him. Their bullying showed young Theodore that the world still saw him as a weakling; in his own words, he was a "foreordained and predetermined victim." That incident prompted him "to join what he would later call 'the fellowship of the doers,'" which at the time meant to him that "if he had exercised hard before, he must do it twice as hard now."[8] By the age of 17, Roosevelt's battle for his health appeared to have been won. He carefully noted his physical measurements at the time, and over a 3-month period he competed in 15 athletic contests and won 14 of them.[9] His asthma attacks became less frequent and less of an impediment in his life. Roosevelt had made a conscious choice to look to himself to make things happen; most important to him (as well as to you and me), he learned that putting in the effort is not enough—doers also need to focus on the results.

Pro-Achievers are all, in varying degrees, members of that "fellowship of doers." They typically say, "If I don't do something to help myself, no one else will."

Martin Luther King, Jr,. believed in the achieving philosophy for himself and all African-Americans. King recalled a childhood incident riding in a car with his father, a respected Baptist minister. When his father inadvertently ran through a stop sign, a policeman came alongside the car and said, "All right, boy, pull over and let me see your license." King's father replied, "I'm no boy." Then he pointed to his son and said, "This is a boy.

I am a man, and until you call me one, I will not listen to you." The policeman was so shocked that he wrote the ticket up nervously and left the scene as quickly as possible.[10]

The image of his father standing up for himself left an indelible mark on King's memory. He developed the attitude that he and his people could change America's racist society by looking to themselves to make something happen and adopting the nonviolent tactics promoted by Mahatma Gandhi. In the years that followed, King faced many challenges that fueled his conviction. In each case, he stood strong, even though his home was bombed and lives were threatened. On one occasion, community officials went so far as to arrest King for driving 30 mph in a 25 mph zone, and hundreds of people peacefully surrounded the jail until King was released. That release gave new hope and confidence to African-Americans, while proving the effectiveness of nonviolent protest. As many were reminded in his famous speech, "Freedom has always been an expensive thing."[11]

Pro-Achievers like Martin Luther King recognize that "saying it" is easy; the challenge is to translate what they say into action again and again. There's no better example than Babe Didrikson.

Mildred "Babe" Didrikson got her nickname because, even though she excelled in track and basketball, she loved to play baseball. She hit home runs like Babe Ruth, so to her delight friends called her Babe. As a child, she promised her father that she would someday win an Olympic gold medal; her best chance to do so was in track. When she competed in the 1932 Olympic games, held in Los Angeles, reporters called her "the world's out-

(Continued)

standing all-around female athlete." During the games she told reporters, "I am out to beat everybody in sight, and that's just what I am going to do." At that time, athletes were permitted to enter only three events. Babe set a world record in the javelin throw, beating the previous record by 11 feet; she broke the world record for the 80-meter hurdles; and she finished second in the high jump. So Babe had kept her promise to her father, and followed through on her statements to the press.

But Babe had made another promise, this one to herself: She wanted to be the greatest athlete who ever lived. After her Olympic victory, Babe tried numerous ventures to capitalize on her growing fame before she decided that golf would be her game. At her first tournament, she told a reporter that she would shoot a 77, and that is exactly what she shot. Even though she lost the tournament, she didn't mope. Instead, she set her sights on winning the next one, and indeed she did. Starting in 1935, she won one tournament after another. In 1945 she was nominated Woman Athlete of the Year, and by 1948 Babe was the top female money winner in golf. Babe's attitude wasn't one of just "trying to do her best." She approached each competition consistently with the attitude that she would do her best and win. She made that commitment not only to the press and to her fans, but to herself as well.

Even though you may have had little chance to get to know someone like Theodore Roosevelt, Martin Luther King, Jr., or Babe Didrikson, you still can spot Pro-Achievers, both at work and among friends. For instance, Pro-Achievers might excitedly tell you about a new idea, then shortly after show you that their idea is being worked on and turned into a reality. At work, Pro-Achievers are the ones who seem to be getting involved with new and different responsibilities—or even getting promoted each time you talk to them.

Or Pro-Achievers could be those people who say they are going to quit smoking, and at the same time start working out three times a week at the gym. Without notice, one week quickly slips into the next, and it's only when the subject happens to surface that you learn that the Pro-Achievers have been living up to their promise for the past three months. Interestingly, Pro-Achievers are not defined by their wealth, educational level, status, age, or sex. Anyone can be a Pro-Achiever.

But saying and doing aren't the only criteria for Pro-Achievers. They continually make a difference by performing at a level that matches or exceeds expectations. They form good relationships with people because they express themselves clearly and never need to be second-guessed. They are able to work independently when needed; but they also work well in a team setting, whether on the job, at home, or on a sports field. To understand how Pro-Achievers operate, we need to examine how they think and how they feel.

LOOKING INSIDE THE PRO-ACHIEVER

> *Pro-Achievers face reality.*

Pro-Achievers have a kind of awareness that Phil Jackson, the Chicago Bulls coach, refers to as "mindful." When you are mindful, you become your own watchdog.[12] When Pro-Achievers "police themselves," they are trying to seek out and deal with the realities of a situation. Pro-Achievers understand that control is required to get what they want, need, or desire. They also understand that controlling their actions is not enough; they must also take control of the way they think and feel about themselves and what they are trying to pursue.

> *Pro-Achievers view problems as challenges.*

Being rooted in a kind of realism that seeks out problems and views them, not as obstacles, but as challenges is what separates Pro-Achievers from Superficial Optimists. For example, when a Superficial Optimist hears that the company has had a successful year, he gets excited and boasts about it to his family and friends. A Pro-Achiever, on the other hand, gets just as excited as the Superficial Optimist, but she realizes that a company's success is no more secure from one year to the next than is a sports team's from one season to the next—and she immediately sets to work on the next year's goals and objectives. Besides not wanting to seek out problems, Superficial Optimists will overlook them.

> *Pay attention to future known events, and be less reactive.*

By taking an honest look at things, a Pro-Achiever is able to be *preactive*. Daniel Burrus, author of *Technotrends* and one of the country's leading technology forecasters (as rated by *The New York Times*), defined the word to describe people who are not just reacting to their environment. Instead, they are taking preaction to future known events. Taking preaction gives a person a sense of control, and a feeling of confidence when doing it." Working with future known events is something that Daniel uses in his personal life as well as when meeting with clients. He lives on a lake in Wisconsin, and like many of his neighbors, he is worried about his cement walls cracking when the lake freezes. Daniel explains how he addressed the problem: "I know this winter the lake is going to freeze (a future known event). So to keep the sea wall from cracking when spring comes and the ice melts (another future known event), I had a pump put in to keep the water from collecting." This example is simple, but it illustrates that when future events can be predicted accurately, you can take control by stopping long enough to face the realities of the situation.

Working with the realistic perspective of the achieving attitude enables you to examine a situation for what it really is and form an opinion about it. The Pro-Achiever and the Negativist resemble each other in their willingness to be critical, but they do so with different intentions. The Negativist's attitude is corruptive because she seeks out the bad then looks no further. Unlike a Negativist, a Pro-Achiever assimilates the information he uncovers and transforms it into something useful to help move the process forward.

Pro-Achievers face realities and believe that much can be learned from mistakes. They look at what caused them to go off track and factor this in with everything they know they have been doing right; then they move forward. Using mistakes to help sort out where to move next is part of multidimensional thinking—a habitual practice for Pro-Achievers.

EXAMINING ALL THE ANGLES

Multidimensional thinking includes thinking forward, backward, upside down, and from different angles. Pro-Achievers also incorporate a special angle: their dual purpose of achieving exceptional performance and making a valuable difference. Indeed, without multidimensional thinking, these two purposes might, at times, seem to make contradictory demands on us. Consider this story of a superstar.

> In the late 1980s, Michael Jordan enjoyed enormous personal success with many high-scoring games—that is, he undoubtedly achieved exceptional performance. But his team frequently wound up losing. While playing for the Chicago Bulls, Michael learned that the basketball was a spotlight, and that he needed to share it with others—not only so that they might shine, but for the team to win.

(Continued)

> The culminating event for Jordan, according to coach
> Phil Jackson, occurred during the Bulls' first champi-
> onship series against the Lakers in 1991. The entire L.A.
> team was collapsing around Michael during the fourth
> quarter, so Jackson reminded Michael of the need to fan
> the ball to his teammate John Paxson on the perimeter.
> "Michael went back on the floor, drew the defense, and
> kicked the ball out to Paxson, who made the winning
> shot for the championship."[13] Coach Jackson said that he
> asked Michael to do something he had never been asked
> to do before: not to make a spectacular play, but to make
> the common, simple one, because that one had the
> greater potential to win the game. In this situation, mak-
> ing a valuable difference (winning the game) *apparently*
> required Michael to forgo exceptional individual perfor-
> mance! By allowing the spotlight to shine on his team-
> mate and his team, Michael didn't improve his statistics,
> but he did increase his stature.

Pro-Achievers look out for others as well as themselves. That perspective is an integral part of multidimensional thinking. We engage
in this kind of thinking in our daily lives when we forgo something
that we would like to do at the moment in order to fulfill the wishes
of people we value or cherish. Our actions may not mean the difference between winning and losing a championship, but they do
nurture the relationships we care about. So when we forgo our own
desires for what others want, we aren't necessarily "giving in" to others or "giving up" something; rather, we are electing to invest in the
relationship to ultimately yield a more enduring sense of fulfillment.

CULTIVATING AN ACHIEVING ATTITUDE

As situations arise during the day and as people you interact with
try to influence how you think and feel, your attitude is constantly
changing. If you consider your basic attitude toward things and aver-

age out the shifts over weeks or months, however, you will uncover an overall attitudinal makeup that helps define how you see the world and yourself in it.

An achieving attitude develops naturally once personal responsibleness has been internalized. Even so, Pro-Achievers are aware of the effects of attitude and work consciously to make some adjustments when things aren't going smoothly—just as professional golfers adjust their swing from time to time. You too can cultivate the kind of attitude that is an asset for achieving what you want. The following pointers will help you stop long enough to assess where you are and where you want to go, with an action plan for getting yourself in gear and moving forward. Along the way, you will come to realize that you have begun working with an achieving attitude.

Taping quotable quotes or fancy phrases to your refrigerator door is not the way. To begin changing your attitude, you must accept not actively changing it. By this I mean that it is not necessary to fight yourself. With the acceptance of control and the integration of personal responsibleness, you will find your attitude evolving naturally into an achieving attitude.

> *To cultivate an achieving attitude, "stop" and assess where you are.*

Stop for a moment to take a very important first step, one that is fundamental to psychological insight: self-awareness.[14] Socrates' injunction "Know thyself" goes beyond being in touch with your strengths and weaknesses, likes and dislikes. It encompasses a kind of self-reflectivity, or introspective attention to your very own experience, sometimes referred to as "mindfulness." Introspection is within your control, and it needs to be done continuously in order to keep up with yourself—who you are, where you are at the present, and where you want to go.

By stopping and taking time to know yourself, you become aware of what you are thinking and saying to yourself and to others throughout your day. Be sure to stop long enough, as well, to get in touch with the assumptions, premises, and beliefs with which you operate. These three factors filter how you see your world and how you interpret what you are seeing—they help shape your attitude.

Viewing yourself objectively, whether at work or at home, gives you the information needed to work on your attitude. Not having this psychological insight can be likened to dealing with a neighbor who is having a problem with his stove. Every time you ask him a question, he tells you nothing except that the stove won't work when he turns it on. If you are inexperienced in this area, you will be just as confused as your neighbor. If you have expertise in the inner workings of stoves, however, you can sort out mentally the possible causes for the problem. By selecting one potential source of the problem, you can establish a strategy for checking out what is wrong. When the "problem" is determining your future, the expertise needed to move in a positive direction is knowledge of self that is accurate, complete, and current.

> *To cultivate an achieving attitude, "stop" and consider how you are benefiting from your current attitude.*

Gaining information about yourself puts you in a pivotal position to assess what benefits you are getting from your current attitude and whether you are effectively "moving the ball forward" toward your goals. For instance, if you have identified that you tend to be negative, then consider the following: Being negative takes about as much energy as being positive—you have to work at either one. At first glance, that statement may appear to be inaccurate, especially if you are in the habit of being negative. First, you're used to being negative; second, there's a lot of negativity around that's easy to latch on to. However, being negative still requires the investment of your energies to find something negative in what is happening around you. Since the investment of energies is a given, and you are in control of how you want to invest your energies, ask yourself, "What benefit am I getting from operating with a generally negative attitude toward things?" On the other hand, if you have determined that you tend to be naively positive, you should ask yourself, "What benefit am I getting from operating with a generally positive attitude toward things?" As a positivist, you may have temporary periods where you feel great, but are you making a difference and moving in a direction that gets you closer to what you want?

> *To cultivate an achieving attitude, "stop" and decide what you want.*

Developing your action plan depends upon investing your energies up front to determine what you want. Make sure "what you want" is driven primarily by what you believe, rather than by what others tell you to do. After all, as an adult, you are in control of deciding what you really want. Combining awareness of self with a wealth of experiences equips you to better think through what you really want and what you need to commit yourself to doing. Clearly define what you want—whether it relates to making important choices about your career or deciding something as simple as what to do for the weekend. Asking yourself, "What do I want?" and honestly defining it for yourself prepares you for the next action step, which involves developing your strategy.

> *To cultivate an achieving attitude, "stop" and determine the parameters of control.*

Developing your action plan also involves determining what you can and cannot control. Among the things that you can control are your assumptions, premises, and beliefs. To begin, write them down. Start checking them out by talking to people you respect, but who think and feel differently than you do about things. Read books about managing and working with yourself, and see the kinds of assumptions and premises that the authors work with. For instance, in *Feeling Good*, David Burns reports that 10 cognitive distortions "cause many, if not all, depressed states."[15] In addition, Dr. Burns introduces the antidote or corrective assumptions to work with.

At any given moment, you can also control your thoughts and feelings as well as what you say to others. So get in the practice of "policing yourself." What you say typically stems from what you have been thinking. So when policing yourself and making "self-checks," you can engage in what one client refers to as a "word-watch alert": paying attention to the words you use, both with yourself and with others. Then check out the validity of your words. For instance, if during your word-watch alert you find yourself thinking, "I'll never get this project done on time," rather than letting that thought go untested and holding on to that tinge of fear, check out the accuracy of your statement. If you don't have a written plan to refer to, you may need to write one out to see if your thoughts are accurate. If your thoughts are faulty, you can discard them. If they are accurate, you can develop some action steps for handling the situation.

Since you have the ability to control your thoughts, get in the habit of re-forming your view of things. The glass is either half full or half empty—both describe the same situation, but you interpret its significance. After all, reality is how you perceive your environment. For instance, a business owner might look at the new year as something to dread, because all the financial books start on zero. Another might see the new year as an opportunity to create a fresh start: a time not simply to achieve short-term goals, but to lay the foundation for achieving longer-term goals. Likewise, being "on the edge" can be perceived as provoking fear because of the chance of falling off, or it can be viewed as being in a position to see a new vista.

> *To cultivate an achieving attitude, now "go"*
> *and think multidimensionally.*

Make multidimensional thinking your habitual way of thinking. You already work multidimensionally when you try to leverage your use of time. For instance, when driving a car, you might play a motivational tape or turn on the radio to learn about news events. But when being assigned a task, you probably think linearly: Energies are typically engaged in thinking about what needs to be done to complete the task. Here are some tips for thinking multidimensionally in this situation in order to shape an achieving attitude—where getting the task finished is not your only focus.

- Stop long enough to assess how the task fits in with the company goals and your personal goals.
- Think about how this task could be another opportunity to "practice" keeping your agreements to yourself.
- Think about other skills you could be working on while completing this task. For instance, many people find monthly reports laborious and time-consuming.
- While working on the task using the computer, you can decide to learn some new functions of your software at the same time. You may even find that your report comes out looking better than ever! (Thinking this way helps you build enthusiasm for what you're doing. It's practicing success readiness . . . more about that later.)

> *To cultivate an achieving attitude, "go" and*
> *implement your action plan.*

A lot of us have had training and experience in formulating goals and coming up with action plans. Now that you have learned to incorporate insights into what you can and cannot control, you are better positioned to utilize your energies effectively. Also, when you make a realistic assessment of the situation, you are better informed about potential obstacles. Keeping yourself focused on the desired outcome and operating with personal responsibleness enables you to act on your plans, knowing all the while that you are in control and can look to yourself to keep agreements. Whatever obstacles lie ahead, you can overcome them without getting discouraged—because you have developed the self-discipline needed to examine setbacks and use the knowledge gained to propel you forward.

STEERING OTHERS TOWARD AN ACHIEVING ATTITUDE

From the interviews conducted for this book, I learned that many people are unsure whether they can influence someone else's attitude; they are even more uncertain as to *how* to go about affecting another person's attitude. Although we can never know for sure what another person's attitude is (that's the individual's secret), we can exert influence that may cause someone to change his or her attitude. Ultimately, each individual is in control of making that change. But if people's attitudes were fixed in stone, why would companies and politicians spend millions of dollars each year on advertising? Once we realize that we do have some degree of control over another person's surmised attitude, we can see that trying to "steer" that person is a worthwhile investment of our energy.

Some of the techniques that work for advertisers also apply to dealing with people on a day-to-day basis. When you want to change the surmised attitude of someone you work with, or even a friend, here are six effective approaches to try.

Use Persuasive Communication

Talking about the kind of attitude that you value and the accompanying behaviors gives others a clear idea of what you want. If they understand and accept what you have to say, people respond accordingly. For instance, if a manager talks about Negativists to his staff and explains how they are "energy drainers," most employees can relate to his description. Employees may also laugh or smirk as they concur with the manager. Behind that reaction is their common understanding of who in their group tends to fit the description. Another common reaction is a sigh of relief: Finally someone with authority is acknowledging the existence of this personality type, thereby giving peers permission to pressure one another for being Negativists. The same holds true for Superficial Optimists.

You can steer the people in your organization toward an attitude rooted in realism by suggesting that they look for and anticipate potential problems. It is important for people to know that they can call attention to potential difficulties without being viewed as "troublemakers" or "whiners." At the same time, if you clarify that you also want some solutions for handling the situation, employees typically come through. You may want to go so far as to explain that if they can't resolve the problem, they should mention that too! Then everyone, including the boss, can get involved in resolving the situation.

By asking good questions, you can capture the attention of your colleagues and encourage them to think about the situation and their position. For example, an editor meets with an author, who has become world-renowned since signing a book contract. The editor's dilemma is that the author doesn't want to finish her book; she has a negative attitude about the whole idea. The author tells the editor that at this point in her life, she makes more money in one day as a consultant and educator than she will in the six months that it will take to finish the book and get a final advance from the publisher.

The editor calmly points out to the author that when she first signed the contract, her fame wasn't at the level it is now, then asks, "Not to be offensive, but when you signed on, was money your only motivation? Or as an educator, were you thinking of how to capture your genius for others' benefit?" This thought-provoking question certainly gives the author another perspective on the value of undertaking such a tremendous task as writing a book.

Set an Example

As one manager put it, "Being an example goes a long way." Basic things such as keeping appointments, returning phone calls, and being well-prepared—all givens for a Pro-Achiever—demonstrate the kind of consideration for others that you expect in return. Listen and understand before responding, so you avoid reacting emotionally rather than thoughtfully.

Beyond your everyday behaviors, you can set an example on a larger scale by proposing an objective, developing a plan to reach it, then carrying through. When one CEO took his company public, he began by joining his management team on a retreat, where he explained his vision and what it would take to go public. He told me, "What is reality to one person may not be reality to someone else. But I really believed we could do it. I wasn't wearing rose-colored glasses when I put this plan together. I wasn't discounting the problems. Many thought they were unresolvable, but I think people were looking at the magnitude of the problems. Looking at the problems individually, I believed that we could overcome them. As problems started getting tackled and solved, the skeptics paid attention. They saw things they thought couldn't be done get done, one by one, and within a short time, everyone was on board. The outcome: we accomplished the unbelievable feat of going public in just nine months!"

Give People Tasks and Exercises

When people engage in tasks, the results help change their attitudes directly. Take golf instruction. David Glenz, the nationally respected golf instructor, explains that every golfer is looking for two things: distance and a straight shot. Novice golfers mistakenly believe that strength makes the ball go far, and trying to convince them otherwise is a tough battle. "Rather than challenge their assumption," David says, "I just give them the following task. I ask the student, using the club that he has in his hand, to make an easy half-swing to the target, which is about half the distance we've actually been trying to go. When I take distance out of the equation, the student relaxes. When he swings the club, he actually hits the ball straighter and longer than when he put all his effort into the swing. When the student expresses surprise, I ask him, 'What are you noticing here?' As the student describes what he's doing, I point out to him that the hardest thing to get across to players is this notion that it's not strength that makes the ball go far; rather, it's the motion that counts." With the proof right before them, David's students are quickly convinced.

Display an Enthusiasm That Matches What You Want

Being an effective instructor or leader goes beyond teaching mechanics; it involves changing people's attitudes. People can become discouraged if they don't see quick results. Recognizing this, the instructor or leader can point out incremental improvements and highlight the things that the person does right. The enthusiasm of the instructor or leader can prevent negative attitudes from developing.

David Glenz has observed that adults, unlike children, are insecure about performing in front of other people. "They get embarrassed by what is really a very normal mistake," he said. So David creates situations where the person can "succeed" even though the outcome is not what is ultimately desired. He explains, "When I ask students to do something different in their swing and they implement it, typically the first shot is not good. The students tend to concentrate on what the ball does, so I bring the focus back to their swing, telling them, 'You did just what we were talking about. Let's do it again.'"

At that point David is working primarily on his students' confidence. By getting them to focus more on the motion and continuing to provide encouragement, David prods them to change their attitude about the swing, the instructor, and the game itself. "It helps," said David, "to be aware of my own attitude toward them and to pay attention to my tone of voice. If I get excited about what they have done, they pick up on it." David believes that guiding attitudes is his responsibility; likewise, leaders in business need to make it their responsibility.

Show Respect

One way leaders can take responsibility for influencing the attitudes of the people they work with is to show respect. One executive, who in his long background with GE helped reshape the company, said that managers need to be straight with their people. "They need to be transparent as it relates to people's livelihood and their careers. Managers need to talk frankly with their people and, when necessary, help them direct and channel their energies in areas where they can be of greater value to the organization."

Avoid "Souring" a Person's Attitude

Showing disrespect can easily chip away at someone's healthy, productive attitude. And the disrespect can be subtle. "All that has to happen," says one president of a major company, "is for a manager always to tell employees what to do. Never giving them the big picture and showing them what role they play within an organization can quickly dampen their enthusiasm and tarnish their attitude. When managers do this, they unknowingly send the message that the employees are dumb, and therefore can be dealt with only by being told exactly what to do. College degree or no college degree, rich or not, adults want to be treated with respect."

They also want to be given feedback. No matter where I travel or to whom I speak, I find that people want honest feedback, but their biggest complaint concerns how it is given. Poorly delivered criticism can change forever the criticized person's attitude toward the criticizer. In a recent study, researchers conducted a simulation exercise in which volunteers were given the task of creating an ad for a new shampoo. Another "volunteer" (a confederate) judged the proposed ads. Actually, the volunteers received one of two prearranged criticisms. One set of criticisms was considerate and specific; the other included threats and blamed the person's innate deficiencies, with remarks such as "Didn't even try; can't seem to do anything right," and "Maybe it's a lack of talent; I'd try to get somebody else to do it." The volunteers who were attacked became tense, angry, and antagonistic, saying that they would refuse to collaborate or cooperate on future projects with the person who gave the criticism. Many indicated that they would want to avoid contact altogether. Their attitude toward the person delivering the criticism was changed by the way they were criticized.[16]

By helping others become aware of and change their everyday outlook, you can steer them toward an achieving attitude as their predominant way of seeing themselves. To ensure that your message is getting across, ask people repeatedly about their dual purpose: "Are you performing at a high level? Are you making a difference?"

Operating as a Pro-Achiever doesn't require asking others to be

superachievers or overachievers. It does involve helping them understand that to enhance their value on a project, whether at work or off
the job, they need to be able to look to themselves to set their own
standards and to meet those standards consistently. It's simply a matter of having "the right stuff."

GOING BEYOND ACCOMPLISHING TO ACHIEVE

"Being on the edge" is often associated with another familiar phrase,
"pushing the envelope." For many people, both phrases conjure up
images of taking great risks, as Chuck Yeager did as a test pilot.
Likewise, for many people the expression "going the extra mile" con-
notes putting extraordinary effort into something. But Pro-Achievers
have a different interpretation. To them, "being on the edge" or
"pushing the envelope" means taking on a challenge and stretching
themselves to move closer to their desired outcome. "Going the extra
mile" is merely operating as they normally do—they are always striving to do a little bit better than is expected.

> *The quality of a people's lives is in direct*
> *proportion to their commitment to excellence,*
> *regardless of their chosen field of endeavor.*
> *—Vince Lombardi*

Pro-Achiever is a state of mind. It's an attitudinal makeup that
determines how people approach their world and all the activities
that go on each day. I'm not referring here to a particular behavioral
style that you may have become familiar with through completing
certain surveys or attending training programs. Rather, Pro-Achiever,
like Negativist, Superficial Optimist, and Entitlist, refers to the lens
through which people see their world. Remember, attitude is passive.
Just as a sea captain has a compass for direction and focus, so you
have an attitude set for personal guidance. Like the captain, you are

in control of setting up your attitude so it positions you to get the best possible outcomes from your investment of energy. Pro-Achiever has a two-part meaning. The prefix *pro-* refers to a person who *supports* looking to himself or herself to ensure that the process of reaching an objective continues to move *forward*. The root word *achiever* indicates that the person operates with the dual purpose of performing at exceptional levels and making a valuable difference— that is, he or she *achieves* rather than simply *accomplishes*.

Consider this scene. Deciding that she might need some additional homeowner's insurance, Mary calls a Midwest-based company known for its "reasonable rates." Mary's initial call to the company is routed to the wrong department. The customer service rep, in a polite and pleasant voice, gives Mary another number to call and then hangs up. Did the customer service rep do anything wrong? In her own eyes, no—she did what she always does. She *accomplished* the responsibilities laid out in her job description. But the service rep could have *achieved* by getting Mary's phone number, having the appropriate representative call Mary directly, then finally following up with a call a short while later to make sure that Mary's questions had been answered. By doing all these things, the customer service rep could have made a valuable difference for Mary and the company as well—after all, there are many places Mary can shop around for insurance! The extra effort may have taken a little more time, but the personal satisfaction gained by Mary—and the customer service rep—would have been immeasurable.

Performing a task at a high level, however, doesn't automatically equate with making a valuable difference. For instance, Harry uses a computer and spends an extra six hours after work to put together a report for his boss. Everything is done beautifully, with color graphs and pages typeset to perfection. The question is: Were those six hours well spent to make a valuable difference, even if it was on Harry's own time? A company promotes—above all else—the need for customer service reps to answer the phone by the second ring, as opposed to the third or fourth. Does that practice make a valuable difference for cus-tomers if their questions are not answered well? An employee e-mails *everything* to her boss in an effort to keep him informed. Although the practice is not time-consuming for the employee, does it actually make a valuable difference in helping the boss stay informed? A cus-tomer coming into a store is unfamiliar with where the children's clothing section is located, and a store employee simply points to where the customer needs to go. Is the employee making a valuable difference? The examples are endless, but the important point is that achieving equates to operating with a duality of purpose: performing at a high level, and making a valuable difference.

Accomplishing Is Operating on Automatic Pilot; Achieving Is Consciously Ensuring a Valuable Difference

When someone goes through the motions, that person is function-ing as if on automatic pilot, without thinking about what he or she is doing. For example, an assistant is setting up a meeting for his boss and all the boss's department heads, just as he has done many times over the past few years. In an effort to save money, this particular meeting will not be held off-site, as prior meetings typically were. The assistant goes about his duties to make the arrangements, and reports to his boss that everything is in order. The boss looks over the memo that is to be sent out to announce the meeting, and cannot find where the meeting room is noted. She inquires about the over-sight, and discovers that the assistant forgot to reserve a room. You might say that the assistant made a simple mistake, but from a Pro-Achiever's perspective, the assistant failed to think through what he was doing and instead simply followed his usual routine.

Sometimes our performance is less than optimal because we focus so strongly on getting the task done that we overlook standards of quality, and even the end result. Time pressure is often the culprit.

But upon reflection, most of us will conclude that doing things right the first time actually saves time and effort in the long run. Faced with having to fold a pile of clothes late in the evening after a tiring day, we may rush through the chore. So the task is done, but it has been accomplished and not achieved. Because the clothes were folded poorly, they may be too wrinkled to wear. In this and similar instances, we may work from a to-do list, focusing simply on checking things off the list. Our energies are directed at getting the task done, with little or no consideration as to whether the task is having any effect on others or whether it's making a difference. Our goal is just to get it out of the way!

Accomplishing Is Doing Things Out of Habit; Achieving Is Making a Habit of Realizing a Valuable Difference

At other times, people get caught unknowingly in the rut of accomplishing because they do things by rote or out of habit and pay little attention to the particular situation. An example of this kind of accomplishing is the friendly waitress who always greets the guests at a table with a smile and cheerful chit-chat. Although this approach may be effective most of the time, if the waitress were achieving she would first assess whether her customers are involved in a serious conversation and thus would prefer attentive but quiet service. Another example is the supermarket cashier who rings up each item without even acknowledging the customer's presence until it's time to accept payment. Any customer who needs something else has to wait until the cashier finally looks up. The cashier isn't being rude; he's just accomplishing his job!

> *Accomplishing is going through the motions; operating from a to-do list; and doing things by rote.*

Whether we call it going through the motions, operating from a to-do list, or doing things by rote, all these people are experiencing the same problem: They are completing tasks without necessarily thinking about the effects of what they are doing.

Accomplishing Is Being Right; Achieving Is Being Effective

People also accomplish when they get caught up in "being right." For instance, a teacher has always taught his material in a certain way. When the class he is working with has trouble grasping the material, his students challenge him. Instead of trying a different approach, he gets caught up in insisting to the class that his way is the right way to teach the concepts. An outsider can readily see that the teacher accomplished because he presented the required material, but he failed to achieve because he did not create a meaningful learning experience for his students.

Focusing on being right can cost the business a customer. For five years, my husband and I regularly visited a German restaurant in New Jersey for Sunday dinner. Although the food was average, the soothing atmosphere with an organ player performing throughout the evening was something we enjoyed after an active weekend. One Sunday evening, the dinner I ordered did not taste right, so I decided not to eat it. The waitress did not check in with us right away. When she did stop by, she asked us the standard, "How is everything here?" I told her I couldn't eat the dinner, because I didn't like the taste of it. She replied, "I served 10 people the same dish a little earlier this evening, and nothing was wrong. Would you like me to wrap it up?" I said, "No, I didn't like it and I'm not planning to eat it, so there's no need to wrap it up." When finalizing the bill, the owner, whom we had talked with regularly at the restaurant, came over to us. As I started to tell her about the dinner, she interrupted me. "There's nothing wrong with that entree. But I took it off your bill, so you don't have to concern yourself over it any further." Was I supposed to be happy about not paying for it? Frankly, I would have preferred to pay for it than to be treated with such indifference.

In seminars, I have asked participants to articulate the difference between accomplishing and achieving. Here are a few responses worth noting:

- Accomplishing is "good enough for government work." Achieving is acceptable to your customer's satisfaction.
- Accomplishing is stating and following a policy. Achieving is resolving the issue and having the customer return for repeat business.
- Accomplishing is being right. Achieving is being effective.
- Accomplishing is doing what is asked. Achieving is making a valuable difference.

At work, an employee who has effectively internalized personal responsibleness and operates with an achieving attitude consistently engages in achieving, because he or she "thinks like a customer and acts with the pride of an owner."

ARE PRO-ACHIEVERS PERFECTIONISTS?

Perfectionists set high standards for themselves and won't settle for anything less, regardless of the circumstances. They don't make any distinction among tasks: Their only focus is to do whatever they do perfectly. Since they don't consider the significance of the task, they often squander their energies trying to perform tasks at a high level when doing so can have only a minuscule effect on whether a valuable difference is realized.

Pro-Achievers, on the other hand, are guided by their dual purpose: performing at high levels *and* making a valuable difference. This duality fosters an awareness of how the tasks they engage in correlate to desired outcomes. That awareness keeps them from becoming perfectionists.

When you put together an outline for your own personal use in preparing for an upcoming presentation, does it matter if the outline has typos and grammatical errors? Watering plants, addressing envelopes, brushing your teeth, dusting, making the bed—these everyday tasks and hundreds more like them don't always have to be carried to the point of perfection.

When Pro-Achievers turn in a handwritten budget report or work from an outline that has grammatical errors and typos, they haven't set low standards for themselves or lost motivation. Paying attention to how best to leverage their energies entails stopping long enough to assess whether the task at hand needs to be completed perfectly in order for a valuable difference to be realized, or whether a valuable difference can be achieved without the necessity of completing the task perfectly. By focusing on the impact of the task (i.e., its contribution to making a valuable difference), Pro-Achievers can establish the performance expectation level necessary and adjust their motivational level accordingly. Pro-Achievers can be flexible and perform tasks at varying levels because they understand control. They are not concerned that they will form lazy habits as a result of lowering their personal performance standards in certain situations.

> *Success isn't what's passable; it's what's possible.*

As one executive remarked about the Pro-Achiever's approach, "You don't just try to get through the day. You get up thinking, 'what can I achieve today?'" Perhaps you approach your day much the same way.[17]

Achieving involves looking for ways to do certain things a little bit better than expected—consistently. Because expectations are changing continuously, whether among bosses, coworkers, customers, friends, family members, or mates, the Pro-Achiever must make an intentional effort to seek out different ways of doing things, to produce results that slightly exceed expectations.

> *Being uncomfortable is a good sign. It indicates that you're pushing yourself to the edge.*

Joining the "fellowship of doers" and becoming a Pro-Achiever does not require a college degree, a lot of money, or a top position. Anyone can do it. To start, you must develop an understanding of control and accept personal responsibleness. When an achieving attitude begins to emerge, you take charge of your own attitudes toward others, your work, and your life. But thinking and knowing are not enough; you need to take action. Taking action requires you to be equipped with skills for staying on track and keeping the ball moving forward. Those skills are introduced in the following chapters.

Here's how you can take control immediately.

1. **STOP** a lousy mood by taking action.
   - Break the task you are working on into smaller parts so you can realize a sense of progress as each part is successfully completed.
   - Do something you enjoy.
   - Think about something pleasant.
   - Talk yourself out of a downswing.

2. **STOP** and ask yourself if you are coming to work with an achieving attitude before the day begins. If not, take control and change your attitude.

3. **STOP** before labeling someone as having a particular attitude, and remember that you can only surmise what another person's attitude is.

4. **STOP** and remind yourself, when others say you can't change someone's attitude, that technically they're accurate. The other person is ultimately the one who changes his or her attitude —but you can certainly have an effect on a person's attitude.

5. **STOP** and think, before starting the next chapter, of one thing that you are currently doing that you could do differently or a little bit better in an effort to achieve.

1. **START** being positive to influence other people's attitudes positively:

   • Clarify the kind of attitude set you admire in others and would prefer that they adopt.

   • Compliment people when they demonstrate an achieving attitude.

   • Team individuals up with others who exemplify the attitude set you admire.

EIGHT STEPS TO TAKE CHARGE OF YOUR LIFE

5

LISTEN FOR WHAT'S NOT SAID

MOVING INTO ACTION: SKILLS FOR THE PRO-ACHIEVER

Tom Walker has been a manager for 15 years at an insurance company that, like many others in the industry, has gone through tremendous changes recently. Among those changes is the company's style of management. Although Tom uses the popular jargon of the new management style, his actions still reflect an old style of management that is autocratic and directive. He is quick to tell people what they are supposed to do, and reluctant to ask for their opinions or to involve them in the daily running of the department. Instead of empowering others, Tom takes on many of the tasks that his people are trained to do, simply because they are things that he has always done.

Recognizing the problem, Tom's boss, Anita, encouraged him to attend an advanced management training program that addressed some of these issues. When Tom returned, Anita met with him to find out what he had learned and what he was planning on doing differently. His response

(Continued)

was, "It's the same old stuff. The instructor was very motivating, but she didn't introduce anything I didn't already know." Tom's reaction to the class surprised and disappointed Anita. She thought to herself, "He's missing the whole point. It's not what you know that gives you the competitive edge and defines your value to the organization; it's how well you can translate your knowledge into action."

Anita's unspoken expectation was that Tom should be working to align his managerial style with the company's new direction and to improve his effectiveness. But Tom missed Anita's message by concluding that the instructor reviewed material he had heard before. Anita's disappointment resulted because, even though she assumed Tom was familiar with the management/leadership tools, she was looking for him to return with new ideas about how to use them. Unless Tom accurately picks up on Anita's message that he needs to start making changes, his job may be in jeopardy.

An essential ingredient in any relationship is understanding the other person's expectations. That step sounds obvious and simple. The only trouble is that not all expectations are articulated, which brings us to the first listening skill for Pro-Achievers—identifying and clarifying unspoken expectations. When expectations are not clearly articulated, relationships are strained because a tremendous amount of energy goes into trying to figure out what the other person wants and how best to work with that person. By learning to listen for more than just the words, you begin to pick up on what's *not* said. When you clarify unspokens, you understand where the other person is coming from and are better positioned to establish expectations that are shared and mutually agreed upon.

WHAT ARE UNSPOKEN EXPECTATIONS?

Meet Lauren Silver, who works as a technician for a telecommunications company that has been undergoing re-engineering efforts. During a divisionwide meeting, the senior manager personally encouraged everyone to come up with ideas for improving the way things operate. Lauren was inspired by what the senior manager said, and because she wanted to go places within the company, she decided to take him up on his offer. She arranged a meeting with him and presented her idea. Much to her surprise, the manager responded by firing one question after another at her. As things started to wind down, Lauren admitted that perhaps the idea she had presented wasn't such a good one after all. She gathered her things and left, thinking on the way out, "So much for him wanting ideas. If he had liked my idea he wouldn't have pounced on me that way."

In my workshops, many participants draw the same conclusion Lauren did. But perhaps the senior manager was trying to send a different message—one that Lauren (and many audiences) missed. Deciphering the message behind someone's behavior is part of learning to pick up on unspoken expectations.

Actually, the senior manager fired a lot of questions at Lauren because he wanted to find out whether she had thought out her idea thoroughly. Also, he knew from experience that if an idea is to become a reality, the person introducing the idea has to have a lot of conviction and stamina in order to overcome the hassles, roadblocks, and disappointments. So his questioning was also intended to discover if Lauren had the level of conviction that was required. Unfortunately, Lauren not only missed the unspokens but also misinterpreted the senior executive's actions to mean that he didn't like her idea. She also concluded, as do many people who have been in similar situations, that the senior executive really wasn't interested in receiving any new ideas. Since Lauren misread the senior executive's unspoken messages, she ended up abandoning what could have been a good idea—and possibly an opportunity to advance her career.

We all anticipate that the people we interact with will behave in a certain way. Some of our expectations are spoken because they are clearly communicated to others, either orally or in writing. When expectations are spoken, you know how best to use your energies. After all, you know "what's expected of you." It seems simple at a first glance, but it gets more complicated, because there are many expectations that remain unspoken. Despite the fact that nothing is communicated orally or in writing, these expectations still operate. They are the unspokens, sometimes referred to as "implicit messages" or "unwritten rules."

Unspoken Expectations at Work

Looking at the workplace, we can see that companies have their own cultures, which house certain "official unspokens." As one human resources executive put it, "They are official in the sense that the operative unspokens comprise the legitimate hurdles that everyone needs to adhere to, whether you are talking about the 'culture,' or norms that exist from one state to another, or from one company to another." Here are a few examples you may relate to.

How long should employees work?

Even though regular hours of employment are usually written into the company's policy manual, employees need to read the signals from upper management and those around them to determine the hours they are actually expected to work. For instance, if a manager comes in at 7 a.m. each day and leaves at 7 p.m., does that mean that all the people below her should do the same? Sometimes employees misread these signals and think yes, when in fact that's not what the manager expects. And the confusion doesn't stop there: What about an employee's dress?

How should employees dress?

Does it matter? Office attire is another subject that is not always included in the policy manual; even though nothing is said, patterns of acceptable dress emerge. For instance, in many companies, nothing in the policy manual prohibits women from wearing slacks or pant suits, yet women who want to advance within the company "know" that they should always wear skirts. Recently, many companies have introduced a weekly "dress-down day." Have you noticed that everyone interprets "casual" differently? Generally, the unspoken expectation regarding how casually employees can dress remains vague for some time.

Talking to people at different geographic locations

When you are dealing with a company whose employees are scattered across many states, you need to be especially sensitive. As one executive explained, certain employees in a southern company prefer to be addressed as Mr. So-and-so, while in the midwestern headquarters business is conducted on a first-name basis.

Going to a job interview

A job interview is a situation in which the things that aren't said can be more important that the things that are. As soon as the candidates walk into the room, they are being watched. The way they make an entrance, their handshakes, the way they sit, the enthusiasm in their voices, and whether or not they ask questions all serve as signals to the interviewer, who has the task of evaluating each candidate on the basis of a fairly brief encounter. Likewise, the savvy candidate watches the interviewer for clues to the criteria that the company uses in the selection process. Both interviewer and candidate are trying to play the role of interpreter—to translate the other person's nonverbal communications into his or her unspoken expectations.

Complimenting an employee's work

Let's explore for a moment the relationship between a boss and an employee. When the boss compliments an employee's work and raves about the job he or she has done, a common unspoken expectation in the employee's mind is that a raise or a promotion will be forthcoming. Another common unspoken among employees is that the boss will never criticize them in front of peers or customers. Just as employees have lots of unspokens, so do bosses. For example, bosses may like to be kept informed of things without having to ask. They may want an employee to think about solutions before bringing problems to their attention. A boss may also have unspokens about how employees should express their disagreement.

When should you disagree with the boss's decision?

One big unspoken that upsets many bosses is employees' failure to pick up on when it is time to "play ball." A senior executive from the insurance industry complained to me about the reaction of his management team when he announced that the company would be restructuring from functioning units to strategic business units, or SBUs. A few managers questioned the decision, and even went so far as to express doubts about proceeding. The senior executive was frustrated by his managers' lack of understanding that once the decision was made, they were expected to run with the decision and make things work. This was not the proper time for people to sit around and discuss whether they agreed or disagreed with the decision—it was time to put the plan into action. Once the game was under way, the executive maintained, his managers and their employees could sit back and question how things were unfolding.

How do you determine if you are not part of the "in" group?

For the many employees who are now working on teams, identifying the large number of unspokens that are operating is ever more essential. Even though team leaders express the need for everyone to work well together, a key set of unspokens center on whether a team member is in the "in" group or the "out" group. Some are:

- The "out" person's view is ignored at meetings, or when the person starts to speak, others sigh or roll their eyes.
- The "out" person doesn't get invited to lunch or social get-togethers.
- The "out" person isn't asked the challenging questions or assigned the exciting projects.
- The "out" person is the last to know about new developments.

Keep in mind that when unspokens flourish, no one is saying anything directly to anyone else. These implicit messages indicate that something is out of kilter in the relationships among team players. Only by clarifying the unspokens can the "out" person take steps to join the "in" group.

Unspokens at Home

Unspokens occur just as frequently with family members at home and in other social settings. In other words, in relationships of two or more people, unspokens will always exist. At home, some commonly occurring unspokens center on knowing how best to be supportive of another, or how best to approach the other person about bothersome things without causing offense. Children pay attention to unspokens when they try to figure out who best to ask, and when, in order to get what they want. We even send unspoken signals to each other to indicate our moods.

"Picking up on what's not said" and "reading between the lines" are other ways of trying to identify unspoken expectations. Relationships are based on communication. Although we generally think of communication as verbal—spoken or written words—people send messages in many more subtle ways. We recognize some of these signals intuitively, but interpreting the expectation behind them requires effort, skill, and practice. When your teenage daughter comes home from school, throws down her knapsack of books, and then goes straight to her room, slamming the door behind her, obviously she's upset. But does she expect to be comforted or to be left alone? Your ability to understand her unspoken expectations is a key to your effectiveness as a parent. The same holds true in the workplace.

MAKE UNSPOKENS SPOKEN—AND STAY ON THE EDGE

Of the two kinds of expectations—spoken and unspoken—which is more powerful? You guessed it—the unspoken. Those who pick up on unspoken expectations and have them clarified or turned into spoken expectations, are working with more accurate information than those who overlook them. It has been said that information is power. If so, those of us who are paying attention to unspokens have more information to work with, and thus more power. Here's how one senior manager described it:

> The person with the greatest amount of information has got
> the control. Reading between the lines and picking up on

what's not said gives you a broad view of the entire playing field and all the variables. It puts you in the pivotal position to see clearly what you are working with, and to determine a strategy for taking control.

Clearly, unspokens can help identify the key factors that are used to achieve desired outcomes in many situations.

When unspokens are spotted and clarified, the "air has been cleared" and we have a good idea of how to interpret what's going on around us. Energies can be directed positively, since there's no need to play guessing games to uncover what the other person really wants. On the other hand, when unspokens are left unclear, the situation can be likened to playing a game of chess: We see the other person's moves, but we never know what she is thinking at the moment or planning to do next.

Undoubtedly, you can recall experiences where you have had to deal with unspokens and the accompanying uneasy feelings. For example, you ask your mate about going out for dinner. The game begins when your mate replies, "I don't care; let's do whatever you want." How do you know the game has started? Because when you think about past experiences, you know that it does matter, and playing the game involves accurately guessing what the other person really wants. If you guess incorrectly, you face some type of retaliation or disappointment on the other person's part. So you continue to probe, in an effort to find some clues as to what your mate really wants to do. Playing this game can consume a lot of time and energy, and can result in a lot of hurt feelings—especially if you fail to guess correctly!

This same investment of energy is needed to feel your way around at work when a lot of unspokens are operating. When your boss gives you little or no feedback as to how you are performing at work, you come home some nights worrying about whether you are doing a good job. When you have a meeting with someone who is difficult to read (perhaps a potential customer or a peer), uneasiness sets in because you are given very little insight into what that person is thinking. So you start to worry about how you and your ideas are coming across. Much of your energy is spent guessing where this other person is coming from.

> *Paying attention to unspokens builds strong relationships and helps get things done.*

Paying attention to unspokens leads to a better understanding between individuals, thereby facilitating the development of matched expectations between people and among team members. When expectations are mutually understood and upheld, the intangible ingredients that nurture strong relationships are given a chance to develop. Those intangibles include mutual trust, respect, and credibility.

Besides building stronger relationships, mutually understood expectations help things get done more quickly and at a higher level of quality, because people have a clearer idea of what is being asked of them. Often, workers have to redo things because they think that knowing "what to do" is the same as knowing "the desired end result." People discuss what is to be done—but only after investing time and energy into answering the "what" do they realize that their efforts will not produce the end result that the person who conceived the idea had in mind. In this situation, as in many others, when unspokens are made spoken, more accurate information becomes available to everyone involved and expectations take shape concerning the tasks to be done and the best way to work together.

GETTING OFF TRACK: MISSING UNSPOKEN EXPECTATIONS

Sometimes we miss or misinterpret unspokens, and when we do, the chances are great that we will get off track and draw faulty conclusions. Let's look at an example of the difference that picking up on unspokens can make.

At an entrepreneurial company in Dallas, Marcy and several peers all report to Ted. As in most entrepreneurial firms, everyone is running around performing multiple tasks simultaneously. Ted is an analytical type who looks calm on the outside, but is anything but calm on the inside! Marcy's peers, who happen to be men, are befuddled and frustrated because Marcy can get Ted's approval in areas where they can't. In conversations they have speculated that it's because she's a woman, or perhaps because she won't stand her ground on issues. Neither guess is accurate.

If you were to compare the way Marcy approaches Ted about problems with the way her peers approach him, you would see important differences. When her peers propose an idea that Ted resists, they are fast to argue with him. Marcy, on the other hand, listens to his objections, probes for more, and then drops the discussion. After a few days have passed, Marcy gets back in touch with Ted and opens the conversation by saying that she has thought about what he said. After reviewing some of Ted's concerns, Marcy proceeds to explain her ideas. Ted follows Marcy's logic, and before you know it, she has his approval. Marcy has recognized Ted's unspoken expectations, which are that his staff should think through ideas before acting, should not react emotionally, and should at least consider what he has to say. Marcy is able to get Ted to buy into her ideas because she has matched her approach to his unspoken expectations. Her peers fall short because they keep missing these messages. When Marcy's peers immediately argue with Ted, they aren't thinking about what he has to say; instead, they are reacting emotionally, and that's a turn-off for Ted. Missing or misinterpreting unspokens has created a lot of unnecessary frustration for Marcy's peers and for Ted.

"The unspoken signal that is easily misunderstood," says psychologist and author Dr. Gwendolyn Goldsby Grant, "is the signal for attention." This problem is as common at home as it is in the workplace. For example, like many men Dr. Grant has helped, Dave comes home grumpy and irritable. No matter what his wife, Carol, does—or doesn't do—it isn't enough. "When placed in a 'damned if you do, damned if you don't' situation, it's easy to want to stand your ground, defend yourself, and get tough." That's what Carol would do; then she and Dave would find themselves fighting each other and not talking for the rest of the evening. Dr. Grant explains, "Rather than fight, that's the time for Carol to put her arms around her husband, give him an adoring look, and say loving things. While it might not be what Carol feels like doing, it's what's needed at the moment."

HOW TO PICK UP ON UNSPOKEN EXPECTATIONS

When interacting with others, you always want to ensure that expectations are clear, so you need to get in the habit of picking up on unspokens and clarifying them. Establishing clear expectations helps put you in the pivotal position of control.

Picking up on unspokens gives you a broader understanding of what is really going on in certain situations. When working with accurate and complete information, you are much better positioned to influence others to achieve desired outcomes. So the "how to" begins with listening on another level for the broader perspective while at the same time listening for what's not said in a conversation. To increase your awareness in this area, keep an open mind and listen with the intent of trying to truly understand what the other person is saying, rather than listening with the intent of judging the other person and his or her ideas. With these insights in mind, let's review a number of effective ways to develop the skill of picking up on unspokens.

Don't just listen; look *for unspokens.*

Observing Your Environment

It's important to get in the habit of observing what is going on at the same time that you are listening to what's being said. This multidimensional approach involves scanning the bigger picture while you focus in on the immediate situation. Rick, a middle manager in the environmental industry, used this technique to get his peers to buy into his ideas. He has observed that when he and his peers get together at a meeting, people are quick to express their own ideas and to argue over them. Eventually, energy levels drop, and that's when Rick jumps in and introduces his idea. At that point, he can appeal to each person in the room because he knows that person's issues, and he can show logically how the idea he is presenting will benefit everyone. If the idea has merit, Rick's peers will agree with him.

In your own work setting, watch how successful people operate at meetings with top management and with the boss. By paying attention to how successful employees present ideas, deal with decisions they don't agree with, or introduce problems, you can pick up some valuable clues about the most effective tactics. While you're at it, watch how those who are not "star performers" handle themselves for hints on how *not* to act. Here's a simple example that came out of a conversation with the president of a successful Midwest-based construction company during an interview for this book. The president told me that his two top performers always ask questions when he is covering a lot of territory during their meetings. He interprets their questions as something positive. He can't understand why his average-performing managers *don't* ask any questions when he is hitting on so many subject areas; their silence makes him question whether they are really paying attention.

Observing people's moods when you need to request something helps give you clues about timing. If what you are requesting is not urgent, you can wait for a congenial situation. For example, an accountant calls one of his clients about an unpaid bill. The company owner seems distraught; she talks about how slow the market is and how she is considering filing for Chapter 11 bankruptcy. So the accountant decides not to bring up the matter of his bill until a later time.

When a matter requires immediate attention, approaching others with the issue of timing in mind may result in a more positive response, because you have considered other people and what they are experiencing. For instance, you may handle a pressing matter by saying, "I know it's bad timing to address this now, but the matter is urgent." The key is to acknowledge the individual and show sensitivity to the timing.

Listening to Word Choices

Listening carefully to word choices is another effective way to pick up on unspokens. Many of the words exchanged between individuals and in groups are unclear. For example, when bosses or customers say, "We have to do this project crisply" or "We need to get our arms around this problem," what exactly do those expressions mean? When your boss or team leader urges, "We need to be committed team players," what is being said?

> *Don't just listen to what's being said. Pay particular attention to the choice of words.*

I have asked hundreds of workshop participants what it means to be "a committed team player," and you'd be surprised how many different interpretations I've received. The various interpretations create different expectations. Many people interpret being a committed team player to mean that they need to get along well with others. Other workshop attendees say that it means doing whatever you have to do to get the job done. Still others think it means focusing on the achievement of a particular goal, and the only thing that can vary is the means for getting there. Who is right?

Right or wrong is not the point here. I am simply demonstrating that commonly used words often are not clearly understood by everyone hearing the message. An employee who is told during a performance review that she is "too aggressive," "too perfect," or "not a good team player" likely does not understand what is meant, because these words are loaded with unspoken implications. The same confusion can occur at home when your mate says that you are "not supportive" or "can't relax." These words don't clearly convey what the person really means. Interestingly, some of us are reluctant to take the next step and ask for clarification—for fear of the unspoken expectation that, at this point in the relationship, we should know what is meant. Therefore, having to ask for clarification could be seen as a sign that we are weak or haven't been paying attention.

When you seek control, you go beyond those concerns because you are interested in working with good information. Since you realize that it doesn't take much to get off track if you reach a wrong conclusion, your personal responsibleness compels you to take it upon yourself to get the important things clarified. In other words, as a Pro-Achiever, you take the lead to make unspoken expectations spoken.

Asking Questions

Perhaps the most efficient and effective way to take unspoken expectations and make them spoken is to ask questions. Let's go back to Lauren Silver's awkward situation with the senior manager. While being barraged with questions, Lauren could have interjected a question of her own to clarify the situation. She could have said, "I'm not sure what you are after. How should I interpret all these questions?"

If she had asked that question, chances are good that the senior manager would have explained where he was coming from.

> *Sometimes the best way to find something out is just to ask.*

Let's say your boss, in a casual conversation after meeting with a customer, tells you that he wants you to write the proposal for this customer "with a lot of energy." Rather than simply dismiss your boss's words, go back and ask what he means. Phrasing the question so it has value to the other person is always an effective way to approach others. For instance, you could bring up the subject by saying, "Rather than assume I understand what you've just said and turn in something that isn't what you had in mind, I need you to explain what you mean by writing the proposal 'with energy.'" The key is taking personal responsibleness for ensuring that expectations are made clear. To do so effectively, remember that it's not only what you say that counts, but also how you say it. By factoring in *what* and *how*, you can make a valuable difference.

Some frequently overlooked but important unspokens concern how best to work together. Interestingly, many of the bosses I have had contact with are receptive and respond favorably to employees who open up conversations about this topic, especially when relationships are new. For instance, today's technology provides a variety of ways to communicate, so you should not assume there is one best way to keep a boss up to date. Some bosses prefer e-mail, others prefer voice mail, and still others prefer face-to-face conversations. What your boss wants to be informed about is another unspoken that can be clarified by asking questions. Does your boss want to hear only good news? What kind of problems does your boss need to know about? Also, most bosses want you to keep them informed voluntarily—another unspoken that is often missed. During "neutral times," explore with your boss how best to handle disagreements.

You may also want to touch on how you can best deal with things that are annoying or bothersome to you or your boss. If you don't address these relationship-building questions up front, you will be navigating your relationship blindly, and a lot of your time and energy will be spent guessing. Guessing incorrectly could have grave repercussions for your career, since it's usually your errors that unmask the unspokens operating in a situation!

Sometimes, unspokens are revealed when people reach the point of total frustration and finally decide to say something. For instance, Doreen approaches her boss, Bill, about the fact that she can't handle all the pressures from work. After their discussion, Doreen walks out of the meeting realizing that Bill doesn't expect her to get everything done every day. Also, if she is feeling overwhelmed and unsure about which project to focus on first, he wants her to come to him for help prioritizing tasks. Doreen and Bill had never talked about these things before; for more than 8 months, Doreen assumed that Bill expected her to do it all. Only by having such an "open discussion" are the unspokens made clear.

As important as asking questions is in the workplace, it may be even more so on the home front. Why? Because we tend to think we can "let love conquer all," or we put things on hold because "we have a lifetime together." With the unspoken expectation that everything will work out over time, we often rely more on trial-and-error methods than we do on talking openly about how to get along.

A good example is the desire to be more supportive of a mate. Barbara and Larry have been married for a little over a year. This is the second marriage for both, and they are committed to making their relationship work. As professionals in similar fields, they both put in long days at work, but Barbara's position requires more travel than Larry's. After they have been apart for a few days, they greet each other with warm hugs and kisses. As they update each other about what happened while they were apart, they find themselves arguing about things that Larry did or didn't do. Barbara thought that to support her husband, she should advise him as she advises her paying clients all day. She thought her free advice was a "perk" she could offer Larry! The only trouble was, Larry wasn't interested. After many arguments and ruined evenings, Barbara finally decided to ask Larry how she could support him in his work. Only then did she realize that she had missed an unspoken: Much to her surprise, what Larry wanted more than anything was for Barbara to listen. He didn't want her to tell him anything about what he could have or should have done; he just wanted her to listen.

Another unspoken that can add a lot of stress in relationships is how best to criticize each other. This essential aspect of communications is commonly ignored. For married couples to explore so negative a subject may seem unnecessary, since love forms the foundation of their relationship, but loving each other is not a substitute for communicating effectively. Taking personal responsibleness and asking how the other person prefers to be approached often leads to a revealing conversation. Couples who have been married for years assume that they know how best to approach each other, but often partners find out how certain things they do can fuel a meaningful conversation and others can stop one in its tracks.

Seeking Out Information from Those in the Know

Closely related to asking questions as a way of making unspoken expectations spoken is seeking out information from those in the know. In any situation, there are certain people who seem to be catching on or who are making a difference. For instance, someone gets approval to do certain things when others don't. A salesperson is making lots of sales when everyone else is complaining about slow market conditions. A coach relates well with all the children on her team when another coach doesn't. Seeking out top performers can be very helpful in uncovering the clues you need to better understand the playing field and the players.

You probably recognize the value of seeking out help from those in the know before you meet a key player for the first time. People who have worked well with this person in the past can supply insights that enable you to go into your meeting with a clearer understanding of how best to relate to the new person.

You may be wondering where behavioral styles and the profiling of individuals fit in. These profiles help uncover a number of unspokens that are important when establishing relationships. Because they are based on norms, the profiles give you a quick picture of people that includes predictions of how they will behave. Using such instruments to determine a person's behavioral style (and your own as well) helps you feel more in control in your interactions, because you know more about how the other person is likely to behave.

Although these behavioral tools are helpful, categorizing or labeling people can be perilous, especially in the light of diverse cultural backgrounds and individual uniqueness. These tools merely provide you with a backdrop. Likewise, asking others in the know can give you added insights. But in the end, getting quality information directly from the person involved is the preferred approach.

Taking Low Risks

Another good way to check out unspokens is by taking low risks. We've all heard that sometimes it's easier to say you're sorry than it is to get permission. This approach is what we are considering here, especially when focusing on work-related issues. The challenge is knowing where and how to take those risks. A guideline for the workplace is: When taking a risk, be certain that your actions meet customer needs while remaining consistent with the goals and objectives of the company.

> *Sometimes it's worth taking a small risk to overcome an unspoken.*

Taking low risks can be used to check out how things really operate in a new job. Ken, an experienced manager, is aware that when you are in a new position, the unspoken expectation is that for a period of time, you can ask "dumb" questions and make some mistakes—it's your honeymoon period. Ken recently accepted a marketing position for a telecommunications company in Dallas. When he started the job, Ken heard through the company grapevine that his new boss was a real "micro manager": He wanted to be kept informed about everything going on in the department and wanted to oversee all decisions. Since this information was a complete contradiction of everything the new boss had said during their interviews, Ken decided to check things out during the honeymoon period by ordering a couple of inexpensive chairs for his office. He submitting all the proper paperwork, but skipped passing the idea directly to his boss for approval—a step that supposedly wasn't necessary. Within two weeks, Ken's boss had learned of the purchase and called Ken on the phone to ask why he hadn't gotten the boss's approval. Ken knew right then and there that the rumor mill was accurate: His boss was indeed a micro manager and all previous bets that Ken would "run the show" were off. Ken learned this lesson by taking a relatively minor risk.

By testing out certain unspokens, as Tony and Ken did, you can gain a much clearer understanding of what the playing field looks like and how best to maneuver around on it. This kind of information helps provide the realistic view you seek as a Pro-Achiever and also helps you recognize what you need to do to take control. If Anne's boss coaches her to understand the nuances of how unspokens operate, she too will have a much better idea of how she can take control when interacting with customers.

Here's how you can take control immediately.

1. **STOP** and assess your relationships with the people close to you at work and at home, and determine where things are unclear. When a lot of unspokens are operating in a relationship, energies are misused, progress is slowed down, and an atmosphere of uncertainty is fostered. Remember, unspoken expectations exist in all relationships, both at work and at home. No one is exempt from the need to be sensitive to them.

2. **STOP** and listen for unspokens during everyday communications. Rather than think of unspokens as something good or bad, accept that they are an integral part of all relationships and they need to be dealt with, not ignored.

START

1. **START** listening for word choices made by others. Be sure to ask questions in order to gain clarification.

2. **START** addressing unspokens immediately. If others are aware that you are reading this book, the following unspokens exist: What new skills are you learning? Are you going to practice them on others? Practice by first addressing both of these unspokens with your peers and staff before approaching your boss.

3. **START** using your newly acquired information to strategize future moves. Once you have picked up on and clarified unspokens, you will want to reexamine your strategy for moving forward. This reassessment is

essential, because achievement always requires trying to figure out what key factors you need to be working with in order to enhance your chances of reaching desired outcomes.

The building of matched expectations requires the incorporation of unspokens. As the next chapter explains, when all parties have a clear understanding of what they are to do and how they are going to work together—when these expectations are matched and shared—energies are directed in productive ways. Stress levels are reduced, relationships are strengthened, and desired outcomes are achieved.

6

GET ON THE SAME PAGE
GET IN TUNE WITH OTHERS

While at work, you get a call from your mate. The call isn't unusual, but what you are hearing is: Your mate has just been offered a new position—in Florida. Immediately, your mind races as you reply, "You know I hate humidity, and Florida is nothing but humidity." Your mate responds by saying, "But sweetheart, this is such a great opportunity. I don't want to turn this one down. Let's talk about it later." Suddenly, you hear yourself saying OK and hanging up the phone.

Your day isn't over yet. Several days ago, you asked a peer in the sales department to give you some sales projections on a couple of products, and he has failed to get back to you. You're really feeling pressured, because these numbers are to be incorporated into a larger budget report. He explains that he's almost finished, and by late afternoon he'll have everything ready. You say fine, but you think to yourself that his lateness is going to put you under the gun, because you really like to proof things carefully before sending them on to your boss. Afternoon arrives, and he hands you the sales projections. After glancing at the figures, you notice that he gave you projections for one, two, and three years in advance. You feel a tinge of anger run down your spine as you explain that all you needed were figures for a single year in advance. Besides saying he's sorry, he tells you, "I thought you would have wanted to see some more figures. One year seemed like so little to work with, and I thought that more numbers would be helpful. If I had known, I could have gotten this to you a lot sooner."

When you recover from that incident, you decide to check your e-mail messages. To your surprise, you get a short note from your boss with an attachment. You go to the attachment, only to find out that one of your customers contacted your boss directly about a matter that you were in the process of handling. Once again, you feel your stress level rising as you ask yourself, "How could my customer bypass me and go to my boss without telling me?"

What do these three snapshot scenes have in common? On the surface, what's going on appears to be a communications problem. If we look more deeply, though, it becomes apparent that the expectations of the parties involved in all three situations are unmatched. Unmatched expectations span the spectrum from simple, everyday exchanges to more persistent or extensive matters. We all have expectations for ourselves and for others; expectations exist in our relationships at work as well as in our relationships with family and friends. Strong relationships are always rooted in matched expectations.

Big or small, important or insignificant, whenever expectations are unmatched, frustration levels rise and desired outcomes are put at risk. Being able to "go" forward is difficult. So what's needed first is to listen for and pay attention to expectations that are unmatched and unmet.

As noted previously, even though you cannot have total control, you can influence what happens around you. In this chapter, you'll learn how to listen for unmatched expectations, and you'll come to understand the four steps involved in turning them into matched expectations packages. When building matched expectations with others, you are operating with a true sense of control and are doing what you can to move a situation forward. So in this chapter, you'll learn how to stop thinking that the problem is simply communications, and will instead go one step further to sort out where expectations are unmatched.

THE MATCHED EXPECTATIONS PACKAGE

A matched expectations package is exactly what it sounds like: a set of expectations that is discussed and mutually agreed upon by two or more adults. Building a matched expectations package involves engaging in an open exchange for the purpose of establishing a mutual understanding. Thus, the matched expectations package is a negotiated agreement as opposed to a one-way exchange in which one person does all the explaining about expectations. By engaging in a meaningful exchange, each party gets to know what the others want and need in an effort to build a relationship. We commonly engage in an exchange of expectations about how to work together when interviewing for a job or when starting to date someone. Everything is new and we realize that each party needs to get to know the other and to clarify what each one is to do. We also work to establish matched expectations during everyday communications, whether at work or at home. In this chapter, let's focus primarily on relationships between two people, whether spouses, friends, or co-workers.

> *Creating a set of matched expectations in any relationship involves clarifying expectations in four key areas: (1) goals; (2) work tasks and roles; (3) work quality; and (4) working relationships.*

Goals

In today's fast-moving, multitasked environment, it's easy to let assumptions and instinct take the place of clarifying and mutually agreeing on goals. Surprisingly, when team members are asked about the goals of their team or the goal of a particular project, many don't know. When they are then asked why they don't try to find out, almost all reply that they are too embarrassed to ask because it is assumed that "everybody knows" and asking might be perceived as a sign of incompetence. In other words, no one wants to turn an unspoken into a spoken or explicit expectation for fear of looking dumb—and yet everyone is investing energy into achieving a particular result that may or may not match the goal.

Work Tasks and Roles

The expectations that surround work tasks and roles get a lot of attention in the workplace. Managers and employees alike have job descriptions and lists of job responsibilities. Still, confusion about work tasks can easily set in when you operate in a fast-paced business environment, where today's high priority becomes tomorrow's scrapped effort. In all spheres of your life, gaining a sense of control requires making sure that expectations are clarified and matched—now more than ever!

Work Quality

Companies have invested millions of dollars to clarify quality-of-work requirements. But even with formalized standards, we still deal on a day-by-day basis with issues revolving around how certain tasks were not performed at the level of quality expected.

Working Relationships

In contrast to the attention paid to work quality, the area of working relationships—or how to interact with each other—has been largely ignored, as if instinct and assumptions are sufficient to get us by. In any group setting but especially at work, you may hear someone labeled as a "people person." The people person is presumed to have some special means of picking up on the wants and needs of others, and even knowing what's best for them.

There's no denying that some people seem to have a knack for being sensitive to others and building a rapport, but that talent doesn't eliminate the need to engage in two-way exchanges of expectations. By the time people reach adulthood, they have amassed a wealth of experiences, from which they have developed preferences regarding common interactions—how they want to be approached when they've made a mistake, how they can best be motivated, and so on. Adults like having a chance to express their preferences and to engage in a meaningful exchange about how best to work together.

Working from "assumptions" is a one-way street, and even a people person can assume things incorrectly. Although the incorrect assumptions may not lead to a disaster, they may detract subtly from the construction of a strong working relationship, or the kind of team spirit that fosters exceptional performance.

BENEFITS OF WORKING WITH MATCHED EXPECTATIONS

Why invest your energies to establish matched expectations? Here are a few of the benefits.

It sets the stage for exceptional performance

In order to achieve, you need to take control and define where "the bar" is set. By knowing clearly what is expected in a given situation, you can lay a foundation from which to start building your strategy for meeting and perhaps exceeding expectations.

It establishes realistic and workable expectations

By stopping long enough, you can align your best intentions with what you can realistically deliver. Then by matching what is being asked of you with what you can deliver, you are better positioned to move forward with realistic deadlines.

It helps leverage energy use

Investing the energies up front to establish matched expectations packages allows you to take control: You are helping shape what is going on around you and ensuring that both parties have a clear idea of what they are to do and how they are going to work together.

When expectations are unclear and unmatched from the onset, a lot of guessing occurs. You operate in a vacuum because you just don't know. If a mistake occurs that leads to a blow-up, only then do you and the other person begin to disclose your misunderstandings and clear the air. All this can be avoided by building the expectations package up front.

It fosters relationships rooted in trust, respect, and credibility

The investment of energy to clarify expectations should be ongoing, so that your expectations package can be modified to keep up with the changes that occur over time. When expectations are understood and agreed upon by two people, their relationship is solid.

Trust, respect, and credibility are interwoven throughout the relationship.

There's no need for resentment

Interestingly, when working with someone who shares your goals and who believes, as you do, in the level of quality needed to complete a task, there's seldom a need for criticism. On the occasions when the need does arise, the criticism is received as intended and the person being criticized quickly takes action to remedy the situation. Since the receiver of the criticism is not resentful, both parties have a greater willingness to be open and honest with each other.

HOW TO BUILD MATCHED EXPECTATIONS PACKAGES

Building matched expectations packages is a four step process:

1. Identify unspoken expectaitons.
2. Communicate and clarify the unspokens.
3. Develop a common understanding.
4. Maintain agreements.

Let's investigate each of the four steps, using a few examples along the way to help you visualize what's involved. After looking at the four steps, we'll put them to work in some everyday situations.

Once you have familiarized yourself with each of the steps, get in the habit of consciously applying them when you are engaging in conversations. You'll feel a greater sense of control, because it helps keep you aware of where you are in the process and what you still need to do. For example, when things don't go as you had planned, the steps help you analyze accurately why things aren't working out and then determine where best to invest your energies to improve the situation. Likewise, when you interact with others, working from matched expectations helps depersonalize the exchange.

Step 1: Identify unspoken expectations

Unspokens exist in every relationship, as we learned in Chapter 5. When there are an overabundance of unspokens and unclear expectations, the relationship is strained. When communicating, you'll want to "stop" long enough to watch and listen for unspoken expectations. You need to develop a special type of radar system to detect the many unstated shoulds and assumptions that exist in relationships.

At work, for instance, many bosses think that employees should put out a 110 percent effort every day and care about the company's success, that employees should admit mistakes, and that employees should come to the boss if they feel overwhelmed by their workload. Employees, on the other hand, often think that if they do good work, their boss will see that and will reward them. Many employees also expect that the boss would never criticize them in front of others, especially peers or customers.

Unless these and the many other unspokens operating in a relationship are identified and clarified, time and energy will be wasted on guessing where the other person is coming from and how best to work together. As it relates to the task at hand, confusion may exist about how things should be done and whether they are being done correctly, on time, and to everyone's satisfaction. When unspokens are not addressed, people draw their own conclusions. A classic example from the workplace involves linking praise to a salary increase. When employees are praised frequently, they interpret the many compliments to mean, "I am doing a good job and therefore I will get a raise." If the boss never addresses the subject of what criteria are used to determine salary increases, the employees conclude that their interpretation must be correct. When they fail to receive the anticipated raise, they become disgruntled. But if the unspoken expectations surrounding praise and reward had been identified, the employees would not have equated compliments from their boss with remuneration.

Follow the next three steps to make unspoken expectations spoken and to create a matched expectations package.

Step 2: Communicate and clarify the unspokens

Once unspoken expectations have been identified, they need to be communicated effectively, and thus converted into spoken expectations. Asking questions is the best way to clarify expectations, especially in a one-to-one relationship. Let's say that you feel that you do not know how best to present ideas to your boss. Since you understand control, you realize that nothing is preventing you from talking to your boss, so you decide to ask about expectations. For starters, you might want to choose a casual encounter, rather than arranging a formal meeting. Open the conversation in a way that sets the stage and explains your intentions. For example: "You know we've worked together for a while, but after attending a training program and doing some reading, I realized that I am not clear about how best to present ideas to you so that I keep your attention and clearly express my ideas so that they are easily understood." Interestingly, I've never met a senior manager who was resistant to such a conversation. They all believe the exchange is worthwhile, because it clarifies up front how employee and boss can work well together.

As you have learned, if unspokens aren't clarified, you can move into an illusory zone of control as a result of working with faulty conclusions. Here's an example: You have high career aspirations. Much to your dismay, you realize that your boss never talks to you about promotions. You invest a lot of time and energy trying to figure out why. As you think to yourself, you conclude that it's because your boss thinks you lack certain technical skills. After reaching this conclusion, you compare yourself with peers who have gotten promotions. You decide that your technical skills and expertise are at least on a par with theirs, and in some cases you have greater expertise. Now you start to get angry because you feel you have been treated unfairly.

Suppose, instead, that you approach your boss directly and address the unspokens regarding promotions. Your boss tells you, "Your career is in your control. The company is no longer going to do the hand holding that it did in the past. If moving up in the company is something you want to pursue, I'll work with you, but it's up to you to take the initiative." That's a very different answer from the one you expected. It might alter your whole perception of your boss and grossly affect the strategy you had put in place. As this example illustrates, it's usually best to go directly to the source when you ask questions.

Step 3: Develop a common understanding

People bring different styles to the way they work; step 3 acknowledges these differences. In a neutral atmosphere, the parties discuss each other's preferences about important expectations for the purpose of reaching a common understanding. Reaching this shared understanding may require some compromises by each party.

Let's return to your conversation with your boss about how to present an idea. Your boss suggests that you think through your ideas thoroughly so that if you were to be asked a series of questions, you would be prepared to answer them. Your boss also prefers to see your ideas in writing, using graphic displays where appropriate. Also, you learn that early morning is the best time to make an appointment with the boss. As you listen to what your boss is saying, you think to yourself that everything being requested is feasible and you confirm this to him. The two of you have just created a set of matched expectations that can be incorporated into your package.

Step 4: Maintain agreements

In several places in this chapter, the word *trust* has appeared. Think for a moment about a friend you really trust. How would you describe this trust? Perhaps you said to yourself that if you asked your friend to keep a secret, he would. Maybe you thought that you could count on your friend to come through for you in a pinch. A common thread running through the concept of trust is that people keep their agreements. Keeping agreements builds credibility in what people say ("my word is my honor") and helps the relationship grow and stay healthy.

The solidifying step in building expectations packages—the mortar between the bricks—is the keeping of agreements. When you accept personal responsibleness, keeping agreements becomes part of your internal makeup. "A commitment is a commitment" and "You've got my word on it" are common expressions used by people who operate with personal responsibleness. When they talk this way, they not only let others know that they can be counted on, but also remind themselves of what they stand for.

There are several valuable ways to work with and manage agreements for the benefit of the relationship. For instance, interactions with others run more smoothly when you refer back to an agreement made previously. Using this tactic can help you ease into what might otherwise be an awkward conversation.

Another advantage of managing from agreements is that it depersonalizes critical messages. In other words, rather than saying to an employee, "Why are you standing around doing nothing," a boss (or a coworker) can say, "Hey, you agreed to get that project done today, right? Well then, where's your commitment to getting it done?" Or, instead of telling your mate "You're always late" and causing sparks to fly, you can address the situation by saying, "Last time, we agreed to be on time. How come you aren't keeping that agreement?" Although this isn't a fail-safe approach for avoiding an argument, it certainly takes some of the bite out of the exchange and keeps it from becoming too emotionally charged.

Managing agreements can benefit the relationship when you are working in an environment where projects and priorities change rapidly and repeatedly. Communicating what everyone had previously understood helps breed confidence in others that you are on top of things. For example, when schedules or plans change, many bosses simply report the most current news without putting it in any context. After hearing news in this fashion, many employees converge at the department's water cooler and complain about how inconsistent management is—management says first one thing and then another. To minimize this waste of employees' energies, managers can announce the change by reviewing what was previously agreed to before introducing the latest news. Many managers operating in fast-changing, quick-paced environments have found that communicating an original agreement up front is a good way to continue to foster trust, which brings us full circle.

IMPLEMENTATION TIPS

Knowing the four steps of the process is only one part of the formula for achieving; the other essential element is being able to implement what you know effectively. To help you put to use the skill of building expectations packages and ensure that your energies are used wisely, let's touch upon a few implementation tips.

Implementation Tip 1

> *True or false? "Treat others the way you would like to be treated."*

There are many underlying assumptions about dealing with others that help shape our expectations. One assumption shared by many is the old adage "Treat others as you would like to be treated." This variation on the golden rule is good to follow when talking about values (not stealing or physically harming others) or when attempting to manage hundreds of people. As it relates to dealing with others on an ongoing basis, however, the assumption is not effective. So, the best response is false. The golden rule doesn't take into account the uniqueness of each individual and the differences in style and preference of the people involved in an interchange.

A more effective assumption to operate with is "Treat others the way they want or need to be treated." This revised assumption is incorporated into the four-step process of building expectations packages. During the exchange, you learn firsthand the other person's preferences so there is no need to project your own preferences onto them. Working with this assumption doesn't guarantee successful outcomes all the time; you still must make judgment calls to distinguish what people say they want from what they actually need. Parents make that judgment call regularly when dealing with their children, as do managers when they interact with their staffs.

As much as we would like to turn performance evaluation into a science with objective criteria and established techniques, it is an art form. There is no one single formula. Being sensitive enough to distinguish what people need at a given moment from what people say they want is a talent that helps place some managers, parents, and coaches in a special league.

Implementation Tip 2

> *True or false? "People should behave in a certain way."*

Another common assumption is best summed up as "People should behave in a certain way." If you overhear someone complaining that the boss should keep employees better informed about changes taking place in the department, or that the boss should give people more direction, you are listening to someone who is working with this assumption. Since other people can't be controlled directly, you can readily see how working with this assumption can stir up a lot of stress and frustration when others don't do what you expect they "should." So once again the best answer is false.

Dr. William Glasser, author of *Control Theory* and best known for his work in reality therapy, explains this assumption in terms of pictures in our heads. He writes, "Most people do not know they are motivated by the pictures in their heads, and have no idea how powerful and specific they are."[1]

Rather than let your picture of the person dominate your thoughts and actions and ignite your emotions, a better investment of energy is to work with the following assumption: "View others as they are, not as they should be." The key word here is view; you don't have to "accept" others as they are. As an example, if your boss is not a good communicator, then why get upset when the boss doesn't keep you informed? When you step back for a moment and view who your boss really is, as opposed to what the boss should be, you may realize that your boss doesn't do a good job of keeping anyone informed. So getting upset is a waste of energy. Rather, because you can influence others, you can use this information to help in the formation of a matched expectations package, one that helps you build a mutual understanding of how to work together better.

Implementation Tip 3

> *True or false? Once your expectations are matched, it's smooth sailing.*

Keep in mind that the four steps represent an ongoing process, not a one-time exchange. Sometimes you need to go through these steps several times before creating a workable package. This is oftentimes what happens, so it's not always smooth sailing. Therefore, the answer is false.

Implementation Tip 4

> *True or false? When two people engage in a discussion about each other's expectations, someone will be right and someone will be wrong.*

When you and another person are engaged in a conversation about expectations, keep in mind that the focus of the conversation is to gain a mutual understanding. Be careful that the exchange does not turn into a point-winning contest. Once more, the best choice is false. This shift in focus is most likely to occur when you are talking with someone you've worked with for a long time or someone you love.

Let's say that you're unsure about how best to be supportive of your mate in terms of work and career. Since you have not talked about this, you decide to ask your mate whether what you do is perceived as being supportive. Your mate replies, "I can't believe you're asking me this after all these years of marriage. I can't believe you don't know."

A polarization is created as the conversation is driven to a more personal level and the issue becomes a matter of knowing or not knowing your mate. When the conversation moves in that direction, you can steer it back toward your original intent by saying something along these lines: "This is not a point-winning contest about who has the answer and who doesn't. It's a chance to make sure we have an understanding. If we don't have a mutual understanding, then it's a good thing the question was raised, because it would be too bad if another several years passed by and I still didn't know." In this way, you keep the exchange from becoming a competitive event.

This chapter has concentrated on the need for matched expectations packages in various forms of partnerships. But building matched expectations packages is important in larger groups as well, especially among teams. After all, employees won't come to understand how to work with one another just because their project group's title is changed to project team. The following chapter explores the matched expectations of high-performing teams.

1. **STOP** assuming that you know how others like to be dealt with.

2. **STOP** assuming that when a conflict arises, the problem is due to poor communications—that's too shallow an assessment.

3. **STOP** working with the assumption that "people should behave in a certain way." A better assumption is that "people should be viewed as they are." Remember, this doesn't mean you have to *accept* them as they are.

START

1. **START** going directly to people to ask questions about how best to work together.

2. **START** strengthening relationships and working more effectively with others by:

- Listening for and paying attention to expectations that are unclear, unmatched, or unkept
- Investing energies to establish matched expectations packages

3. **START** treating others the way they "want or need" to be treated. When interacting with people you work with daily, you won't be effective if you treat them the way you prefer being approached. Remember, it takes "different strokes for different folks."

7

STEP THREE

THINK LIKE A TEAM PLAYER

COACH: We've got a tough season ahead of us, and the job of selecting a starting lineup has not been easy, but everybody can't be out there on the field. I've made my decisions, so let me announce who has made the team. Charlie, John, Kevin, Bill . . .

Later, in the locker room . . .

JOHN: Congratulations, Bill. Terrific that you'll be on the team.
BILL: Thanks, John. I can't wait to tell my wife. I'm really very excited about the season, and I'm looking forward to playing with you. Hey, maybe we could go out and celebrate—how about next week?
JOHN: Sounds good to me. Tuesday night OK with you?
Bill: You're on. I'm going home to tell my wife the good news!

MANAGER: Well, we have another tough project ahead of us. One of our most demanding customers wants us to work on some innovative technological applications. Kevin, I'm going to put you on this project along with Charlie, Joe, Susan, and Kerri. I'll expect to see a plan from you next week. Now let's make this project a success.

Later, in the coffee room . . .

KEVIN: Another assignment! I already have so much on my plate—I don't see how I'm going to have the time to be on this team too.

CHARLIE: I know what you mean. I've got the same problem. Wait until I tell my wife that I'll be home even *later* now for the next two months. She'll be thrilled.

KEVIN: I get the same stuff at home too! When I get home, I'll have to prepare Linda for what's down the pike. Gotta go—see you later.

Making the team in sports elicits a very different reaction from being selected for a team at work. In the first scene, being on a team is viewed as a reward; in the second, it's perceived as just another assignment, not something to be excited about. In fact, in business the outstanding performer's ability to excel may be hampered by too many assignments. Yet many companies (you may work for one) still try to use sports as a metaphor for their business teams. Employees instinctually know that a business team is not the same as a sports team. Even though sports have been a big part of my world, there are some major differences between what I experienced in the world of athletics and in the business world.

In this chapter, we will explore what team members in business can do to work more effectively together. Specifically, we will address:

- What characterizes a team, anyway? How are business teams different from sports teams? Are teams the same as committees?
- What, if anything, does an employee need to do differently to be an effective member of a team?
- Is it true that in order to be effective team members, employees need to focus solely on the "we" and forgo any emphasis on self?

In addition, the chapter will shed some light on what is needed to move teams from successful to exceptional levels of performance. This transition requires learning the six maxims of interdependent team thought, and understanding the need to work with a matched set of team expectations.

WHAT CHARACTERIZES A TEAM?
Sports Teams Are Not Business Teams

How players get on board is one important difference between sports teams and business teams. In sports, players make the team on the basis of performance in tryouts or qualifying competitions; the criteria are clear and linked directly to the objective. In business, players are assigned to teams for a variety of reasons. Skills, training, experience, and past performance are usually considered. Sometimes an assignment is made for developmental purposes or because a boss wants to give an employee some visibility. Often, a player is assigned to a team simply because of availability. The clearly established qualification system in sports helps promote mutual respect among team members from the start, whereas in business respect and credibility aren't granted automatically because the assignment process seems arbitrary. Since the backgrounds and skills of players assigned to a workplace team may be imbalanced, more energy must be expended at the onset to get players to accept one another.

Another distinction between business and sports teams is that athletes are not bound by hierarchical structures. Even though businesses have tried to deemphasize rank, many employees still sit up a little straighter and take notice when the top executive walks in the room. In business, job titles symbolize greater or lesser responsibility, authority, and power over others within the organization. In sports, players tend to view themselves as having similar status.

Here's another difference: The performance and contribution of an athlete can be evaluated more readily than that of a business team member. The results of an athlete's efforts are seen almost immediately; they are also recapped in the game's statistics. In business, a person works on a task, then passes the project on to the next step, often to another department; rarely does the person receive any feedback on whether the work contributed to or detracted from the end result. For the same reason, athletes cannot talk their way into the winner's circle, but business team players can—and do— talk their way into success. And sometimes a long time passes before management recognizes an employee's incompetence—or unique talents.

A final distinction here concerns winning and losing. When a sports team loses, its ranking in the league is affected but it is still in the game. In business, however, teams have to win just about every time in order to remain in the competitive pool. Losing could cause the team to close down or force it to lay off some people.

Despite these (and other) differences, the idea of teams continues to be all the rage in business. Each employee is now referred to as a valuable member of a team. Project groups have been relabeled project teams, a sales force is now a sales team, a support group has become a support team, and so on. But employees realize that a team isn't a team just because a leader utters the word or hangs posters on the office walls. Notwithstanding all the attention given to teams in books, articles, videos, and TV coverage, many employees are still wondering what distinguishes their unit as a team, rather than as a group or committee.

A Team Is Not a Committee

Until a few years ago, I too wondered what distinguishes a team from any other group of individuals. So I spent more than nine months conducting an independent study on the ingredients of successful teams and teams that perform exceptionally. My interviews with hundreds of people, ranging from human resources directors to team leaders to proponents of self-directed teams, revealed that a team has three distinct characteristics that separate it from a group or a committee.

1. A team has a clearly defined goal. The goal can be assigned to the team or the team can formulate it.
2. The set of players that has the goal is the same set of players that is charged with achieving it. In other words, the team's goal will be achieved through the team's own actions.
3. The players must operate with a high degree of interdependency to achieve the goal; they are not able to achieve the goal individually.

Clearly, by these three criteria, a committee is not a team. A committee makes recommendations, but its members do not carry out those recommendations, nor are they accountable for the results. A group, on the other hand, is distinguished from a team because group members do not have the degree of interdependency that exists on a team.

Effective Team Players Don't Sacrifice Self

Talking about self when discussing teams is not at all incongruous, because teams are composed of individuals. Also, when people are thinking multidimensionally, the team and self coexist harmoniously. To be an effective team player, however, you need to look to yourself to give up some control, while at the same time investing energy to adjust your expectations for yourself. Achieving a larger goal involves shifting from relying exclusively on yourself to relying on others; hence it entails giving up some control. As I learned from the hundreds of people interviewed in the study, adjusting your expectations begins with incorporating six maxims of interdependent team thought:

1. *Recalibrate your criteria for personal reward.* Feeling a sense of personal fulfillment when involved in a team effort requires adjusting your criteria for what constitutes a rewarding experience.

2. *Check your ego at the door.* Thinking multidimensionally, you realize that keeping the team's interests in mind doesn't require you to give up your own interests. But you need to make sure you don't put your self-interest ahead of what is best for the team.

3. *Detach self-interest from the flow of information.* To be an effective team player, you must be willing to share all information freely, rather than manipulating information for your personal benefit.

4. *View all players as having value.* By working with the attitude that everyone is someone's hero and has the potential to bring some value to the team, you can foster the kind of respect that is needed for team members to work effectively together.

5. *Be a self-starter.* A team is defined by its actions and it comes about because of members' willingness to give to the team. Self-initiation is constantly looking to yourself to give to the work and to the team, without waiting to be asked.

6. *Speak collectively.* Get in the habit of discussing activities using the collective pronoun we, to include the entire team rather than only yourself.

One director of training succinctly captured what many of the people interviewed said: "When you are on a team, the focus shifts from an inward focus to an outward one. Besides paying attention to yourself, you need to pay attention to how you are affecting others. Your attitude affects other people, and their attitudes can affect you as well."[1] Let's examine the impact of the six maxims.

Recalibrate Your Criteria for Personal Reward

Changing your criteria for personal fulfillment begins with understanding the criteria you currently use. First, you need to recognize the tremendous amount of satisfaction you derive from actually "doing" the work. When you rely on others, as in a team situation, they take over part of the doing, so the emotional reward is divided among the participants. But once you move emotionally beyond the notion that performing the work is the *only* source of reward and internalize the team's goal, then you will feel a sense of fulfillment when the goal is realized.

Working on a team can provide some other rewards not available to the person who works alone. Interacting with others on an ongoing basis gives you the opportunity to learn new ideas, new perspectives, and new skills from members of your team.

Check Your Ego at the Door

Check your ego at the door before entering any meeting or engaging in other interactions with team members. You make this adjustment because you don't want to let narrow-minded interests, including self-aggrandizement, sabotage the achievement of the team's goals.

In my interviews for this book, I asked people how they knew when their ego was getting in the way. Some interviewees said that it was intuitive. Others said that they could detect their ego coming into play when they experienced a certain feeling building up inside—primarily in the chest and neck area. Still others admitted to a combination of feelings, and a shift in thinking. One top executive explained that the way he keeps his ego in check is by being a good listener and asking good questions. By investing all your energy into what someone else is saying and addressing the situation at hand, you'll have little energy left to think about how to promote yourself.[2]

Whatever sensing system you rely on to pick up on your ego, keeping it in check requires a conscious effort. When first serving on a team, stop long enough to clarify for yourself any personal agendas you may have. Then, when you sense that your ego wants to take over, stop talking. Next, start investing energies to ask yourself the following two questions: "What's my purpose right now? What do I want, both in the short term and in the long term?" Answering these questions will get you properly focused and back on track.

Detach Self-interest from the Flow of Information

Everyone recognizes that the person who has the information has the edge over those who don't. Often, fear of losing some of that edge leads to a reluctance to pass along good ideas. As an achiever, you understand that having the information is only one part of the control formula; taking control also encompasses putting what you know into action. Be willing to share information in a team setting because, in all likelihood, few people will act on your information. However, if someone else in your company successfully uses your ideas, keep your ego in check and remind yourself that it is for the good of the team.

Working effectively on a team is easier once you learn to detach yourself from the information. For instance, when you introduce ideas, imagine them being thrown into a pot. Then as people pick apart "your" ideas, or even reject them, the experience won't seem so personal. As one executive said, "It's important to remember that your idea is a building block and not the structure. The structure is built from the collective."[3]

> *Use ideas as the building blocks, not the structure.*

Keep your focus locked on the goal, while simultaneously remaining open to multiple ways of achieving the goal. This tactic helps you avoid the tendency to quickly label ideas from others as being right or wrong, good or bad. Another good information detachment habit is paying attention to *what* is being said rather than to *who* is saying it. Focusing on *what* is being said helps you remain open-minded and keeps you from being too quick to judge others.

Interestingly, holding back information or not passing it along immediately is never a characteristic of an exceptionally performing team. In exceptional teams, people are willing to let go of information; they communicate with one another continuously. The belief that one team member could benefit from knowing what another knows, even if it seems irrelevant, prevails over any personal feelings of insecurity. As a result, everyone is kept up to date and no one is left out of the loop.

View All Players As Having Value

Although you would like to think of all members of the team as being equal, they are not. Some people have greater expertise in certain areas. Some members are at greater risk because the tasks they are working on are more crucial to the team's overall success. Every task is important and has its place, but not all tasks carry equal weight. Therefore, suggesting that everyone's role on the team is of equal importance is misleading and strains credibility. The key is to focus not on equality, but on the value each person can bring to the project to ensure that the project reaches a desired outcome and achieves what it was intended to do.

As one executive explained, "Viewing people as having potential value encourages you to use what control you have to figure out where team members can make a positive difference. Let's say that a member of your team lacks technical skills. If the project requires technical expertise, then you might immediately conclude that the team has a problem. But by taking the time to figure out what each player can do to add value, including this one player, the team may discover that this person's value is as a sounding board. In my experience, however, if a team member doesn't bring any value, then saying that he or she is of value is an insult to the individual, because everyone knows otherwise."[4]

> *Every team player is somebody's hero.*

Viewing others as having potential value and treating them with respect is enhanced when you keep in mind what I learned from a group leader at a Ford production plant in Ohio. He told me that every one of the people on his line is somebody's hero. He pointed to a man about 10 feet away, and told me that this gentleman had a three-year-old grandson who viewed his grandpa as the most important person in his young life. So while this man won't be moving up the corporate ladder, he is a hero to someone, and he needs to be respected.

Be a Self-starter

Team relationships demand constant giving without expecting to receive an immediate return, although the giving creates the momentum for receiving. Just as a married couple might say, "It's up to us to make this marriage work," so each member of a workplace team must take personal responsibleness for ensuring that the team carries out what it agrees to do.

If you and others are self-initiating, then you won't fall into the trap of "monkey see, monkey do." A typical water cooler question is "Why should we concern ourselves with all this team stuff when top management isn't doing it?" But top management's inaction is not a legitimate excuse for team members to stop contributing to the team effort, nor is it a reasonable explanation for why their current team isn't working. It's up to you and each member of your team to take charge and do what's necessary to make the team structure work.

This attitude of taking charge and looking to oneself to think about what's said and to make something happen is shared by a number of managers. In a national study of managers,[5] those managers who were among the most highly rewarded groups placed high importance on what top management *said*. The less successful groups placed greater importance on whether top management's *actions matched its words*. Although expecting actions to match words was practical in the past, today doing so can foster the detrimental wait-and-see attitude. As someone who operates on the edge, you recognize that in rapidly changing environments, there is frequently a time lag before all the actions can catch up with and match the words. So, when you know that top management's directional changes are for the greater good of the company, you don't let management's failure to match actions to words bring you down or "legitimize" your own inaction. As someone who is a self-starter, you look to yourself to take what has been said and make it happen.

Speak Collectively

Collective or plural pronouns offer a system of checks and balances to make sure that your focus is directed at the team and that you are keeping your ego from getting in the way. Once you have internalized the idea that the goals of the team are realized through the contributions of others, you will discuss what is happening in terms of we. If you continue to speak in terms of I, then you are not paying attention to your word choice. Besides speaking from habit, you may be focusing on yourself, and your ego may need to be put in check.

Also, keep in mind that those who are listening to you will question your motivations, and some people will think that you are self-centered because you don't acknowledge the presence and contributions of others.

Likewise, if you haven't swung the pendulum from I to we, then as problems arise, you will tend to address others using you rather than we. When you tell someone, "You didn't do so-and-so," the shift to second person distances you from the responsibility or blame. When you are working on a team, personal responsibleness for what you say includes substituting we for I and you.

When Expectations Are Not Met

Whether in a team or any other kind of business relationship, conflicts are inevitable. Perhaps one person fails to deliver as promised; or perhaps things are not handled the way another person thinks they should be. In any relationship, there are times when we face the need to give or receive criticism. The next chapter demonstrates that criticism isn't an ugly word after all; rather, criticism is essential to personal growth and to achieving exceptional performance.

Here's how you can take control immediately.

1. **STOP** thinking that if other people on the team don't do something, you're excused from having to do it as well.

2. **STOP** letting your ego enter into conversations. To help you practice being a good listener, ask questions that pertain to the individual, and avoid always using the word *I*.

START

1. **START** getting everyone to focus on what expectations or rules need to be established to ensure that people work effectively together to achieve particular goals.

2. **START** talking to everyone on your team about the six maxims of interdependent team thought, and decide together which ones need to be addressed.

3. **START** clarifying expectations and how best to use them in your particular team, department, or division. Remember, as someone who has accepted personal responsibleness, you may find that this is one area where you want to *start* taking initiative.

8

STEP FOUR

CRITICISM DOESN'T HAVE TO HURT

A l, director of the company's research and development group, has prepared a presentation on the new products being developed by his team. Several customers will be touring the plant tomorrow, so Al is rehearsing his speech before an audience of one.

> AL: Well, Patricia, what do you think of my speech?
>
> PATRICIA: I think it's really informative.
>
> AL: OK, thanks. But what do you think about my delivery? My boss said that she wants the talk to be upbeat for the customers.
>
> PATRICIA: Well, I do think you should smile more, and you could be more expressive when you talk . . .
>
> AL (harshly): What do you mean "be more expressive"? It sounds like you want me to come across like some kind of cheerleader. I don't agree with you—it's just not my style.

In this scene, Al and Patricia could as easily be a married couple as two peers working on the same project. Regardless, the scene exemplifies criticism and the ambivalence it provokes. Al chose to rehearse before Patricia because he realized that getting someone else's viewpoint could help him improve his presentation; also, he apparently valued Patricia's opinion and trusted her to be honest with him. Yet when Patricia's comments were critical, Al responded defensively.

Like Al, we all have a love-hate relationship with criticism: How often do we seek out the opinions of others and tell them we expect them to be honest with us, only to feel hurt when we don't like what they say? Although none of us enjoys being on the receiving end of criticism, most of us realize that we *need* criticism to improve and to achieve the outcomes we seek.

Most of us recognize that we don't always see ourselves as others do; in fact, we operate with blind spots. So we rely on other people to point out what we're missing in order to avoid falling into the illusory zones of control. Operating with too little or inaccurate information puts desired outcomes at risk. The information provided by others may be just what we need to move toward the outcomes we are ultimately seeking and to grow personally as well as professionally.

This chapter shows you how to benefit from information delivered in the form of criticism and how to avoid responding defensively. In addition, the chapter offers some insights on how not to personalize criticism. The first lesson in how to benefit from receiving criticism is an understanding that criticism doesn't have to fall at the ugly end of the communication spectrum.

WHAT HAVE YOU BEEN FORMALLY TAUGHT ABOUT CRITICISM?

Just saying or hearing the word *criticism* can create uncomfortable feelings, upset stomachs, and headaches. Criticism's bad reputation most likely originates in childhood, when we linked "being criticized" with punishment and verbal abuse.

> *Criticism can be as motivational as praise. It can strengthen relationships, help bring about change, and improve performance.*

Criticism's bad reputation has rarely been challenged, and the subject itself has been grossly overlooked as an area of study. It comes as no surprise that many bosses think that the only way to motivate others is through praise. And it's no wonder that so many of us are confused and uncomfortable about the subject of criticism.

Perhaps it's best to pause for a moment to address a key question: What kind of criticism are we talking about? Is it the kind of criticism that is exchanged during a performance review meeting? Or is it the kind that surfaces when you have made a big mistake? How about when someone tells you that you dominated the discussion at the last meeting and didn't allow others to participate? Or is it the criticism that comes from your mate when you forget to pick up some milk on your way home from work? Actually, we're talking about all these kinds of criticism: formal or spur of the moment; from supervisors, peers, or subordinates; at work or at home; from people who know you well or virtual strangers; trivial or substantial.

To sort out our understanding of criticism, let's dispel four myths that surround it and attempt to gain an enlightened view of the subject. In the process, our goal is to adopt a fresh perspective on criticism.

Myth 1: Criticism Can Sometimes Be Positive

In an era whose catchphrases include "Be more sensitive to others," "Seek personal fulfillment," and "Coach and influence others," criticism is often considered an objectionable, or unmentionable, word. To make it seem more palatable, criticism has been renamed "constructive criticism," "positive feedback," and even "caring confrontation." In the workplace, many organizations think they can disguise criticism by calling it something else. But employees are quick to see through the name changes.

Criticism, at its core, will never be positive and was never intended to be. So let's begin by working with a realistic premise:

Criticism is negative. Trying to hide that fact is an act of deception. But the negativity of criticism doesn't have to be interpreted as bad. Criticism and praise can be viewed as representative of a yin-yang relationship. The positive element, praise, is contrasted with and complementary to the negative, criticism.

> ### *Criticism is negative.*

Let's imagine a world with only one of the complementary parts: At your place of work, management sends out a memo to all bosses stating that they can no longer criticize any employee; managers must rely exclusively on praise in dealing with their people. What would happen? In all likelihood, the praise would lose value over time and would mean very little to the employee receiving it. Alternately, those receiving the praise would develop egos that would be very difficult to work with; these employees would have a distorted view of their worth to the organization. (Think of the many employees who for years were given good performance reviews by bosses who didn't take the performance review process seriously.) In addition, the continuous use of praise would cause performance standards to suffer—something that could be devastating to the organization—because the unspoken message of praise is that people are doing well and should continue what they are doing.

Conversely, criticism carries the implication that behavior needs to be changed. This implication is the source of some of the stress that accompanies being on the receiving end of criticism. Whatever your boss (or someone else) is criticizing you for, the implicit or unspoken message is that you should change your behavior in some way. If you don't agree either with the criticism or with the corrective action that the giver of the criticism thinks you should take, things could get a little tense.

On the other hand, would you trust a boss who uses praise exclusively and never tells you anything negative? Would you respect a boss who never told you about the areas where you could use some improvement? Would you view your boss as a credible leader? Most audiences, when asked these questions during presentations, are quick to respond no. They are saying that for managers to build trust, respect, and credibility, they need to communicate with honesty—consistently.

Just as praise is ineffective when used exclusively, so is criticism. What's needed is a mixture of both. The best proportions for that special mixture vary from one individual to another. When the effective use of criticism is mixed properly with praise, employees have an accurate understanding of the value they bring to the organization and what they could be doing better. They also are motivated, because they recognize that their boss cares about them and the contribution they are making.

Myth 2: Criticism Is Destructive and Should be Avoided

Myth 2 reflects the belief of many well-meaning but misinformed prospective givers of criticism. Criticism *can* be destructive but need not be; criticism *cannot* be avoided, only postponed.

Because the exchange of criticism is so uncomfortable for both people involved, some of us put off saying anything negative in the hope that somehow the situation will correct itself, and the whole thing will just go away. Managers in today's fast-paced environment have at their fingertips a lot of excuses to avoid giving criticism. One popular excuse goes something like this: "I just can't say anything. After all, my people are working so hard—it just wouldn't be fair." Another excuse revolves around not having sufficient time for criticism along with tremendous daily workloads: "I want to say something, but I can't find the time to do it right." The manager never seems to get around to meeting with the employee, so the conversation gets put off until it's forgotten. Then, at the performance review, the situation may resurface, taking the employee completely by surprise.

> *Regardless of your status in life, you can't escape criticism.*

When you think about it, criticism is inescapable. When you operate with the assumption that human beings aren't perfect, then you and everyone else are vulnerable to criticism at some point. Experience has taught us that criticism can be destructive. Not only can the ineffective use of criticism rattle a person's self-confidence, it can destroy self-esteem. For instance, a soft-spoken woman from New York City told me that when she was a child, her mother repeatedly told her that she was ugly. Her most devastating moment, surprisingly, came when she was an adult—on her wedding day. The young woman was immensely pleased with the wedding dress she had picked out. As she was admiring herself in the mirror, her mother walked by and commented about how unbecoming the dress was on her. The woman admitted to me that she couldn't work through her insecurity on her own after that, and to this day she still gets professional help.

When I first heard this story, I couldn't believe it. But after thinking about it further, I realized that many parents misuse criticism, though usually to a lesser degree. Take, for instance, the parent who says to a child at the peak of frustration, "Why can't you be more like your brother?" Hearing such a comment over and over can certainly have an impact on a young person.

All of us can recall destructive uses of criticism. As much as we would like to forget these instances, we have episodes that are etched in our memories. As Dr. Norman Vincent Peale said, "Believe you are defeated, believe it long enough, and it is likely to become a fact."

Just as criticism can be used for destructive purposes, so it has a positive use—and that's the one we are seeking. This kind of criticism points out what we are not doing correctly, and gives us insights as to what we need to do differently to achieve desired outcomes. Hearing someone point out a negative and then talk about what we should be doing instead is motivating—and exciting.

That's right, exciting! Of course, no one likes being criticized. But as an achiever, you need not linger on the criticism and the discomfort or pain it causes you. Instead, you can zero in on what you need to do to ensure desired outcomes. For example, you are unable to get some numbers to add up correctly when trying to balance your checkbook. Your mate comes over and points out your error and what you need to do to correct the situation. When you're finally able to get everything to add up, you are thrilled and relieved. Similarly, in the scenario at the start of this chapter, Patricia served as Al's eyes, pointing out that he wasn't smiling throughout his presentation and that he needed to be more expressive. Her viewpoint was valuable because it helped ensure that Al's presentation would be well received.

In other words, the kind of criticism we are talking about here involves pointing out something negative for the purpose of encouraging another person to bring about a change in behavior designed to achieve desired outcomes and help the person grow personally or professionally.

At work or at home, criticism is being misused when someone blurts out, in a rage, "You idiot, how could you be so stupid? "You just weren't thinking, were you?" or any of thousands of similar comments. What's the suggested change in behavior? There is none. What's the purpose here? Most likely the criticism giver's purpose is simply to vent his or her frustrations and possibly to hurt the receiver's feelings. This type of criticism is not what we are after.

Well-considered and well-delivered criticism, however, has a *constructive* aspect—the outcome it produces. If, after hearing the negative (i.e., criticism), the receiver takes the opportunity to act on the criticism and ends up doing something better or growing personally or professionally, then the criticism has been con-structive.

Myth 3: The Giver is in Control of the Criticism Process

Contrary to popular belief, it is the receiver, not the giver, who is in control of the process. Because the giver initiates the criticism, it is tempting to think that the giver is the one who has control during the exchange. But think back to a time when you were planning to criticize someone you cared about. You see? All along you've known, instinctually, that the receiver is in control. Why else would you have spent hours thinking about the upcoming conversation?

> *"No one can make you feel inferior without your consent."*
> —*Eleanor Roosevelt*

When giving criticism, many people are concerned about how the receiver is going to respond. The receiver can—and often does—challenge the giver by asking for specific examples. The receiver also decides whether to agree or disagree with the criticism. A receiver who disagrees can reject what the giver is saying and decide not to take any corrective action.

No doubt, a receiver's lack of willingness to take the desired action can breed a lot of frustration for the giver. For instance, an employee agrees to pass along information to the boss in a timely manner, but continually fails to do so, allowing the boss to be caught by surprise repeatedly by others outside of the department. Or an employee promises to proofread all letters before sending them out, but fails to do so. The boss soon hears about it from customers, who complain about various typographical and grammatical errors. The examples are limitless!

Besides being in control of whether or not to act on the criticism, the receiver is in control of whether the words being uttered are allowed to pierce through and hurt. In other words, the receiver can control the reaction to criticism. (Some ways to avoid personalizing criticism are discussed later in this chapter.)

You may be wondering exactly where the giver's control lies. The giver is in control of the preparation phase of the criticism process—the period of time prior to delivering the criticism. Giving valuable criticism—or, as a client of mine once called it, "instructive criticism"—requires a lot of thought. Besides considering how the receiver is likely to react and how best to deliver the criticism, the giver has to think about which specific examples should be cited, what the desired behavior change is, and when and where the criticism ought to be presented. The familiar statement "Think before you speak" should be adopted as a slogan by all givers of criticism. Once the giver starts to speak, the control shifts to the receiver.

Myth 4: It's Harder to Receive Criticism Than to Give It

Popular belief would have it that it's much tougher to be on the receiving end of criticism. Ongoing research on criticism continues to support the original finding that it's just as tough, and in some cases even tougher, to give criticism as it is to receive it.[1] Givers are commonly concerned about ensuring that the criticism is received as intended without hurting the other person's feelings.

> *It's just as difficult to give criticism as it is to receive it.*

Receivers, on the other hand, find it difficult to avoid personalizing the criticism or reacting defensively. Many receivers worry about whether the giver still believes in them, and whether the criticism will resurface at a later time and be used against them. They think to themselves, "What if my boss brings up my situation at the staff meeting, two weeks from now, embarrassing me in front of my peers?" Or they think, "What if the criticism comes up again at my performance review meeting?" These "unspoken" concerns among employees add a lot of stress—especially in environments where rumors float around about another downsizing effort.

Receivers of criticism often conclude, out of habit, that the giver is having a wonderful time unloading on them. This isn't true. As the receiver, you should keep in mind that the giver is having just as much trouble in delivering the criticism as you are in receiving it. Also bear in mind that it's not necessary to "like" criticism. When you adopt an achieving attitude, you are rooted in realism so you recognize that mistakes will occur and that criticism serves a purpose. The challenge is understanding the control that is yours as the receiver, and learning how to use it to your benefit when you're being criticized.

EXERCISING YOUR CONTROL AS THE RECEIVER

> *Learn to view criticism as another source of needed information to help in your pursuit of control and desired outcomes.*

Imagine that you have been designated to present the company's proposal to a potentially large customer. You, your boss, and two of your peers have spent many hours putting the proposal together. The potential customer opens the morning's meeting with some small talk. Let's zoom in and hear what he says to you.

"So you got your degree from Arizona State. I've heard ASU is a big party school. (Big laugh.) You must have had a great time! Anyway, I've had a chance to review the proposal that you submitted, and I'm not sure it's comprehensive enough—at least when compared with proposals submitted by other vendors. By the way, your fees are considerably higher than theirs."

As the receiver of criticism, how would you respond to this customer's remarks? Would you take the comments about your college personally? Would you take offense at being compared with your competitors that way? Would your reaction be any different if your mate, who was knowledgeable in this area, said these things to you? As an achieving individual, you understand that control involves taking action. It's not enough to know that the receiver is in control—you want to take that understanding and use it effectively. For example, as the receiver, you are using control when you determine how you want to listen, and even if you want to listen. You have control over what you want to listen for—whether you want to put more weight or emphasis on *who* is giving you the criticism as compared with *what* is being said. The choice is yours. Out of habit, some of us may automatically zero in on *who* is delivering the criticism. If it happens to be a peer who is a known enemy, the chances are great that you won't listen at all. Instead, you may immediately "tune out."

As you listened to the conversation above, you may have become irritated because you didn't like the constant references to "you." If the customer was using a sarcastic tone of voice, that may have ignited your emotional fuse as well, causing you to react negatively. As the receiver, you are in control of whether you are paying more attention to *how* the criticism is being delivered or to *what* is being said. You can easily get your emotions stirred up when you focus more on the *how* than on the *what*.

> *When you're receiving criticism, listen to understand, as opposed to listening to argue and judge.*

You are in control of your interpretation of what is said and whether it is a criticism. For example, when the customer makes a comment about Arizona State University, you can receive it as a criticism—an insult to your choice of colleges—or you can interpret the remark as a poor attempt to open a conversation. Likewise, you can get even hotter under the collar if you interpret the customer's comment about high fees as a personal criticism.

> *As the receiver of criticism, keep an open mind.*

Using your control to your advantage involves keeping an open mind and paying attention to *what* is being said. Don't let a person's style of delivery or choice of words put you off immediately and cause you not to listen. At any point, you can reject the criticism—or the giver's recommendation for correcting the situation. Utilizing your control wisely also entails viewing criticism as helpful information. Information is power. Your job is to make sure that you are getting enough information, so you have a clear idea of how best to ensure that something positive will result.

To get valuable information you need not only to keep an open mind but also to keep the giver comfortable. Let the giver finish leveling the criticism. Then raise questions so that you are clear about what is being asked of you. By keeping the giver comfortable, you are able to get the information you need to help you reach the outcomes you desire.

THE 10 COMMANDMENTS OF CRITICISM

1. Don't be thrown by a giver's manner of delivery—givers think they are right. Otherwise, why would they be approaching you? Remember, however, that they only "think" they're right. It's not necessarily true.

2. Keep an open mind. You can reject the criticism at any point.
3. The receiver colors what's being said.
4. The ability to accept criticism varies, depending on who is delivering the criticism.
5. If the giver is attempting to deliver instructive criticism, it is the receiver's responsibility to make the giver feel comfortable.
6. The giver is just as uncomfortable in delivering the criticism as the receiver is in getting it.
7. Avoid personalizing criticism; instead, look at constructive criticism as a resource for achieving your goals.
8. In most instances, reacting defensively or becoming argumentative is ineffective; this kind of behavior precludes any meaningful discussion.
9. Receiving criticism is uncomfortable because the giver is pointing out something negative or expressing some form of disapproval, and criticism implies that you will need to make a change.
10. As the receiver, you need to look beyond the words to the intent of the criticism.

What's key here is to identify the value to be gained from making an effort to act on the criticism. You no longer need to feel helpless! Hold your emotions in check, stay focused on sorting out the information and the intent behind the criticism, and keep the criticism in proper perspective so you can benefit from what is being communicated.

HANDLING CRITICISM EFFECTIVELY

The accompanying flowchart is designed to help you deal with the criticism itself and the person delivering the criticism. This chart doesn't tell you what to say; rather, it guides your thinking and encourages you to ask questions. Step 1 acknowledges your natural tendency to look at *who* is delivering the criticism. Step 2 focuses your attention on the criticism itself. The questions here are directed at ensuring that something positive can be gained from the criticism. Step 3 takes into account your emotions. Each question helps you examine how you feel about the criticism and whether you want to take any action.

STEP I – RECEIVER CONTROL CHART[2]

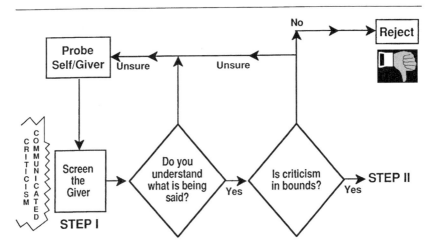

Step 1: Screen the Giver

Zeroing in on who is delivering the criticism is a natural response that can instantly color what is being said. *Your job is to get past who is giving the criticism.* Envision a laser beam, and direct it beyond who the person is—tone of voice, choice of words, posture, and so on. Focus on the following questions.

Do you understand what is being said?

Asking yourself this question helps you get beyond some emotional land mines. If the giver yells at you, for example, your focus may

STEP II – RECEIVER CONTROL CHART

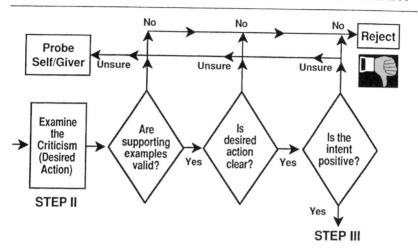

STEP III – RECEIVER CONTROL CHART

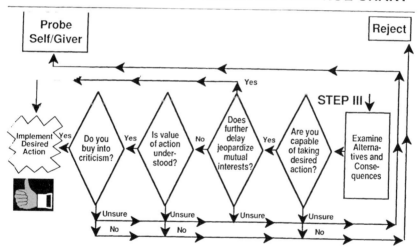

shift more toward the person's volume or tone of voice than the content. Likewise, if the giver dishes out certain emotionally charged words, you may suddenly tune out and miss what is really being communicated. Naturally, your willingness to hear what is being said depends on your past experiences with the giver and the quality of your relationship. If you don't like or respect the giver of criticism, the chances are great that you will ignore what is being said. This first question encourages you to keep an open mind and move past the *who* to *what* is being said. Since you are in control, you can always reject what the giver is saying. You do, however, want to uphold good habits—and keeping an open mind is a good habit to nurture.

Sometimes, even when you listen to the words, you can be confused about their meaning. For example, during a performance review would you understand if your boss said that you were "too perfect"? At a meeting would you understand when someone told you, "The proposal is fine, but it needs some more punch" or "You need to handle yourself a little less aggressively"? One employee I spoke with was asked by her boss—who also happened to be a woman—"Is that the way you're going to wear your scarf?" What is the meaning behind these criticisms? If you are unsure about the meaning, go back and probe. The best person to probe, in each example, is the giver. A key point is that taking control as the receiver entails making sure you understand what the criticism really is.

Is the criticism in bounds?

This question touches on two important issues—timing and content. Timing concerns appropriateness and receptivity. Being criticized in public, or having someone scream at you with foul language, may ignite your emotional fuse and cause you to reject whatever is being said on the grounds that the person has no right to approach you like that. When the setting is inappropriate, your receptivity to the criticism decreases.

There are days when everything seems to go wrong. Then, just when you think you can call it a day, your boss walks in to tell you about a mistake you've made. Rather than speak first and regret it later, use your control to tell the boss that the timing isn't good right now and that you'd like the discussion postponed until tomorrow morning. Exercising your control in this way is not unusual. People often say, "Hey, this isn't such great timing right now—can we talk about it later?" or "I'm up to my eyeballs right now—can you get back to me?" All you are doing is factoring in your timing at the moment, just as you do the giver's.

Content deals with the expectations package between two people, and whether the criticism is within the boundaries of their relationship. For example, if your boss were to tell you that you were spending too much time at work and neglecting your family and your health, you might reject the criticism. Why? Because you start thinking to yourself that your personal life is your own business. If your doctor were to tell you that you were working too many hours and need to spend more time relaxing and being with your family, you might have a different reaction to the criticism. Similarly, a boss's suggestion, however well intended, that you get additional schooling or an advanced degree, could be rejected on the grounds that that's your own issue to address. If you are unsure whether the criticism is in bounds, once again you should go back and probe the giver.

Step 2: Examine the Criticism

This step is the most crucial. The questions raised here need to be addressed and answered. This is the step where you carefully examine the criticism and the desired action.

Are supporting examples valid?
You need to determine whether the criticism you are receiving is accurate. To check out the accuracy, look for two things. First, the giver should be able to supply specific examples to support the criticism. As the specific examples are cited, you can ask yourself silently whether you think the examples match up with the criticism and whether they are valid.

Reggie works in the training department of a major computer company. At his last performance review, Reggie's boss pointed out that Reggie was not as organized as he needed to be. The boss used the rollout of a new management course to justify her criticism. A couple of months after the performance review meeting, Reggie was asked to take on an assignment that was outside his normal duties. His boss wanted him to put together a technical conference for senior managers. Reggie agreed and, on top of his normal duties, found time to organize the weekend-long event.

In preparation for the meeting, Reggie asked the presenters to supply him with technical papers. All but six of the presenters turned in their papers on time. Reggie and his staff couldn't go to press and put together the large, bound books for the meeting until those six papers were received. Putting the books together was the last thing that Reggie needed to get done before the conference began on Saturday. In an effort to hasten things, Reggie asked his assistant to phone the six people and ask them to turn in their reports by Wednesday. All of them agreed, and all but two complied. On Wednesday, Reggie called the two managers personally to convince them to turn in their papers. The first manger came through with his report on Thursday; and the second manager turned in hers on Friday morning. As soon as the last report was received, Reggie's staff hustled to put the large meeting books together for the conference, which was now only one day away.

On Saturday, all the senior managers gathered for the conference. Reggie's boss, who was nervous as could be at the onset, began to relax as soon as she saw things start to come together smoothly. The conference went great, and the next week Reggie's boss stopped by to tell him what a terrific job he had done putting the event together. Before Reggie could say thank you, his boss interrupted him and said, "But I saw everyone scurrying around on Friday afternoon doing last-minute things. You know, if you were a little more organized, as we discussed during your recent performance review meeting, you and your staff wouldn't have had to do all that last minute hustling." When Reggie heard the comment, he was quick to reject the boss's criticism! Rather than immediately writing off the criticism, Reggie would have been better off keeping an open mind and running through all the steps in the flowchart. He might have gained some insight about what his boss found important, or what the boss *didn't* see around the office.

If you're operating with an achieving attitude, you recognize the importance of developing and integrating good habits. Look beyond the criticism itself and inspect what's being said in a broader context. By getting in the habit of objectively inspecting "information," you are taking control to ensure that if any benefit can be gained, you will find it. (Remember that you can reject the criticism at any time.)

Is the desired action clear?

The specific corrective action needed is the most important information you want to take away from your conversation. If you don't know specifically what to do, you'll end up guessing. If you guess incorrectly, more criticism will probably result.

An important caveat comes with knowing the specific desired action to take.

Meet Lisa, an editor at a major magazine based in New York City. Lisa is a member of Women in Communications, a prestigious organization of influential women in PR, advertising, publishing, and other fields. Several years ago, Women in Communications was having a

(Continued)

meeting in the city, and I was fortunate enough to be invited as the evening's speaker. At the end of my talk I met Lisa for the first time. She came up to me in tears. I was taken aback because I knew the talk I gave wasn't *that* moving! Lisa's tears had to do with what was happening in her life, and she began to explain her situation.

For four years, Lisa had worked for one boss. During that time, she had often asked him to verify whether he thought she was doing a good job. In each instance, he put a grand smile on his face and gave her a fatherly look of approval as he reassured her that everything was fine. Six weeks prior to our meeting, Lisa was told that she would be reporting to a new boss, Maura. During that six-week period, Lisa did her best to get to know and work with Maura. At 4:00 in the afternoon on the day of the Women in Communications meeting, Maura called Lisa into her office to give her some feedback about her performance. Maura told Lisa in blunt, uncushioned terms that she was not a very good writer and that her ideas for the magazine were very self-centered. Hearing these criticisms in such unabashed terms caused Lisa to lose control and burst into tears. (Now I understood the tears in her eyes after the meeting!) Lisa asked Maura if they could get together the following morning rather than finish their meeting with her so upset, and Maura agreed that it was a good idea.

Lisa and I strategized for about 30 minutes before calling it a night. The one thing she promised she would do—and she did—was to call me afterward to let me know how everything turned out. Her experience holds an important lesson for all receivers of criticism.

Lisa initiated the next morning's conversation by saying, "Maura, thank you for the feedback. It's something that I've wanted to have, though I must admit that I don't agree with you." (I told Lisa that I didn't think rejecting the criticism was necessary, but Lisa said it was a matter of pride.) She continued: "I know that's not the purpose of our conversation. To begin with, you told me that I am not a very good writer. What is it that I could do differently that would make me a better writer in your mind?" Maura started to explain herself, and Lisa listened quietly in order to make sure she had a clear understanding of what Maura was looking for. Regarding the subject of "self-centered ideas," Lisa asked Maura to help her understand how she could shape ideas more clearly so they were perceived as having the magazine's best interests in mind. Once again, Maura explained where she was coming from.

The one "receiver lesson" that needs to be pointed out here—since that's our focus at the moment—is that when it comes to knowing the specific behavior desired, make sure you understand it from the *giver's perspective* and not your own.

A common mistake is assuming that the corrective action is embedded in the criticism. Imagine that your boss tells you that your attitude is bad and needs to be changed, or that your style is far too aggressive, or that you need to be a better team player. These criticisms tell you what you have done wrong (in your boss's eyes), but they do not tell you how to correct the problem.

A second mistake that can get you into trouble is trying to determine on your own what the corrective action should be. Remember, if the action you choose is not what was wanted, you are vulnerable to more criticism. As the receiver, you are responsible for finding out, as Lisa did, exactly what the giver is looking for. Lisa understood that she was dealing primarily with perceptions. To eliminate any guessing, she needed to know how her boss perceived the situation, and what she wanted.

Lisa's example illustrates another key control factor—you can go back to the giver at a later time to discuss things further. When you are not offered any concrete ideas as to what the boss wants from you, take some time to formulate what you think the corrective action is, then ask your boss if you are on target. The most important point is to make sure that you invest your energy in knowing specifically what the desired behavior is.

Is the intent positive?

Sometimes the giver's intent isn't positive. Before accepting the criticism or deciding whether to take any corrective action, you need to sort out the giver's intent. This issue is addressed by the next question on the flowchart. Sorting out the intentions behind a criticism is a good way for you to exercise control as the receiver.

Sometimes the giver's intent is unclear. For instance, you turn in a report and a coworker remarks, "Well, this looks OK for someone who whipped a report out really fast." Or during a casual conversation with a group of peers, someone laughingly blurts out, "Yeah, we all think you're a real character." In each of these situations, you can ignore what was said—after all, you are in control. You also can respond defensively and run the risk of having others come back and accuse you of not having a sense of humor. But the best tactic is to examine the giver's real intent by asking, "How would you like me to take this?" Another way to inspect what is being said is to comment, "Moving forward, how do you want me to interpret this?" or "I'm not sure—what's your purpose right now?"

When you probe, you are asking the giver to take what is unspoken and make it spoken. Because criticism can be destructive, I've asked hundreds of people (as part of a national study and subsequently at workshops) what they look for when trying to determine the intent behind criticism. Although all said that they can tell when the giver's intent is questionable, most people admitted that they have a hard time identifying specific signals. A few clues are mentioned repeatedly:

- The giver fails to look you in the eye (especially if the giver generally does look you in the eye).
- The giver deliberately uses words that will upset you.
- The giver compares you with an identified, known enemy.
- The giver talks in generalities.
- The giver offers no corrective action.
- It remains unclear who is to benefit from the criticism.
- The giver approaches you in a situation where you are likely to be upset by the criticism.
- The giver is quick to cut off your response.

If one or more of these clues are present, and if circumstances allow, you can ask for a further explanation of what's going on, to ensure that you are not misinterpreting the giver's intentions. When asking for clarification, be careful about your tone of voice. A challenging tone could easily add fuel to the fire. Keep your purpose clearly in the forefront of your mind. If you are not satisfied with the response and feel that the giver's intent isn't positive, you can consider other courses of action, including rejecting the criticism.

Step 3: Examine Alternatives and Consequences

To be able to sort through the giver's intent and logically inspect the criticism, you must keep your emotions in check. Step 3 of the flow-chart helps you work with your emotions and sort out what is happening in the larger picture.

At times, questioning the criticism and engaging in a conversation with the giver on the spot is not the most effective thing to do. For example, imagine coming home and, instead of being given a warm greeting, you are hit with a series of criticisms. Rather than growling and fighting back—and possibly starting World War III— you can take control of yourself at that moment, say nothing, and nod as you walk past your mate to get yourself settled.

To help use your energies productively, consider the broader circumstances surrounding the criticism, which includes assessing emotional levels. Factoring in this broader perspective helps you determine how best to respond. Remember, when emotions are stirred up, it's easy to lose your focus, and win the battle but lose the war.

Past experiences suggest that with certain people and under certain circumstances, it's best simply to accept what is said at the moment, rather than try to "set the record straight" or "have your turn to speak." Knowing how best to handle yourself in these situations hinges on your ability to accurately pick up on unspokens. Asking yourself some key questions can help you interpret what is going on during a criticism exchange and can sharpen your sensitivity to the situation.

Are you capable of taking the desired action?

Even givers with good intentions often fail to consider this important question: Is the receiver capable of taking the desired action? As the receiver, you need to address this question or complications are sure to occur further down the road. When considering this question, ask yourself if you are capable of doing what is being asked of you—and if you want to do it. As a result of your accumulated experiences, you can accurately determine whether the changes being asked of you are the kinds of changes you want to make.

> Simone is a client who is facing some tough management issues. At the end of one of our meetings, she focused her attention away from the work scene and zeroed in on her marriage of 10 years. She said to me, "I'm very happy in my marriage, so don't get me wrong. I love my husband dearly, but he is such a bump on a log. Trevor never gets excited about anything. Right now, we are in the process of having our dream house built—and wouldn't you think he'd show a little enthusiasm? Absolutely not. He displays

no emotion at all. It's so frustrating." After explaining the situation, she asked me for my opinion. I reminded her, "We breed a lot of frustration in ourselves by thinking that people should behave in a certain way. Attaching expectations onto others affects those we love the most, and in your case, that's your husband. The first thing you'll want to do is bring a big-picture perspective into focus. By doing so, you'll be viewing him as the person he is."

After mentally reviewing past scenes, Simone quickly realized that her husband rarely, if ever, displayed any emotions. So logic would hold that the purchase of a new house would not necessarily create visible excitement. I pointed out that Trevor's not showing emotions shouldn't be taken to mean that he was unhappy with their house or unhappy with her. Simone stopped me at that point and said, "That's exactly what Trevor told me. He said that his being unemotional has served him very well in his career and throughout most of his life, so he really isn't interested in changing." Now Simone needs to absorb what Trevor is telling her because, in essence, he is saying that he doesn't want to change.

Trevor's willingness to tell Simone what was important to him and how he felt about her criticism certainly put their conversation on a different level. If he had said nothing, Simone may have drawn some faulty conclusions about his actions. For instance, let's say she continued criticizing Trevor for not getting more excited about this major event in their lives. From his lack of enthusiasm she could have concluded that Trevor didn't really want their new home and that their dream pursuit was no longer mutual. With the project no longer a team effort, Simone might have decided that she would have to deal on her own with any problems that arose. If Trevor's unwillingness to change had gone unexplained, Simone could have ended up becoming resentful and wishing they hadn't started such an ambitious project in the first place.

As the receiver, you need to assess whether you are capable of and want to take action. Thinking this through may require some deliberation—and more time than you have right then and there in the midst of a conversation. An option here is to request a recess: Ask the giver if you can get back to the conversation at a later time.

Will further probing, delays, or resistance jeopardize personal or mutual interests?

Good timing is important in many situations, and being on the receiving end of criticism is no different. When you are being criticized, you need to hold on to the big-picture perspective. Specifically, what is at stake if you delay taking action on the criticism beyond the point considered reasonable by the giver? What is at risk if you resist taking any action at all? In making this judgment, you should instantly factor in everything that you know about the giver—the spoken and unspoken expectations, the intensity of the giver's delivery at the moment, and your observations of the current situation and prior similar situations.

Pam recently had to give the issue of taking action a lot of consideration. She was engaged in a three-way conference call with her boss and her boss's boss regarding a proposal they were putting together for a potential client. The big boss pointed out that he didn't like the way the pricing structure had been put together. Pam's boss interrupted to apologize for what appeared to be some errors in the pricing structure. He explained that Pam had been given the corrected figures while preparing the proposal, but she had neglected to include the changes. Pam could feel her emotional fuse being lit as a combination of feelings swelled inside her, because her boss's criticism of her was totally inaccurate.

After stepping back and examining the situation, Pam

decided not say anything. She realized that correcting her boss in front of his boss was likely to create more of a problem situation than was already there. Pam quickly reminded herself of the unspoken rule that you need to pick your battles—and this was one battle best left behind. Besides, if she still wanted to address the unjust criticism, she could do it better when she and her boss were together in the office. As it turned out, her decision to remain silent was an effective one. Her boss thanked her and explained that extenuating circumstances had developed that prompted his reactions.

Before you begin thinking about who's right or wrong here, keep in mind that timing is an art form, not a science that yields consistent, predetermined outcomes.

Is the value of the desired action understood?

As mentioned earlier, the likelihood that you will make a lasting change in your behavior is slim if you see no value in the change. In other words, like all adults, you are not inclined to initiate permanent changes in your ways just because someone has told you to do so. You may go through the motions at first, but over time you will most likely revert to your old habits if you don't understand what value is to be gained. If the giver does not explain to you, during the criticism exchange, why it is important to make the necessary changes, and if you don't see the importance yourself, then you owe it to yourself and the giver to find out. Ask the giver to help you understand why making certain changes is beneficial. Think on your own about whether you perceive the value to be gained as valid and meaningful. If not, probe the giver again, rather than being quick to reject the criticism.

If you see some value to be gained in what the giver is pointing out, you need to check out your emotions by asking the final question.

Do you buy into the criticism?

Asking yourself whether you buy into the criticism gives you a chance to reflect on the whole situation and to check out your thoughts and feelings. To begin with, if you don't have a clear understanding of the specific action to take, you can't legitimately buy into the criticism. In this case, probe further to uncover the desired action. Reexamining the criticism gives you a chance to reflect on whether you focused more on how the criticism was being delivered than on what was said. It also gives you an opportunity to evaluate the giver's intent, the situation surrounding the criticism, and how credible the criticism is.

The timing of the buy-in question merits some consideration. Over the years, you have developed a "typical response" to criticism. If you typically respond more emotionally than others when criticism is first presented, then perhaps it's best to heed the advice, "Things will look better in the morning." You may need time to let things settle. Even if you are not typically emotional, when you are tired, angry, or in a bad mood, you may let your emotions win out over any rational thinking. Taking some extra time to digest the criticism may help you avoid moving into one of the illusory zones of control. On the other hand, getting emotional may be exactly what you want to do. Perhaps you're tired of dealing with the same issue and not getting anywhere, and you need to let others know how strongly you feel. Keeping an open mind as to how you should react is crucial. Once again, you are in control as the receiver, and you can decide to reject criticism at any point.

HOW TO AVOID RESPONDING DEFENSIVELY TO CRITICISM

One of the main questions that arises in the course of my work with executives is how to avoid responding defensively. Let's first explore the trigger points of a defensive response and then learn how not to take criticism personally.

Learn Your Trigger Points

Responding defensively is not automatic. Let's take a moment to examine what many of us do to prompt a defensive response. To begin, it's not uncommon to view criticism as a confrontation, as in "I have to go confront so-and-so about this issue." Viewing criticism as a confrontation sets up a playing field in which only one side can win. This view is mistaken; criticism and confrontation are not synonymous terms. The giver of criticism is pointing out something that is rooted in negativity. The purpose is to get you to change your behavior—to do something better, achieve a desired end result, or grow personally or professionally. Keeping this understanding of criticism in mind can help you see the situation differently and prevent you from listening in an argumentative or judgmental way. When you listen to argue or to judge, you are automatically creating a right/wrong, agree/disagree condition. Putting a lot of emphasis on whether you agree with the criticism can also spark a defensive response. Another trigger for a defensive response is paying more attention to *who* is delivering the criticism, and *how* it is being delivered, than to *what* is being said.

Having a better idea of what triggers a defensive response is helpful, but what you may want to know is how to keep yourself from saying things that you may later regret. Perhaps the best advice is to think about certain people who arouse your emotions more than others, and make a mental list of those people. Then prepare a non-defensive response in advance. When you meet up with one of the people on your list, you will be less apt to react in a way that is disappointing to yourself.

> *As the receiver of criticism, you are in control of whether or not to respond.*

The response you prepare might begin with closing your mouth and saying nothing! That's right, you say nothing. Already you have kept yourself from saying something you might later regret. Don't fall into the habit of thinking that when someone tells you something, you have to respond. Remember that as the receiver, you can stop and say nothing.

Another tip: The giver, who has always seen you get upset in the past, may not understand where you are coming from when you remain silent and may draw false conclusions. (Your boss may view your silence as a sign of insubordination.) To avoid any misunderstandings, you need to clarify your nonresponse to the criticism. Try something like this: "We've been through some battles before because of my quick responses. Sometimes, I have spoken too soon and regretted it later. So to avoid saying something I'll regret, and making things more difficult for both of us, I'd like just to listen to what you have to say and think about it before responding. Is that agreeable to you?"

The phrasing is up to you, but your explanation should include three important items. The first is to clarify where you are coming from, the second is to show some respect so that the other person will want to buy into your suggestion, and the third is to ask for the other person to go along with your approach. Explaining yourself by covering these three areas shows respect for the other person, and at the same time gives you an opportunity to take control and stay at your best. There's no trick to using this technique effectively; it just takes personal responsibleness and a little practice.

Don't Personalize the Message

Learning to avoid personalizing criticism takes practice too. You need to think about what is going on and then employ some appropriate skills. People have different views about what "personalizing the criticism" means. One meaning is obvious: People say that when they are criticized, it hurts. Stop for a moment and think about that meaning; maybe the hurt feelings that accompany criticism aren't so bad. Certainly, you've heard the expression "The truth hurts." Perhaps the only way certain receivers are motivated to change is by first experiencing hurt feelings.

Another common interpretation of "personalizing the criticism" involves a heightened level of feelings that impairs thinking and the ability to engage in a meaningful exchange. In essence, people "emotionalize" the criticism. If this description fits you, you can take some specific actions to deemotionalize the exchange. Besides relying on quick charges—techniques that are used instantly in high-pressured situations for greater self-control (see Chapter 10)—you should bear in mind three deemotionalizing factors.

The first factor concerns your personal level of confidence. Like the weather, confidence fluctuates from one day to the next. Criticism is easier to handle when your confidence level is high than when it is low.

Likewise, confidence is linked to the number of successful experiences you have had. When you are criticized for something but can draw upon successful experiences to the contrary, it is easier to reject the criticism. The opposite is also true. When you lack a frame of reference to put a criticism in perspective, that criticism can have a bigger impact and hurt you more deeply.

To avoid personalizing criticism, consider your level of self-confidence in the particular situation. If it's low, give yourself a little "permission" for having made a mistake. At the same time, to help build your confidence, make sure you have a clear idea of what specific action you need to take to correct the situation and start building successful outcomes.

A second powerful deemotionalizing factor to draw upon is maintaining a big-picture focus. When you are being criticized, immediately consider the big picture and ask yourself if *anyone* is perfect, including you. No one likes making mistakes, but doing so is inevitable. The best you can hope for is that the mistakes that do arise will be little ones, and their effect will be minuscule. Large mistakes or small, the point here is that in the big picture mistakes are a given, and even though you may not like them, you need to give yourself permission to make a few. At the same time, by examining every error and learning from it, you make a second mistake less likely to occur. Keeping an open mind and seeking to learn from mistakes turns criticism into a valuable tool for enhancing performance and for building relationships that are rooted in trust, respect, and credibility. A valuable and valid big-picture perspective to hold on to is that the person cared enough to say something!

The third defusing factor has to do with getting into the habit of inspecting what others say. Developing good habits is essential. If you accept praise from someone without inspecting it, then when someone criticizes you, out of habit, you won't inspect the criticism very closely either. Instead, you will personalize it.

The three deemotionalizing factors work together. Consider your level of confidence at the moment of criticism; if it is low, that's all the more reason to inspect what is being said. Next, put what is happening in the context of the bigger picture. Besides giving yourself "permission" for having made a mistake and being human, keep the following big-picture perspective in mind: When people feel stretched to the limit, the easiest way for them to handle the urge to criticize is to say nothing at all. The fact remains that someone, however awkward or abruptly, took the time to say something to you,

> *Absorb the mistake and remember the lesson.*

When you are on the receiving end of criticism, simply saying you're sorry and admitting you're at fault is not enough. As Benjamin Disraeli, a nineteenth-century philosopher and educator, said, "Apologies only account for that which they do not alter." If you are going to operate consistently with duality of purpose, you need to inspect the criticism and have a clear idea of what to do about the situation, then make the necessary corrections swiftly. When you invest your energies this way, you are incorporating the habit of absorbing the mistake and remembering the lesson. Although the idea of making criticism work for you is obviously valuable in the abstract, putting it into practice can be difficult, especially when you have lost your focus. The following chapter examines what you need to know in order to stay focused.

Here's how you can take control immediately.

1. **STOP** thinking that criticism equals "people bashing," and is something bad.

2. **STOP** thinking that you can avoid being criticized.

3. **STOP** thinking that when you are being criticized, you have no control. Rather, remind yourself that, contrary to popular belief, once the criticism is delivered, the receiver, has the control, not the giver.

4. **STOP** expecting givers to be eloquent. Most givers have had no formal training, so their delivery will probably be crude at best!

1. **START** viewing criticism as "information" that can be of potential benefit. Your job is to inspect it. Pay attention to what's being said and make sure you have:

   • Enough information
   • Good-quality information

CHAPTER EIGHT

2. **START** using your control as the receiver to:

   - Ask questions to ensure that you know the specific desired actions from the giver's perspective
   - Ask questions to make sure that the intent of the criticism is clear
   - Ask questions so you know the value to be gained by taking the necessary actions

3. **START** listening to understand, as opposed to listening to argue and judge. Remember, the easiest path for the giver is to hold back and say nothing at all.

9

STEP FIVE

KEEP YOUR FOCUS

"Keep your eye on the ball."
"If you don't know where you're going, any road will take you there."
"It's not over till it's over."
"Start with the end in mind."

These familiar expressions all pertain to an important aspect of self-discipline: staying focused. What does staying focused mean? I posed that question to several CEOs who oversee many diverse activities and deal with high risks. Although some mentioned having a clear direction, concentrating, keeping a perspective, and achieving goals, no synonym conveys all the implications of the word *focus* as it occurs in our everyday vocabulary. These executives stated what focus meant to them, and to each it was a little different.

Dennis Gormley, when he was CEO of Federal Mogul, said that in order to stay focused, we first need to *get* focused. "Getting focused relates to having a clear sense of direction and purpose for what we are doing. In business, that translates into a need for all employees to think about the actions they take, and whether or not those actions are geared at making money or saving money. When we stay with that focus, it becomes clear that people who work in quality control departments, for example, need to be thinking of how to eliminate their jobs. Why? Because we want all our managers and employees alike to integrate quality into everything they do. When they do, then there is no need for the quality control department to exist."

Bob Annunziata, CEO of Teleport (pending its planned merger with AT&T), also took a big-picture view. To him, focus signifies a personal pursuit that cannot be attained. "Staying focused is a never-ending quest for improvement. If I get there, I'll probably still say I'm not there. The same holds true for the successes we experience in this company."

Sandra Goecken is CEO and president of the Goecken Group, a parent firm with four operating companies. In our interview, she talked about the many things going on in her life. "Recently I have been working on launching a number of major marketing campaigns. Besides Wireless Works, where we are working on some mutual joint ventures, we are engaged in a national marketing campaign to make consumers aware of Global Media Net and Personal Guardian. There's Personal Safety Wear to keep up with as well—we just had some huge sales. There are all these companies to deal with, plus my newborn child, and the fact that I am consciously working on losing the extra pounds I gained during my pregnancy. I *have* to stay focused."

From what you have learned in this book, you probably recognize that these people are using the phrase "staying focused" multidimensionally. A common mistake is to think of staying focused as a sort of road map: The end result equates with the city we select as our destination; the route we are going to use to get there is symbolized by the various roads we choose. Although this analogy is easy to understand, it is faulty because it conjures up a one-dimensional image. When disciplining ourselves to stay focused, we are engaging in a multidimensional pursuit.

The pursuit begins by stopping long enough to develop our sense of direction and our plan for getting there. When we are about to launch into something, it's easy to have a sense of control and to feel confident about ourselves because we know where we are going and how we will travel. The pursuit becomes more difficult as we move into the action where we strive to achieve a short-term gain. While in action, we are continually investing energies to ensure that we keep things in perspective. We are also maintaining high levels of concentration, and at certain points along the way we are keeping our commitment despite unexpected setbacks or disappointments. When moving into the action state, we check out our focus by establishing goals along the way. These goals serve as checkpoints to confirm that our focus is well targeted, that our energies are being directed productively, and that forward momentum is being created. As Pro-Achievers who always operate with duality of purpose—performing at exceptional levels and making a valuable difference—thinking multidimensionally and ensuring that energies are being directed productively are things we do on an ongoing basis.

INTRODUCING THE 2M SIMULTANEOUS FOCUS

Staying focused is a challenge, given mile-long to-do lists and today's hectic pace. To help you deal with this challenge, let me introduce a multidimensional approach that consistently factors in two dimensions—the *2M simultaneous focus*. The first M refers to the macro, and the second M refers to the micro. Today, having a big-picture, or macro, focus is essential, but it is not enough; nor is it effective to limit your view strictly to the micro. Some people are visionary, oriented to long-term goals, but their macro view leaves them too far removed from day-to-day realities. At the other extreme are myopic people, those who endanger their desired outcomes by concentrating solely on the minutiae.

Melding the macro and the micro is essential to staying focused. You want to bring both into view simultaneously; then you can give each equal weight or emphasize the perspective that's advantageous in a particular situation or at a particular time—that is, the perspective that allows you to leverage your energies most productively to ensure that a valuable difference is realized.

Think of the 2M simultaneous focus as the zoom lens on a camera. Consider a typical tense situation: You are being criticized. Your first reaction is emotional—in the micro or immediate situation, you are upset at yourself for having made a mistake. Refocus the lens and the macro view takes shape. You are a human being and imperfect; therefore, making mistakes can be considered a natural and inevitable aspect of life. Also, by learning what you can from the criticism, you enhance your ability to achieve future desired outcomes. So, you zoom back in close for the micro view to get a clear understanding of the criticism and the corrective action needed.

In the realm of criticism, both perspectives carry roughly equal weight. Think about a different situation. You have just learned that your health is at risk. Instantly, your perspective shifts. The daily issues that arise at work and at home are transformed into trivial matters, to be dealt with as best you can. You become engrossed in viewing your life from a big-picture perspective. All your focus is on getting well. Here the macro and micro perspectives do not have equal significance.

In other circumstances, concentrating on the micro focus may be best. For instance, when an important deadline is approaching, a macro focus on all the things remaining to be done may cause your head to spin, making it difficult for you to concentrate on any one task. If you zoom in to a micro perspective and identify a single task or activity that can be done in the hour before your next scheduled meeting, extraneous thoughts tend not to enter your range of view, enabling you to concentrate.

As an achieving person, you are already in the habit of thinking multidimensionally. The 2M simultaneous focus builds your awareness of the micro and macro perspectives in all situations. The application of this skill are numerous and varied. This chapter explores how you can use the 2M simultaneous focus to handle four conditions in which staying focused can be difficult:

1. Too many changes and too many changing priorities
2. Too much to do and too little time
3. Too little attention
4. Too much emotion

TOO MANY CHANGES AND TOO MANY CHANGING PRIORITIES

Sometimes we wish that things would stand still. Everything is going great at work, our family relationships are wonderful, everyone is healthy and happy. But soon reality sets in, and we must remind ourselves that life never stands still. We've been living with change all our lives—it's nothing new. Two conditions prevalent today can make it difficult for us to maintain our focus: the rapidity of changes and the frequency with which priorities change.

> *Priorities change; be ready to change with them.*

Victor Friedman is the founder and vice president of Computer Generated Solutions, a successful entrepreneurial company headquartered in New York City. When asked how he handles today's changing priorities, Victor said, "I prioritize my work constantly. I come in to work with the traditional 'to-do list,' but as the momentum of the day picks up, it changes. I'm prioritizing after I finish each task and before I move on to the next, and I'm prioritizing while I work on each one."

Randy Bolstad, head professional at Willow Crest Golf Club at Oak Brook Hills Hotel and Resort in suburban Chicago, also frequently adjusts and reconsiders his priorities. When shuffling priorities as unexpected events arise, Randy takes his personal life into account. He explained, "A lot of people I know separate their work life from their personal life. I don't do that. So when something comes up that I have to think about how to handle, I factor in my family. For instance, we run a lot of tournaments. If I get a call that I'm needed at the pro shop on my day off, I might bring one of my daughters to the club and have her take a swim while I check up on the emergency." At the time, Randy didn't realize that he was practicing the 2M simultaneous focus, but he was.

Like hundreds of people interviewed for this book, Victor Friedman and Randy Bolstad were putting each task, each interaction, and each investment of energy in proper perspective by raising two questions: "What do I want to do right now?" and "Does what I am planning to do fit the sequence order of priorities?" Answering these two questions helps you take the task at hand, which represents the micro, and position it in the macro picture among numerous other tasks. While in the macro picture, you can more easily weigh that task's importance against other tasks in order to determine whether your energies are being utilized productively. Remember, being efficient is not enough—you need to be effective and make a valuable difference.

Finding Your Bearings

Life resembles a ticker tape in which events keep occurring as the tape rolls by. By viewing events as unfolding along a ribbon of tape and thinking about where your control lies, you can better under-stand how the 2M simultaneous focus can help you keep your bear-ings.

Phil's personal ticker tape is shaped by his workday. From a micro perspective, there are certain things that he wants to get done prior to going to work and others he wants to get done at work before noon. As Phil goes about his morning activities at home, his son cuts himself. Then on the way to work, Phil gets a flat tire. As he is dealing with the tire, he gets a call from the office on his mobile phone telling him that his early meeting has been can-celed—the meeting for which he put in four hours of preparation time yesterday! The ticker tape keeps mov-ing, as Phil is hit with one event after another.

Using the 2M simultaneous focus, Phil steps back to assess the macro picture; it becomes apparent to him that the events appearing on his ticker tape are not within his control. This is just one of those days. Since he has no control over what is happening, Phil needs to exert more control over himself in the micro; things aren't going as planned, so he can't operate on automatic pilot, as he often does while commuting.

In the micro perspective, Phil could allow himself to get upset or angry by these setbacks. But by zooming out to a macro perspective, Phil realizes that these events are simply inconveniences—five years from now they will most likely have been forgotten. At the same time, he rec-ognizes that the cancellation of his meeting is a positive turning point (changing the flat tire could have made him late for it) and that he should be glad his son is OK, and so is he!

> Tina's personal ticker tape has been filled with many changes over the last two months. She has accepted a new, top-level job in a completely different industry from where she was before; she has also remarried and moved into a new home; and she is helping her son adjust to new friends as he goes from elementary school to middle school. Although the events occurring on Tina's ticker tape are mostly ones that she chose to deal with, she still feels a bit overwhelmed and tired, and finds concentrating on specific tasks difficult.
>
> Tina could think that she has a problem, but after using the 2M simultaneous focus to shift to a macro perspective, she realizes that the difficulty concentrating and physical fatigue she is experiencing are "natural." By holding onto the macro view of the future she is shaping for herself, she'll keep from misdirecting her energies and getting off track.

Regardless of whether the events on your ticker tape are desired (as in Tina's case) or uninvited (as in Phil's situation), a substantial investment of energy is needed to adjust to them. How you react to the events of your life, whether you create them or not, is also within your control.

Gaining Perspective

Dealing with changing priorities that are initiated by others in the workplace is especially challenging because those changes make keeping your focus more difficult. People generally adopt one of two perspectives in responding to changing priorities. The first perspective involves taking a micro view of their work and their role within an organization. Micro-thinking employees find it more difficult to shift gears when priorities change. Typically, they use the number of items completed as a major criterion for determining whether they have put in a good day. Therefore, when a high-priority item they have been working on for four hours is suddenly a cold issue, their frustration level peaks. They think, "I've wasted the whole day on this project, and for what? Can't management figure out what it wants to do?" At some point, these people begin to lose confidence in management because they think management can't make a decision that lasts.

The second perspective, more macro in scope, is associated with greater flexibility. Macro-thinking employees view the changing priority as management's attempt to use resources wisely: "Given the limited amount of available resources, it's a good thing management is willing to pull out and invest our energies in an area where we can make a greater difference." These people are usually less upset when the project they were working on is killed. By operating with the macro perspective, they see changing priorities as having less to do with self and more to do with how the change will benefit a larger whole. The big-picture perspective also reminds employees that changing priorities are inevitable and a natural offshoot of operating in a fast-paced, unpredictable environment.

TOO MUCH TO DO AND TOO LITTLE TIME

No need for any examples here! Having too much to do in too little time is one condition that most of us deal with daily. As a matter of fact, a 1995 national study revealed it to be the number-one emotionally charged situation for managers in the workplace.[1] As a Pro-Achiever, you recognize the big-picture reality that things won't go back to the way they were in "the good old days," so you must adjust the way you perceive the situation.

"A tough reality," says one successful sales force program manager for Hewlett Packard in Atlanta, "is dealing with the fact that I will not get everything done in a day." How does he give himself permission to not get everything done? "How can I not give myself permission? I've learned through the years that while I kept trying to separate work and home life, in reality everything is integrated. Problems, changing priorities, and having too much to do occur at work *and* at home. If I've done my best in juggling everything, even the things that didn't get done, I'll sleep at night."[2]

> *Pressure is a fear of not having enough time or resources available to live up to your expectations or those of others around you.*

Even if we have learned to juggle, as this sales manager has, having too much to do can create a sense of being out of control, because pressured feelings mount with each task that gets added to our already overloaded to-do list. Today, pressure can be described as a fear of not having enough time or resources available to live up to our own expectations or those of others around us. Sometimes the pressured feelings are so great that our focus gets blurred and we don't know which task to tackle. While we try to figure out our next move, a familiar, panicky feeling intensifies as we recognize that we need to get so much done. Regaining our focus and our sense of control requires separating our emotions from the tasks themselves. The 2M simultaneous focus is helpful in handling these intense pressured feelings.

Coping with Pressure

Pressured feelings can be fueled by thinking repeatedly in the macro picture. For instance, saying to yourself or to others, "I have so much to do," generates pressure because it instantly reminds you of all the work that needs to be done in your day. In this instance, using the 2M simultaneous focus involves taking your lens and zooming into the micro picture: Ask yourself, "Given the amount of time available, what is one thing I can do that will make a valuable difference and, at the same time, make me feel better about myself?"

> *To keep things in perspective, ask yourself,*
> *"How important will this be in five years?"*

Conversely, you can add a lot of pressure by thinking only in the micro, such as when you are facing a deadline. To regain your focus, take your lens and zoom to the macro. Ask yourself: "Is this task a life-or-death situation?" Unless you work in the medical or law enforcement fields, most of the deadlines you face don't have such dire consequences. Likewise, try asking yourself, "How important will this task be five years from now?"

Another question can help put the deadline in perspective while positioning you to do your best. Ask yourself, "What is the worst that can happen if this deadline isn't met?" If you can live with the answer, you can move forward with less pressure.

Defining What's Important

Not having enough time in a day to get everything done is a common complaint. How many times have you insisted that the reason a particular assignment didn't get done was that you didn't have enough time? When the Hewlett Packard manager hears this excuse, he responds, "You've had all the time there is." Usually, his sales reps give him a bemused look, before realizing what he's really saying. Then the sales manager adds, "Remember, time is a constant, and you've had the same amount as everybody else. You simply didn't make this assignment a priority. There's no reason to make any excuses about time. You're in charge of how you spend your time— so keep in mind, once you spend it, it's gone."

If we need to direct our energies toward how we spend our time, let's try an exercise. Take 15 seconds to think about how you organize yourself when you're faced with having too many tasks to complete and not enough time to do them all. Remember, there's no way to get any more time—that's the wrong focus. So how do you go about establishing priorities?

When I ask workshop participants this question, they reply that their priorities are set according to "what my boss wants," "who is yelling the loudest," "what's most urgent," "what the customer wants," and "what I feel like doing." Most people say that they set priorities not simply according to what's urgent, but also according to what's most important.

> **Think about what you consider important,
> and what others think is important.**

When workshop participants mention importance, everyone in the room nods in agreement. But what is really meant by "most important"? On the surface, the meaning may seem obvious; but from a multidimensional perspective, deciding what's important is not an easy task. Who determines what's important? If you reply, "I do," is that compatible with today's team-centered, customer-focused business environment? Consider the macro picture of the 2M simultaneous focus. When you determine what's important in isolation, you may overlook what the customer thinks is important. Likewise, what's important to you might not be as important to other members of your team. So you can't determine what's important by yourself; you need to coordinate what you think is important with what others around you think.

Don't overlook seeking guidance from the boss. In team-centered environments, it's not always clear how team members should use the boss. But your boss can be a big help when it comes to setting priorities. However, we've all heard tales about employees who ask for help from their bosses only to be greeted unenthusiastically. Likely, those employees overlooked an important unspoken expectation regarding how best to approach their bosses.

Rachel, an administrative support person, told her boss how upset she was because she couldn't deal with her long list of work priorities. She asked him, "What should I do first?" He responded by noting specific things Rachel should be working on. As he spoke, his mannerisms were abrupt and rather cold. Rachel walked out of his office thinking that the boss didn't seem very interested in helping her. Later, she found out that what she had thought wasn't accurate: Her boss didn't mind "helping" her; what he did mind was having to do all her thinking. In other words, if Rachel had presented her situation and then reviewed how she planned to address the problem, her boss would have been much more receptive. Interestingly, his viewpoint is shared by a lot of managers!

You can use the 2M simultaneous focus to think about your tasks. While factoring in that your boss assigned the task, part of the micro picture, zoom out to the macro picture and remember that it's important to examine whether the completed task will meet customer needs and remain aligned with the goals and objectives of your organization. Also look at whether this task, when completed, will make a difference and move the department closer to its goals. While you're at it, see if the customer will be better off in the long run.

Handling Tasks That Are All Labeled Top Priority

After using objective and subjective methods of determining what's important, you may still find yourself with several tasks that are all "top priority." Knowing that several tasks are urgent and have to be done at once can produce a tremendous amount of pressure. Often, you'll hear someone say, "Well, I've got to dig in and work late so I can knock all these things off my list." This is the linear approach that many people use: As soon as one thing is done, the next task begins.

From a multidimensional perspective, completing what has to get done can be likened to making an elaborate breakfast of eggs, toast, bacon, and coffee; the challenge is to have everything ready and hot at the same time. Sequencing priorities involves looking at each micro task and weighing how much control you have over its timing, what has to be done to complete it, and what effect each step will have in the end. Some tasks have fixed times, like giving a presentation at a conference, completing your taxes, and attending a wedding. They serve as focal points around which other tasks can be planned. As one successful manager at IBM said, "The thinking is a complex integration process that requires filtering and weighing each situation as if you were putting together a flowchart, like we do when working on a major technical project."[3]

Two practices can help you sequence tasks when all have high priority:

- Create a perfection-to-acceptability scale.
- Solicit help from others.

First, think about the level of quality that each task requires. A lot of internal pressure comes from assuming automatically that each task has to be done perfectly. Assumptions from the past often play a part in setting standards of perfection—assumptions such as "Anything worth doing is worth doing right" and "If you can't put 100 percent into something, don't bother to do it at all." These assumptions can serve you well when you have two or three priorities and when time and other resources are available to enable you to reach these high standards. When eight or nine priorities are staring you in the face, however, you can't possibly do each one perfectly. Besides, when you focus on the macro picture, you'll find that some tasks do not require perfection. So, don't get wrapped up in being perfect for the sake of being perfect, when what is needed is to make a valuable difference.

> *When all priorities are number one, adjust
> your expectations level.*

The perfection-to-acceptability scale gives you flexibility to examine each task according to the level of expectation you will set for yourself, given the amount of time and other resources available to you to complete it. When the time allotment is limited, you need to set your rating lower than "perfect" on the scale. No one likes to do sloppy work—that's not what's being suggested here. Rather, the objective is to learn to accept control for establishing performance standards that meet or slightly exceed the expectations of others. Since the number of priorities will most likely still be there tomorrow, you need to build some flexibility into your performance routine, giving yourself permission to vacillate from perfection to high levels of acceptability. Sometimes "a good plan today is better than a perfect plan tomorrow."

It's not uncommon to hear people explaining that they could do a better job if they only had more time. The trouble is, there is no more time. Time is fixed, and our plates will remain full. So the best use of our energy is to adjust our expectations.

The second practice involves soliciting help from others. Besides getting help from the boss, try going back to the customer and checking out if the task can be redefined or reworked in some way. You can also solicit help from others on your team. In today's team-centered environments, it's acceptable for team members to go directly to other team members for help—assignments don't always have to go through the boss first. Learn to look at others as resources to help achieve a common goal. You are not diminished just because you are not working directly on a task. Stay focused on getting the task done.

As one human resources director said, "I lose focus when I have too many requests from too many senior managers. Because you are good at one thing, you are expected to do a number of things. Sometimes, I don't have the option of saying no. So what I do to maintain my focus is not get so tied up with administrative things. Rather, I will reach out to others—they could be my peers or people on my staff. Then I'll keep my mind on whatever process I'm working on. That's where I can make the greatest difference, because it's where my greatest strength lies."[4]

> *Motivate yourself to engage the help of others by thinking of your value.*

One way to motivate yourself to engage the help of others is to consider yourself as worth so many dollars per hour. You can then decide who is better positioned to handle a task—you at your hourly dollar rate or someone else who works at a lower rate. For easy calculating, let's say that your time is worth $50 per hour and your assistant's time is worth $20 per hour. The task at hand involves getting some figures together for an upcoming report. Are you better suited to search for that data or is your assistant? Granted you may be able to find the data more quickly and input it more readily at the computer, but your time is better spent putting the report together. Your assistant can do the necessary research—even though it will take longer than doing the task yourself.

TOO LITTLE ATTENTION

Being a good listener has always been valuable in the workplace, whether you are a manager or an employee. It is even more valuable in today's complex work environment, in which relationships with others are far more important than simply giving orders and expecting people to respond. Since the autocratic leader has become unpopular and respect for authority figures cannot be presumed, we need to promote relationships bound by mutual trust and respect. This bond is something that must be earned. One way to build the bond is to be a good, attentive listener.

> **Don't underestimate the importance of being a good listener.**

Being a good listener entails not only listening well (that is, hearing and understanding what the other person is saying), but also conveying to others that they have your attention so that you are *perceived* as being a good listener. By giving others your full attention, you send them a clear message of respect. This message is conveyed because you are giving of your *time*, a valuable resource that is in limited supply. After all, how many of us will give the time of day to people we don't respect?

With the multitude of things to do each day, combined with all the thoughts that keep swirling in our minds, it's easy to let our focus become blurred and to come across as not listening. Too often, we jump quickly into the macro picture and formulate our response without considering (on a more micro level) how we are affecting others. Here are two familiar examples of people who may be listening well, but who fail to be perceived as good listeners because they overlook one perspective.

> Paul goes to an experienced manager with an idea that he is very excited about. Before he can finish explaining the idea, the manager jumps in and says no. The manager's macro perspective is that she has heard the idea many times before, and experience has shown that it is unworkable. The manager fails to see the micro perspective. For Paul, this abrupt treatment implies that the boss isn't interested in hearing his ideas.

(Continued)

> At home, Carlos stops listening to his wife when she starts talking about an editorial she read that day about the death penalty. He is convinced he knows her views so well that he even knows what she is going to say next. Although Carlos is feeling good about himself at the macro level, he overlooks the micro—the irritation and frustration his wife experiences because he cuts her off and doesn't give her the attention she sought.

Sometimes when we jump into a macro picture, the anticipation of what others are going to say colors our lack of attention with a negative attitude. For instance, Connie was invited to give a second presentation to one of her clients, since her first effort was so well-received. The only problem was that Connie was assigned to work with a new corporate contact, Jim, who was not excited about using a different speaker from the one he wanted. As they talked on the phone about tailoring the content of the new presentation, Jim began arguing over things Connie had not said. At one point, Connie replied, "A lot of presenters would address the subject of stress at this point, but I think we should stick to the main subject of criticism." Jim interrupted. "You don't want to talk about stress. Our audience isn't interested in that subject. I don't know why you want to move in that direction." Clearly, the idea Jim was criticizing Connie for was contrary to what she had actually said. It was what Jim thought he heard—or what he wanted to hear, since he already had a chip on his shoulder.

Likewise, our lack of attention to what is occurring in the macro picture can demonstrate an insensitivity to others, especially when we overlook their time constraints as listeners. People may say that they are busy and can take only a few moments. But we are so intent on communicating our point that we fail to consider that the few moments allotted to us have long since expired. The attempt to influence our listeners falters because they have stopped hearing anything we are saying; instead, they are thinking only about how disrespectful we're being at the moment.

Becoming Aware of Whether You Are Listening

If you know you have a short attention span, or have a lot of things happening at once, make a conscious effort to listen. As noted previously, being perceived as listening attentively sends a compliment to the other person and is seen as a sign of respect.

A big complaint among employees is that their bosses don't listen. Not surprisingly, employees want the undivided attention of their bosses. During a conversation they are disappointed if the boss begins entering information into a computer or signing documents, if the boss suddenly interrupts the conversation to write down some unrelated thought, or if the boss begins taking incoming calls. Any kind of personal grooming during a meeting can also be a turnoff, such as filing or trimming nails. Not only do employees question whether the boss is listening; the grooming activity tends to trivialize the conversation.

> *Create routines to check up on whether you're really listening.*

As a manager, you can create certain routines to ensure that you are listening, and to reassure employees that they have your attention. Start by clearing your desk or at least closing any files. If possible, hold your phone calls. If you must take a call, let others know up front so your actions aren't misinterpreted or taken personally. Take notes. Writing down key ideas is an effective way to keep your mind from wandering while demonstrating your interest in what the other person is saying. Be aware of your posture. One executive told me, "Late in the day, it's hard to stay focused and listen intently to what others are saying, especially if people are bringing up ideas that I've heard before in one form or another. To monitor myself, I make sure that I'm sitting on the edge of my seat and that I'm leaning forward, as opposed to slumping in my chair. Also, I repeatedly remind myself that even though I've heard the idea before, the environment we are working in is different now."

Most managers have been told at some point that getting out from behind the desk is a good way to build rapport. But it can serve another purpose as well. As one midlevel manager with the Immigration and Naturalization Service explained: "It's a good technique to help you stay focused on your goal, which is to be a good listener. Although every conversation doesn't warrant using this technique, when you do use it, it is very effective."[5]

As a final check of whether you're being attentive and focusing on the micro perspective, rephrase in your own words what you think the other person is saying before adding your own comments. If the employee nods in agreement with your interpretation, then you know you're focused.

All these tactics work equally well outside the workplace. Typically, conversations at home take place with something else going on—cooking dinner, cleaning, washing dishes, watching TV. When the issues are serious or when your mate is upset, being sensitive about supplying your undivided attention is important, because it demonstrates that you value your mate as a person as well.

Becoming Aware of How You Are Listening

Another micro focus to be aware of is whether you are listening to argue and judge or listening to understand. When you are listening to understand, you ask questions and try to get past the words in order to figure out *what* the other person is trying to communicate. You can rely on two clues to indicate when you are listening to argue and judge. First, pay attention to your own self-talk. If, while the other person is talking, you are continually thinking, "That's not accurate," "I disagree," and "It didn't quite happen like that," you are listening to argue and judge. Second, pay attention to the first words to leave your mouth when you do respond. If you verbalize similar phrases of disagreement or if you simply say no, you are listening to argue and judge.

> *Listen to understand.*

That is not to say that listening to argue and judge is never appropriate. Do not fall into the illusion of control and begin thinking that one listening technique is right and another way is wrong. Each has its place. Take, for instance, your search for where to send your children to camp: You listen to all the features that each camp has to offer, and throughout the presentations you are appropriately judging which camp best suits your needs. Your focus should always be on which listening technique is most effective given the circumstances at the moment. The key is to be aware of how you are processing information and of whether your approach helps you handle a situation more effectively.

Paying Attention to Your Effect on Others

The third important consideration when listening is paying attention to how you are affecting others. Here's a telephone scenario: You call someone to discuss an important matter, and the person at the other end of the line sounds upset. In the micro perspective, you have this issue to discuss. If you are operating with a macro perspective simultaneously, you become aware that your call has come at a bad time for the other person. If the matter you want to discuss can wait, you may suggest arranging to call back at a more convenient time. Once gain, your focus is the same: to keep the big picture in mind so that you can accurately interpret what's going on around you in order to respond appropriately to the situation at hand.

> *Pay attention to how quickly you solve other*
> *people's problems.*

An important and less ovbious area to be sensitive to is *how quickly you respond to issues or problems as they are raised.* Two executives I interviewed said they learned the hard way that their ability to instantly zero in on the main source of a problem isn't always well received when employees have been wrestling with the issue for several days. The executives explained that their ideas or recommendations are sometimes interpreted as emotional responses, and therefore are accorded less credibility. Or they are viewed as quick fixes designed to outsmart others in the room.

To defuse the issues of personal competition and emotion, shift everyone's focus to the broader issue at hand, and the challenges that lie ahead, making sure you communicate everything in objective terms. Or, when you can, ask questions that help others come up with the solution themselves. Being a good listener in today's fast-paced, chaotic times is crucial. If you're not getting good information, you are putting desired outcomes at risk.

TOO MUCH EMOTION

Sometimes, experiencing too much emotion can cause you to lose your focus and your ability to achieve desired outcomes. Take a few minutes to read through these two situations and consider what they have in common.

> The last time Jack approached his boss, Charlene, with a problem—some of the support people in production were uncooperative—she dismissed his suggestion that they bring in outside vendors. In anger and frustration, Jack made some disparaging remarks about how the company

STEP FIVE: KEEP YOUR FOCUS

provides inadequate support to employees. Charlene withdrew from any further conversation, causing Jack to leave the meeting wondering what Charlene thought of him. Now Jack's heavy workload is causing him to fall behind on a major project, one that he would be able to complete on time if his immediate tasks could be handled elsewhere. He wants to ask Charlene to reassign some of his minor projects to others in the department, but he thinks that she might respond negatively to his request. If she does, he's afraid he might lose his patience and say something he later would regret. So he puts off meeting with her.

Just days before Pete and Melissa are scheduled to leave for a family reunion, Pete learns about an important meeting that he must attend. He will have to fly out a day later than planned. He asks Melissa to accompany his mother on her flight and she agrees. Melissa then realizes that she will have to spend several uncomfortable hours confined with her mother-in-law, who is negative and critical of others. As Melissa worries about putting up with her mother-in-law during the trip, the headaches she has been free of for several months return.

In both of these situations, emotions become the central focus and drive what actions people take. Jack's fear is paramount so he postpones meeting with his boss until the project is seriously behind schedule; now facing a greater fear—that he will miss the project's deadline—he knows he must talk to Charlene, but still he avoids her. Melissa's worrying makes her sick over something that *may* happen. Both Jack's and Melissa's actions are driven by their emotions; and those actions keep them from moving in a positive direction.

"Sometimes we get stuck, and all we focus on is our feelings," explains psychiatrist Harry Croft. "Furthermore, we block ourselves from thinking about the source of those feelings, and instead all we experience is the emotion. We keep feeding our feelings by constantly reminding ourselves how we feel about a certain person or situation, and we look for examples to support how we feel. For example, every time a certain coworker's name is mentioned, we cringe as we call to mind all the things we dislike about this person. Likewise, every time we run into our coworker, we feed ourselves information to support our view. In the macro picture, we're helping to feed the negative attitude that we already have. If someone asks why we dislike this person, our typical response is, 'I just do.' The basis for our reaction is the accumulation of negative emotions. Our negative attitude colors the way we perceive the coworker's actions, and probably how we react as well. Sometimes the actions that we take in these situations cause us embarrassment."

Margaret finds working with Sharon, a peer in another department, extremely difficult because Sharon always turns work in late. Finally fed up with having to rush to get things done because of Sharon's lateness, Margaret approaches her about the matter. As Margaret explains her frustration, Sharon listens politely and, much to Sharon's surprise, she doesn't argue—in fact, she's empathetic. The conversation ends with both of them agreeing to have Sharon notify Margaret as soon as possible if a project is going to be late. Even though an expectations package has been agreed upon, Margaret is skeptical.

Three days later, a project comes in late. Margaret is furious because she never heard from Sharon—as she had expected she wouldn't. Margaret calls Sharon and starts criticizing her for not calling in advance. After they exchange some harsh words, Margaret learns that Sharon did indeed try to reach her, but the voice mail system was down so she left a handwritten note on Margaret's desk. As Margaret locates the message among a stack of papers, she realizes that she is actually the one at fault. She treated Sharon unfairly by not trying to find out what happened before assuming the worst. Here again, emotions and a negative attitude colored the situation and caused Margaret to lose her focus.

We've all done things like this from time to time. After all, we are only human. In this type of situation, we need to use our control by taking an objective view and looking beyond the reaction prompted by our emotions. When we do, we have greater control, and are less apt to react rashly and jeopardize what we are trying to achieve.

Most of us recognize that when we get too emotional, our focus can easily become blurred and we may act in ways that are contrary to what we want. Our thinking is adversely affected, so we make poor decisions. We have many expressions to remind us of how we lose our focus when we become too emotional: "I'm so upset that I can't see straight," "I'm so angry, all I see is red," "I got so choked up," and so on.

What does it take to keep emotions from getting so out of control that we fall off the track? Two important tactics can help you to use your energies more productively. To illustrate, let's take a close look at one common emotion, worry. After all, there's lots to worry about in today's environment. Once you learn to handle worry, you can apply the same tactics to other emotions.

The following tips may sound familiar to you. Bear in mind that the focus isn't on whether you know what to do. Rather, the focus is on whether you are using these tactics on a regular basis—effectively.

Inspecting Your Emotions as Clues for Action

For the past 20 years, I've asked workshop participants if they worry. Everyone raises a hand and admits to worrying at least sometimes.

When I then ask how many people think that worrying is bad, a majority of hands remain raised. But is worrying necessarily bad? Worrying can be bad if we direct all our energies to the act of worrying. When this occurs, our focus has shifted from taking control and doing something positive about the situation to emotionalizing the experience.

> *Worrying, if properly controlled, can be an asset.*

But worrying can be an asset if you view it as a signal requiring further investigation. When an adult worries, it's most likely for a good reason. With the benefit of the experiences you have accumulated over the years, you sense that something is wrong or has been overlooked. A good way to look at worrying is as if it were a flashing light on the dashboard of your car. The only difference between your worrying signals and the lights on the car's dashboard is that the dashboard lights are clearly marked to indicate the problem. Your worries are not so simple. You need to do a little more investigation to find out what's causing your signals to light up.

Imagine that you are worrying about an upcoming meeting. You ask yourself what's causing you to worry, and your mind starts searching for possible causes for your uneasiness. "Handouts for the presentation" comes to your conscious mind, and you consider whether this is the root of your worries. You sense a familiar signal indicating yes, that this is what is causing you to feel uneasy. By probing further, you realize that you have not followed up with the production people to make sure that the handouts have been duplicated. Next you need to consider your parameters of control in the situation. You ask yourself whether you can do anything about the handouts, and the answer again is yes. You develop a workable plan of action, and almost instantaneously the worried feelings begin to dissipate as you start to put your strategy into action.

What's important to focus on here, whether your concern is nervousness, worry, or anxiety, is acknowledging your feelings and using them as clues for gathering more information—in contrast to ignoring them or letting them control your actions. Check out the source of your feelings by repeatedly asking yourself, "What's causing me to feel this way?" Your answer will provide the kind of information you need to gain an action-centered focus that moves you closer to your goals.

Controlling Your Underlying Thoughts

I'm sure you have noticed how rarely your situation improves after you tell yourself to stop worrying about something. Even when the advice comes from someone who cares about you, it seldom helps. Ironically, your emotional condition is likely to worsen. You misdirect your energies and your focus when you try to control your worrying. Putting your energies into trying to control your emotions at that moment is ineffective. Rather, you should focus your energies on controlling what you are thinking.

All kinds of emotional reactions are sparked by what you are thinking. Keep the macro picture in mind—that worrying, like other emotions, is just a reaction. It may appear to be spontaneous, but it isn't: You have to think about something to worry. When you ask yourself what's causing you to worry, ideas begin to surface that you can investigate. Instead of investing your energies to deal with your worrying, focus on the thoughts that are linked to your feelings.

> *To control your emotions, pay attention to what you are thinking.*

Other emotions can be dealt with in the same way—by paying attention to the thoughts that underlie them. For example, when you say, "I'm under so much pressure right now," have you noticed that your body responds accordingly? To handle the feelings that are transmitted throughout your body at that moment, pause long enough to move from the macro perspective to the micro. While focusing on the micro perspective, write down every task and responsibility that comes to mind. Often, you are surprised because your list reveals that the situation isn't quite as bad as you had pictured it. Once again, a wise investment of your energies is to deal with what you are thinking in an effort to better manage your feelings.

Obviously, handling emotions is a complex subject. After combining these tips with your other experiences and insights, you may still be having difficulty achieving desired outcomes. You face reality, and the reality is that managing your emotions requires an investment of energy and the use of a variety of skills. One group of skills that you can rely on are the quick charges introduced in Chapter 10. Quick charges can be used instantly to enhance self-control in high-pressure situations. When you combine quick charges with the skills learned in this chapter, you can position yourself to deal effectively with any situation.

There are other techniques that can help you stay focused and perform at your best. They are called "Quick Charges" and you will read about them in the next chapter.

Here's how you can take control immediately.

1. **STOP** listening inattentively.

2. **STOP,** when engaging in a conversation, and ask yourself, "Am I giving this person 100 percent of my attention, or am I losing my focus and allowing myself to think about other things?" If you are losing focus,

check out whether you heard the last thing said by re-phrasing or summarizing the discussion.

3. **STOP** trying to directly control your emotions. Instead, invest your energies to assess the quality of your think-ing. Your thoughts help "spark" your emotions.

4. **STOP** long enough to examine whether your immediate actions are aligned with the macro picture before tak-ing on tasks. Even though the tasks themselves may be properly aligned, your sequencing and timing could be off.

START ▶

1. **START** to pay attention to how you are listening: Are you listening to argue and judge, or are you listening to understand?

2. **START** paying attention to being focused on accomplish-ing desired outcomes.

10

KEEP YOUR COOL

Sheila, an attractive salesclerk for a major European clothing designer, is attending to a customer who walked into the New York City boutique over an hour ago. Her boss, Nancy, is in the back room, coding a new shipment of clothes. While Nancy is doing the coding, she observes Sheila working with the customer. After Sheila shows the customer a number of outfits, the customer walks out of the store without buying anything. Nancy immediately casts her eyes on Sheila, and she can tell from her expression that Sheila is very disappointed. Sheila's disappointment is linked to the fact that she works primarily on commission—the company pays her only a small hourly wage. When that customer walked out, she took Sheila's hopes for a sale with her.

During the six months they have worked together, Sheila and Nancy have gotten along fabulously. Nancy, a seasoned veteran in the fashion industry and the store's manager for the past five years, sees herself as Sheila's mentor. Realizing how badly Sheila feels, Nancy decides to see if there's anything she can do to make her feel better.

Walking from the back room, she approaches Sheila, saying, "How did things go with that customer?" In a disheartened tone, Sheila replies, "OK. You know I tried . . . (sigh). It's just so disappointing that she didn't buy anything after all that effort." Nancy, continuing to comfort Sheila, concludes the conversation by saying, "As long as you did your best, Sheila, that's all you can ask of yourself. There'll be more customers. Don't feel bad."

Sheila tries to put a smile on her face as she returns to her duties. About 10 minutes later, another customer walks into the boutique, and Sheila greets her with a smile. The customer is interested in one of the most expensive dresses, but her size is not on the racks out on the floor. Sheila heads to the back room, where Nancy is, to find the dress in the customer's size. As Sheila approaches, Nancy asks her for some help, unaware that Sheila is assisting a customer. Instead of simply telling Nancy that a customer is waiting for her outside, Sheila snaps at Nancy, saying that she has to help her customer first. As Sheila continues to search for the dress, she reflects on what just happened. With each passing thought, she feels worse and worse—not only for losing the sale to the last customer but, more important, for snapping at Nancy.

I'm sure you can relate to this scene—all of us experience disappointments each day, regardless of what line of work we're in. You might be thinking that Sheila needs to work with the damage control dimension to take control of herself and let go of a bad situation so it doesn't ruin the rest of her day. But Sheila's problem goes deeper than lacking good rebounding skills to get back on track: Sheila doesn't know where the "track" is.

Sheila, like many of us, needs to become aware of what it means to be at her best at a given moment. To perform at high levels and make a valuable difference, we all need to learn how to take control and invest energies to do our best when the situation demands it. This chapter peels apart what "doing your best" really means, then introduces you to several *quick charges*—techniques that can help you instantly rise to your best in high-pressure situations.

DOING YOUR BEST

Surprisingly, many people lack an awareness of themselves when engaging in everyday activities. As a result, these people are unclear about what it means to do their best. For example, Sheila wrongly equates doing her best with the amount of effort or energy she exerts in a situation. She thinks that when she puts in a lot of effort, she should achieve a result of proportionate value. In this particular situation, because Sheila put in a lot of time with her customer, she figured she should have gotten a sale that would have made it "worth her while."

Sheila is not alone in her belief that results should be proportional to energy expended. A number of professional and amateur athletes I have worked with think the same way. Consider a professional golfer who practices for hours on the driving range in preparation for an upcoming tournament. The golfer plays poorly, and in a moment of frustration he exclaims that he can't believe how badly he did, since he practiced so long and hard. Similarly, if an employee works all weekend on a proposal only to have her boss respond that the proposal is too weak to accept, the employee might fire back, "I can't believe this. I spent my whole weekend on the report and you shot it down!"

If you equate doing your best with obtaining results and the results aren't there, it's easy to get discouraged and to assume, as Sheila did, that something is wrong with you. But this assumption is faulty because it doesn't factor in events that are outside your control. Perhaps Sheila handled her customer as well as anyone could have, but the customer left the store because she suddenly remembered an appointment. The customer leaving the dress shop had nothing to do with Sheila or the way Sheila treated her.

The amount of energy expended in a given effort is part of the formula for doing our best, but the results are not proportionate. Still, many of us, like Sheila, get so disappointed and discouraged when the results aren't there that rebounding becomes more difficult. Similarly, a number of us focus on our rate of success. If the results don't come fast enough after we invest a lot of energy, we tend to give up or drop what we are pursuing—whether it's learning to cook, use a computer, or play an instrument.

Doing your best often requires taking multiple approaches. The results are generally not directly under your control. You can control the amount of energy you expend, so that is an important factor in doing your best. You can also take control by determining the resources available and the most effective ways to use them to achieve the desired outcome. In other words, "doing your best" means that in any given situation you perform optimally—energies are properly invested as you summon up whatever resources are available to achieve desired end results. A simple formula captures all the elements:

> *Doing your best = energy input + being at your best + staying at your best.*

Let's examine each element of the formula.

Energy Input

The amount of energy you expend depends on your day and the things happening around you. On days when everything seems to flow naturally, whether at work, at home, or on the sports field, performing up to your expectations seems to require a minimal investment of your energies. Try those same activities on another day, however, and doing your best may require a tremendous expenditure of energy. No one else necessarily can see a difference—it's just that things don't flow the same way. You know things are different, because you're working really hard to get results.

In today's fast-paced environment, you can easily find yourself running from place to place and task to task. In order to position yourself to achieve, you want to make sure you stop and think about what you are doing. Using your energies wisely is an essential part of taking control. Beyond expending energies to perform the task at hand, you need to invest energies to determine your parameters of control and the control levers that you have to work with. Then, invest your energies in deciding whether to move into action.

> *Even though you have control, you may elect not to invest your energies to take action.*

Sometimes you have all the control you need, but for one reason or another you decide not to take action. For example, your boss says something inaccurate in front of you and one of the company's best customers. In a flash, you size up the situation—you can correct the boss if you choose to, but you decide not to invest those energies and say anything, because you could "win the battle and lose the war." So you elect not to exercise that control option. When it comes to energy input, doing your best entails effectively leveraging your energies to achieve the best returns. In the process, you need to recognize that you are your own most important resource.

Being at Your Best

Being at your best requires an ongoing awareness of yourself, and your minute-by-minute performance. This self-awareness can be compared to an internal radar system that is constantly sending you signals, telling you that at a given instant you are performing at your optimal level. Understanding what it means to be at your best goes beyond having knowledge of your strengths and weaknesses, or your likes and dislikes; you need to invest your energies to be aware of whether you are at your optimal performance level before and while engaging in an event.

> *How do you know you've had a good day?*
> *Teddy Roosevelt said, "when you have used*
> *every minute wisely."[1]*

Do you recognize when you are at your best? Over the years, thousands of people in my workshops have been asked to identify when they are at their best. I've found some interesting results. Most people respond by saying they are energetic, sharp, productive, happy, feeling good. In one sense this is valuable information, but in another sense it is worthless because it does not relate specifically to people's performance in a given situation. If you use only generalized indicators, you won't know soon enough when you are moving away from your optimal performance level, and your ability to rebound and get back on track is impaired because the signals are too vague. Working with specific signals helps you pinpoint how you are actually affecting a situation.

Let's look at an everyday work situation: a one-to-one conversation with your boss. Which specific behaviors or sensations indicate to you that you are at your best? Here's a sample listing: "When I am at my best, I am aware that I easily recall information, I express myself clearly and succinctly, I pick up cues from my boss and accurately interpret them. I am aware that I am listening to what my boss is saying and trying to say. I enunciate my words softly and my tone of voice is appealing. My posture is good and my deodorant is working." The signals you "screen" in are your own, but they must be specific. Being specific is important because, after all, how can you feel good about yourself and operate at your best if you don't know specifically what you are looking for? How can you get back on track if you don't know where the track is?

The salesclerk described at the beginning of this chapter did not know where her personal track was. To determine whether she was at her best when dealing with the customer who did not make a purchase, Sheila needed to become aware of specific signals. For instance, when assisting the customer, was she being a good listener? Was she accurately picking up on unspokens, such as the customer's facial expressions as she looked at various garments? Was she effectively handling the customer's objections? Was she carefully selecting her words? Was she asking appropriate questions? Was her tone of voice friendly and appealing?

> *Being at your best varies with every activity.*

The set of signals you use to determine whether you are at your best varies with the activity in which you are engaged. For instance, when you are playing tennis, the signals that you are in top form may include keeping a firm grip, anticipating your opponent's moves, accurately sizing up your opponent's weaknesses, and having a confident feeling in your chest. Mentally, you may be aware that you are concentrating only on the play at hand. When you are cooking a special meal, the signals that you are at your best may include having good sequencing and timing, readily finding the utensils you need, anticipating what needs to be done, and also enjoying what you are doing. You may notice that your mind is calm and void of interference.

The signals I've identified here are merely samples; they are not all-inclusive. You may focus on a number of different ones. The important thing is to put in place a built-in feedback mechanism that tells you how you are doing as you engage in a task or interact with others. As Aristotle said, "We cannot be in error about something and have knowledge of it at the same time."[2] Having knowledge of yourself in a given situation gives you a greater sense of control, which is translated into a feeling of confidence. The confidence comes when you are getting specific signals telling you that you are at your best at the moment.

Having a keen sense of when you are *not* at your best is also important. Interestingly, reversing the signals you work with to tell you when you are at your best doesn't necessarily give you the insights you need to learn when you are not. Go back to the situation of talking one-on-one with your boss. What signals might tell you that you are moving away from your optimal level? Perhaps as you are trying to listen to your boss, your mind is flooded with thoughts about whether your responses will be accepted. Maybe you fumble for words as you try to express your ideas, or you hear yourself using the same phrases again and again—phrases such as "you know" and "right." When you move outside your optimal performance zone, you may begin to perspire or your hands may feel cold and clammy. Staying focused on the purpose of your conversation may become increasingly difficult as your mouth gets dry or your voice cracks. The list goes on and on.

When you become aware that you are moving away from being at your best, you need to take control and act on that self-awareness by calling on specific skills to help you return to your optimal level. At this point, you are drawing on the third element of the formula for doing your best.

Staying at Your Best

> *How can you get back on track when you don't know where the track is?*

Being at your best entails developing your awareness of yourself; staying at your best involves using skills to keep yourself performing optimally. The skills that you can use to gain greater control over yourself and your circumstances—that give you an instant boost back to your optimal level—are called *quick charges*.

Quick charges can be used instantly, and without detection from or dependence on others. Quick charges are the trade secrets that many athletes rely on to maintain their competitive edge. Quick charges give you the ability to turn a mistake into "part of the dance," and if you use them well, no one around you will ever know that you missed a step. People who can continually come back strong from one tough situation after another, and who don't let past failures affect present or future successes, quickly earn reputations as "real pros." These are the people in business, as well as sports, who always seem to have the situation under control. They react to tough challenges with aplomb.

To work effectively with the damage control dimension, you need to have a full set of quick charges at your disposal. Remember, flexibility is an element of control. Flexibility is especially important for rebounding. If you have only one recovery skill—say, for letting go of a mistake—and that skill doesn't work for you in a particular situation, what are you going to do to get back on track? When you lack options, you become stuck in the rigid zone. So part of your strategy for staying at your best involves learning and practicing a variety of quick charges, which you then can use effectively in tough, high-pressure situations.

PUTTING QUICK CHARGES TO USE

Quick charges are neatly packaged skills that are easy to remember and useful in a wide variety of situations on and off the job. Remember, no one can tell when you're using them. You select for your repertoire those skills that appeal to you. You can also modify the quick charges introduced in this book to fit your needs more specifically—my clients do this all the time. The balance of this chapter describes some tough everyday situations, in which thousands of people over the years have benefited from using quick charges. Pause for a moment to complete this exercise before you read on.

Exercise 1: How Well Do You Handle Yourself?

Determine how effectively you handle yourself in each of the following situations.

1. How effective are you at staying calm in a tense situation?

Ineffective   Extremely effective

| 1 | 2 | 3 | 4 | 5 | 6 | 7 |

2. How effective are you at thinking before you speak?

Ineffective   Extremely effective

| 1 | 2 | 3 | 4 | 5 | 6 | 7 |

3. How effective are you at letting go of a negative situation?

Ineffective   Extremely effective

| 1 | 2 | 3 | 4 | 5 | 6 | 7 |

4. How effective are you at maintaining your confidence when on the firing line?

Ineffective   Extremely effective

| 1 | 2 | 3 | 4 | 5 | 6 | 7 |

5. How effective are you at dealing with intimidating people?

Ineffective   Extremely effective

| 1 | 2 | 3 | 4 | 5 | 6 | 7 |

6. How effective are you at eliminating stomach knots?

Ineffective   Extremely effective

| 1 | 2 | 3 | 4 | 5 | 6 | 7 |

7. How effective are you at leaving the problems from work at work?

					Extremely	
					effective	
Ineffective						
1	2	3	4	5	6	7
⊥	⊥	⊥	⊥	⊥	⊥	⊥

Staying Calm in a Tense Situation

> *To stay calm, use the breathing quick charge.*

When you get upset, your body responds with the opposite of what it really needs: Your breathing tends to become rapid and shallow, ultimately resulting in your brain receiving less oxygen. The dearth of oxygen may lead to a lack of focus and a dulling of thought processes. You may not realize this is happening, but when it does, you are more likely to say something rash or do something foolish. That's why the *breathing quick charge*, even though it is a basic technique, is a valuable tool to help keep your emotions in check and your thinking clear.

Do you sigh when you feel pressured? The *breathing quick charge* capitalizes on that sigh by combining your breathing with relaxation of your muscles. To use the *breathing quick charge*, inhale deeply through your nose and hold your breath for a second or two, then exhale very slowly through your nose. Combine your exhalation with a relaxation of your whole body, starting at the top of your head when you first start to exhale, and working your way down to your toes. Repeat the process two or three times to instill a smooth rhythm of breathing.

There are numerous situations where you may want to practice the *breathing quick charge*. Because this quick charge helps you calm down, you can use it before making your opening remarks in a presentation or before responding to a question in an interview. Many people practice the *breathing quick charge* to help them fall asleep at night. When you're having trouble falling asleep, your breathing tends to be rapid and shallow. When you repeat the *breathing quick charge*, your breathing becomes more rhythmic and you can fall asleep more easily. The *breathing quick charge* can be used alone or with other techniques as part of a strategy to handle certain difficult circumstances.

Avoiding the Tendency to Speak First and Think Later

Some of us subscribe to the assumption that we can always be forth-right—that is, we feel free to "tell it like it is." Working with this assumption discounts any interest in paying attention to unspokens and disregards the need to be sensitive to timing, to those present, and to the consequences of what is being said.

Here are two quick examples to clarify what I mean. You and your mate are having dinner with your boss. You are explaining something that happened at work and your mate, who "tells it like it is," jumps in to say, "That's not how you described the situation to me." Your mate has spoken without considering that you may be trying to put the situation in the best light possible, for your boss's benefit.

Or you are trying to explain an idea to your supervisor and before you finish, he interrupts you, saying, "That's not going to work." Your supervisor has failed to consider that you may be proposing a workable variation on a formerly infeasible idea; even if your idea won't work, by dismissing it without hearing you out, he may be discouraging you from presenting ideas in the future.

If you, like the supervisor in this example, typically jump right to the point as soon as you *think* you see it, you may want to change that habit. Some people have modified this practice from "calling it the way I see it" to "being clear and up front with others in an effort to avoid any hidden agendas." Note that this modified assumption implies a lesser degree of urgency.

> *Even though your emotions are valid, you have control over them.*

The assumption that we are free to tell it like it is also implies that our emotions play a part in the decision about when to speak up. When we allow our emotions to spring us into action, they sometimes override our sensitivity to the unspokens operating in the situation. Do you have to act according to how you feel? From what you've learned in this book about the parameters of control, you realize that even though your emotions are valid, you don't have to act on them every time. The next time you feel yourself moving outside your optimal performance zone because your emotional fuse is lit, try the following three-step approach.

1. Keep your mouth closed. By keeping your lips pressed firmly together, you avoid saying anything you may regret later on. As you read this now, the recommendation may seem trite. But in a high-pressure situation, the urge to say something right then and there can seem overwhelming. Just picture yourself in a meeting where people are criticizing the ideas you are presenting and their reasoning is inaccurate. Closing your mouth and saying nothing isn't easy then.

2. Breathe. While keeping your mouth closed, practice the *breathing quick charge.* During the slow, smooth exhalation through your nose, ask yourself the following questions:

- "Did I listen?" Did you hear not only the words being said but what the speaker was trying to get across? Are you listening for unclear or unmatched expectations?
- "What do I want right now?" Sometimes what you want is to protect your ego, and in doing so, you may find that you

are suddenly dealing with a situation other than the topic of discussion.

At this point, you may be confused. How can you be asking yourself all these questions while you are engaged in a highly charged situation? The answer is simple. You think much faster than you can speak. It's said that people think at about 600 words per minute but speak at 150 to 200 words per minute. You're filling that extra time by addressing those questions.

3. Speak softly. When you do speak, speak slowly and in a quiet voice. A slow pace and low volume help you to keep your emotions in check.

Letting Go of a Negative Situation

As we've seen throughout this book, when we invest energy to take control of a situation, we are trying to increase our chances of achieving a desired outcome. We do not always succeed. Being criticized for something or having someone point out a mistake we've made is uncomfortable and disconcerting. Even when the outcome was not within our control and we have the support of others, we may become disappointed or discouraged, as Sheila did in the scenario that opened this chapter.

When you don't achieve a desired outcome, you want to harness your energies to rebound from the temporary setback. The *wastepaper basket quick charge* can help you return to your optimal level. Many of us have had training with visualization techniques. This quick charge builds on that visualization training to help you achieve the specific goal of rebounding instantly from a negative situation.

To use the *wastepaper basket quick charge*, begin by envisioning a sheet of posterboard. Take up to 15 seconds to mentally scribble on the posterboard whatever negative thoughts you are having at the moment. Let's say your boss pointed out some simple mathematical errors you made in a report. As you walk back from your boss's office to make the necessary revisions, you take 15 seconds to mentally write down, "How could I have been so stupid? Why didn't I double-check my figures? I could have caught that." (Many people can beat themselves up pretty good in just a few seconds!) Whatever is on your mind at that point gets scrawled on the posterboard. At the end of your timed period, you envision yourself taking a very big paint-brush and painting a large X across those negative thoughts. Then picture a big wastepaper basket. Take the poster, crumble it up or tear it in pieces, and dump it into the waste basket. Then light a match and burn the whole thing.

> *To let go of negative situations instantly, use the helium balloon quick charge.*

If you are really pressed for time, such as when you are in the midst of a presentation, the *helium balloon quick charge* may be the energizer of choice, because it's an even faster way to let go of a negative thought. Instead of filling your head with negative thoughts, picture a balloon being filled with helium. As the gas is pumped into the balloon, include your thoughts. Then release the balloon and let it fly away, taking your negative thoughts with it.

Even after you have "absorbed the mistake and remembered the lesson," there can be a lot of emotional debris lying around. You may be tempted to reach for a snack or a drink to ease your tension. These quick charges let you acknowledge your feelings and deal with them instantly, so you don't carry them into your next effort. There is no need to involve anyone else. If you are visually-oriented, the *wastepaper basket quick charge* and the *helium balloon quick charge* will probably work very well for you.

If you often talk to yourself during stressful times, you might want to try the *"So what? What now?" quick charge*. Practice the following two steps:

1. "So what if . . . ?"
2. "What now?" or "What am I going to do about it?"

Let's consider an off-the-job example this time. You let your emotions get the best of you in an argument and say something nasty to a friend. To practice the *"So what? What now?" quick charge*, you say to yourself, "So what if I lost my head? So what if I don't look so good now?" Once again, you go through a mental litany of things you feel like saying to yourself for a set period of time. Limit yourself to 30 seconds in most cases. Save the bigger time expenditures for the really big mistakes. At the end of the timed period, you follow up by asking yourself, "What now?" or "What am I going to do about it?" Raising this question shifts you from acknowledging your feelings and what has happened to thinking about your parameters of control and how to deal with the present situation.

You realize that your friend heard and understood your hasty words. There's no way to erase them. So you fall back on the 2M simultaneous focus to reestablish perspective. In the micro picture, the only control you have is to apologize. As you zoom out to the macro, you think about controlling yourself better from now on. You may think specifically about how you got to that point in the first place and consider the signs that could have helped you recognize, and avoid, a loss of control early on.

Now let's see how the *"So what? What now?" quick charge* can be used to help you rebound from the mathematical mistakes you made in that report to your boss. You might say, "So what if I missed those errors myself? So what if I look a little careless or unprofessional?" Then you have to ask yourself "What now?"—in other words, you address what you are going to do about it. Here again, you can't erase the mistakes. At this point, the only control you have in the micro is to quickly make the corrections. You can affect the situation by taking control to manage or influence your image. For example, you may decide to hand-deliver the corrected report to your boss and thank her for pointing out the errors. At the same time, you may try to assure the boss that this is not how you normally operate, and that you will work hard to make sure it doesn't happen again. To help minimize the chances of repeating this error, you can invest your energies to figure out some checkpoints for making sure your reports are accurate before they're turned in.

The *"So what? What now?" quick charge*, the *wastepaper basket quick charge*, and the *helium balloon quick charge* can help you use your energies wisely.

Keeping Your Confidence from Slipping

How do you keep your confidence from slipping when you're actually on the firing line and worried that you're going to make another, similar mistake? In other words, you've let go of the negative situation—perhaps you elected to use the *helium balloon quick charge*—but now you're starting to worry about goofing up again. Worries could surface as you write up another report for your boss, or as you engage in another conversation. If your worries reach the point where you can detect your confidence cage being rattled, try using the *stay-in-the-present quick charge*.

> **Stay confident with the stay-in-the-present quick charge.**

The *stay-in-the-present quick charge* helps you quickly size up where your control lies. Here's an image to help clarify what I mean. You're staring at a glass of milk after you've spilled some on the floor; that position represents your worrying about something that has happened. Taking a moment to assess your parameters of control, you quickly conclude that there is nothing you can do to alter the past so you have no control here. You tell yourself, "What's past is past." Next, picture yourself worrying about possibly losing your balance and spilling more milk as you prepare to carry the glass into the next room. Do you have control over what might happen? Not really. Again, a quick analysis of the parameters of control reminds you that you have no control here either; after all, the situation hasn't happened yet. All you *can* control is what is happening at the present moment. So in this example, you would invest energy to make sure that you keep your balance as you are about to take each step. Operating in the present should be your focus as well, because the present is the only place where change can be controlled.

Imagine that while reworking the report for your boss, you start to feel uneasy as your thoughts move away from the revisions and toward how stupid you were to have turned in a report with mathematical errors. Now you have lost your focus and your energies are being misdirected. To regain your focus in the micro, use the *stay-in-the-present quick charge*. Think to yourself that worrying and getting upset over something that happened in the past is dwelling on things that are beyond your control. Likewise, getting anxious about making another careless error is a waste of energies, because it hasn't happened yet. Instead, "stay in the present" and invest your energies in the key factors that can help you ground yourself and, at the same time, give yourself an opportunity to reach a desired outcome.

Handling Intimidation from Others

Another tough situation that can cause you to leave the optimal performance zone is being intimidated. Intimidation can come in many forms, from another person or from a small group. A common form of intimidation results from the way a person looks at you. Think of the familiar expressions "if looks could kill," "piercing eyes," and "stares right through you." These expressions are reminders that the eyes are powerful nonverbal communicators. That's why you've probably been taught to look someone squarely in the eyes while talking. But when your boss or an important client is giving you a stern look that could be interpreted as either a look of disapproval or merely an intent look, looking that person in the eyes can be very difficult. On the other hand, your failure to do so may be interpreted as a sign of distrust, or having "shifty eyes."

> **To avoid being intimidated, use the look-between-the-eyes quick charge.**

When faced with a situation like this, try the *look-between-the-eyes quick charge* to help regain your focus. Look straight at the person as you speak, but instead of actually staring into the eyes, look at the bridge of the nose, right between the eyes. The person cannot tell the difference. However, the effect on your confidence can be remarkable, as though a wall had been built between the two of you, protecting you and giving you "your space." In high-pressure situations, that can be the little boost that you need—some space to regain your composure and think on your feet.

This quick charge works fabulously in a different kind of intimidating situation—when you have to make a presentation in front of a group. I can personally attest to its effectiveness, since I regularly stand in front of audiences, making speeches and presentations. When I am faced with a highly critical crowd, I look around the room with my gaze stopping on the bridge of each person's nose! No one can tell that the confidence you or I exude is linked to this quick charge.

Intimidation can come from unlikely sources, such as family

members. Clients have told me that using the *look-between-the-eyes quick charge* when they are determining whether to make a major family purchase is a lifesaver. Parents say they can keep their cool more easily and think more rationally during emotionally charged discussions with their kids. Parents of teenagers swear by this quick charge.

When intimidation comes in large doses, such as when someone is very upset and starts dumping frustration on you, try using the *"Excuse me?" quick charge.* (You may already be using this one from time to time—and if you are, you know how effective it can be.) Rather than snapping back with, "You have no right to talk to me this way," or "How dare you," you practice this quick charge by waiting until the person is taking a breath of air in mid-conversation. Then you say, "Excuse me?" in a questioning tone of voice. The tone you use here is extremely important. The unspoken message is "Will you please repeat that?" If the question sounds more like a declaration, then the unspoken message may be interpreted as "How dare you!" Using a confrontational tone during a heated exchange can add fuel to the fire.

When you say "Excuse me?" in an agreeable, questioning tone of voice, the person picks up on your message and starts repeating what was said. Remember, at this point the person is still emotionally charged, and ranting at you. Typically, the person repeats the comment, starts to listen more consciously to the words, and as a result changes his or her approach. Those of you who have successfully tried this technique also know that you can't use the *"Excuse me?" quick charge* repeatedly with the same people, because they begin to catch on and are affected less and less by it.

> *Eliminate stomach knots with the untying-stomach-knots quick charge.*

Handling Knots in Your Stomach

Sometimes just the thought of having to get up in front of everyone and talk at a meeting is enough to tie your stomach in knots. For many, getting knots is a frequent occurrence. How do you eliminate them? Try the *untying-stomach-knots quick charge*. I developed this quick charge as a result of my experiences in platform diving. Each day, during my practice sessions, when it was my turn to "hit the tower," I would get that familiar feeling in my stomach, and it would stay with me for the first few dives. In order to start untying the knots, I learned to do the following.

First, take a deep breath and hold it. While holding your breath, tighten your abdominal muscles for about three seconds—this is called an isometric contraction. (Interestingly, while you are contracting your muscles this way, you are still able to talk normally. So once again, no one can see that you're using a quick charge.) At the end of the three seconds, exhale, and as you do, imagine the muscles in your stomach loosening as your tensions are released with your breath. During the relaxation of the abdominal muscles, some people like to envision their stomachs being coated with a smooth layer of Pepto-Bismol. Coating the stomach soothes and comforts you, allowing your stomach knots to loosen and untangle. Users of this quick charge have found that they have a new friend to rely on besides their Rolaids!

Leaving the Mental Problems from Work at Work

You too have a life outside your career. The trouble is, enjoying that life is hard when your mind is stuck on problems at the office. Now that you understand control, you realize that making rules for yourself—such as "When I'm home, I don't worry about my job"—is just promoting a slide into the rigid zone. What happens if you come up with a great idea to solve a problem when you're at the dinner table? Are you not going to allow yourself to write it down? What's important is to remain flexible—to have the ability to turn work off and on when you choose to do so. When you want to shut work off, but just can't, you don't have control.

> *Control is leaving the problems from work at*
> *work when you choose to.*

As easy as it is to suggest, leaving work problems at the office when the end of the day rolls around is very difficult for most Americans to do. Findings from two national studies in the United States and Canada conducted by the American Management Association and Bright Enterprises revealed that 36 percent of the men and 22 percent of the women said they were very good at leaving the problems from work at work. That left the majority of people in the study in the position of having at least some trouble with the issue.[3]

How about you? Are you good at turning the job off and on when you choose to? Being able to look to yourself to create your own breaks is extremely important. The division between work and home is blurry enough these days. For the many people working out of their homes, the issue can be even more complicated.

> *To stop thinking about work, use the anchor*
> *quick charge.*

To position yourself so that you are in control of your own work, as opposed to being controlled by it, try using the *anchor quick charge.* The anchor quick charge is rooted in the same phenomenon that takes place when you listen to "golden oldies" on the radio. Certain songs flood your mind with fond memories and associations of days gone by, and they can change your mood in an instant. A song acts as a symbol for something else. To use the *anchor quick charge*, you create your own symbol—to signify the end of the working day and the start of your personal time.

To select your symbol, consider the things you do every day before leaving work. Do you shut off your computer, lock your desk drawer, or water your plants? Now select the one "anchor" that you want to make the official sign of the end of your workday. What if you want to review the day as you travel home? Then select pulling into your driveway or stepping off the subway as your anchor. The only requirement is that you choose one anchor and stick with it so you instill it with meaning.

If you work at home, you can designate certain areas as work space and others as leisure space. Let's say you've turned the guest bedroom into your home office. Each time you step over the threshold into that room, you've entered a separate space and you're at work. Likewise, shutting the door to your office at the end of the day can be your anchor to signify that you've left work and you're home now.

When you use the *anchor quick charge*, consistency is crucial. At first, you may have some trouble making a definite break. Since you're paid to fill your mind with bright ideas, letting go of them isn't always easy. When you are first establishing your anchor, try following it with some activity that you look forward to at the end of the day. Doing so can help your mind switch more readily from work to leisure, until you have incorporated this skill. After you have practiced the *anchor quick charge* for a while, leaving the problems from work at work becomes easier.

To see if work is controlling you, or the other way around, periodically check up on yourself. A good test is to not bring your briefcase or laptop computer home with you one night or, if you have a PC at home, to leave it untouched for the night. Of course, be careful if your boss sends you e-mail that you're supposed to read at night. (I've heard of a few bosses who do this!) If you feel uncomfortable going home without your "lifeline," then it's time to ask yourself if you're really in control of your work. Try this test from time to time on typical days, not when you have a big deadline coming up.

Your reentry into your home can be a little unsteady when everyone in the family has been out during the day, at work, at school, or wherever. To ensure a smooth transition, get everyone in the family to participate in the *stress report quick charge*. Children especially like this quick charge. Find a corkboard and display it somewhere in the house where people can see it as they come in. Tack the names of all family members across the top of the board. As each family member comes home, he or she tacks up a colored piece of paper from a pile at the bottom of the board. Each color is assigned a meaning, signifying a particular mood and physical state. You might choose the meanings that correspond to familiar traffic signals: Green means a good mood, a great day, and everyone can go ahead without fear that you'll snap at any moment. Yellow means that everyone should move with a little more caution around you; that you've had a few things fall apart on you today or you're a little tired. Red underneath your name is an immediate tip-off that you've had it "up to here" today, and people had best not cross you. Hopefully, as the evening wears on, you can cool off into the yellow, then green zones.

The *stress report quick charge* helps avoid a clash where one family member "barks" at another, only to have to apologize and blame his or her mood on problems at work. Although this quick charge doesn't promise that people will suddenly get along beautifully and that eruptions won't break out from time to time, it does at least give people an early warning of what they're dealing with when they come home!

Imagine yourself incorporating these quick charges into your daily routine. As you are ending your day, you build your to-do list for tomorrow. Before leaving your office, you take a reenergizing break with one of the relaxation techniques described in Chapter 12. Pleased with yourself and refreshed, you drive home, reviewing the events of the day as you go. You pull into the driveway and shut off the car, setting off your *anchor quick charge*, then go inside and tack up the green paper under your name on the *stress report quick charge corkboard*. Here's one last tip to help ensure that your evenings get off to a good start: Instead of the standard "How was your day?" get in the habit of asking family members, "Did anything new or exciting happen in your day?" Substituting this question helps people avoid rehashing the problems from work and school that they want to avoid bringing home. If only new or exciting events are discussed as you greet one another, the rest of your day can remain undisturbed in your mind.

Incorporating Quick Charges

As you read about these quick charges, you may realize that some of them are familiar to you. All the better. Refer back to the original ratings you gave yourself in Exercise 1 and decide whether any one of those ratings improved with the use of certain quick charges. With your understanding and acceptance of personal responsibleness, you are positioned to start integrating these techniques into your repertoire of skills. If you have difficulty using quick charges the first few times, you won't give up, because you understand that when you try something new, you won't get it perfect right away. As with all skills, the more you practice quick charges, the easier and more natural they become.

During the learning phase, disappointing results may catapult you into a self-criticism session—an internal conversation in which you're both the giver and receiver of criticism. If you ever find yourself "tearing yourself down," read on to learn how to effectively handle this unique form of criticism. The next chapter examines how you can work with yourself to feel empowered, ready to move forward with greater confidence, after a self-criticism session.

1. **STOP** long enough to assess whether you are at your best when talking to others. Imagine yourself having a radar system in place, feeding you back signals as to whether you are operating at your optimal performance level.

2. **STOP** thinking that you have to act the way you feel.

3. **STOP** talking the next time you get that familiar urge to "set the record straight." To regain your focus, use the breathing quick charge. Before you speak, make sure you have clarified what you want and have captured what others were trying to say.

START

1. **START** using either the "So what, What now?" quick charge, or the wastepaper basket quick charge when negative thoughts run wild in your mind, causing you to feel terrible about yourself.

2. **START** using the look-between-the-eyes quick charge the next time you're going to talk in front of a group of people. This technique will give you the space you need to remain confident, so you can think on your feet.

11

STEP SEVEN

WORK WITH YOURSELF, NOT AGAINST

*More players lick themselves than are ever licked
by the opposing team.*

Connie Mack

WHAT IS SELF-CRITICISM?

Are you good at writing reports and proposals? Are you a good speller? Good at math? Good at sports? If you answered no to any of these questions, you were engaging in self-criticism.

Self-criticism is different from self-evaluation. With self-evaluation, you are assessing yourself objectively. The process includes both the positive and the negative. You are examining your behavior and motives for the purpose of determining their value in relationship to a desired end result. Self-criticism, on the other hand, emphasizes the negative. Like other kinds of criticism, self-criticism portends action or change—and the negativity is what spurs you into action. That is, provided you know how to empower yourself with self-criticism.

Self-criticism is a unique, mostly silent exchange that pits you as the giver of criticism against you as the receiver. Almost anything can spark this internal dialogue, and no words, it seems, are too

284

harsh. As the giver, you know everything there is to know about the receiver. Since you know all your own weak spots, your words can really pack a punch—unless you stop yourself long enough to consider this revealing question: If you had a friend who talked to you the way you talk to yourself, would that person be your friend for long? Probably not.

Here are a few more questions that shed light on self-criticism: Do you work from the assumption that human beings are not perfect? Do you, then, tolerate the mistakes of others? The chances are great that you answered yes to both questions. But when *you* make mistakes, are you as tolerant and forgiving of yourself? Probably not. Why the double standard? Why go harder on yourself than you do on others? Most likely, because you realize that you can make changes in yourself more easily than you can influence others to change. Actually, there's some clear evidence to indicate that people are very tough on themselves. Research findings from 1985 to the present indicate that more than 77 percent of survey respondents classified themselves as being "extremely hard" or "very hard" on themselves.[1] In this chapter, we'll examine how to create your own "honesty forum" and work *with* yourself. You'll discover that it's OK to be hard on yourself—as long as it's deserved, and as long as it spurs you into action, leading you closer to your desired end result. To learn more about the process, take a look at the way two different people handle self-criticism.

Carrie and Phil Williams are young, aspiring, career-oriented newlyweds working for different organizations. Both are in sales and, by coincidence, for the past week, both have been devoting a lot of their time to preparing sales presentations to give to their respective clients.

(Continued)

Having made their presentations on the same day, they meet for dinner at their favorite restaurant to compare the outcomes. Carrie gets the ball rolling.

"After I finished my presentation, my boss pointed out a few errors I had made. He was right. Oh, I'm so upset. I worked so hard preparing for this. How could I be so stupid as to forget to point out facts about the product? My brother was right. I'm just not cut out for the business world, especially sales. I never thought sales was really the job for me, and I guess I was right. My boss will probably never give me an opportunity to be the lead person again."

"Well, you're not the only one hurting," Phil puts in, picking up the ball. "I guess when it rains it pours, because I blew it, too. I put so much time into this presentation—how could I blow it the way I did? In college, I always made great presentations. How could I have forgotten to allow time for questions? I can't let that happen again. You know, next time, I'm going to ask someone to flash a time card or something to cue me as to how much time I have left. Speaking of next time, when I call my boss in the morning to talk about salvaging our client, I'm also going to ask him to watch my next presentation so he can let me know where I'm going wrong."

By analyzing the differences in how Carrie and Phil engage in self-criticism, you can turn your conversations with yourself into an asset—creating our own "honesty forum" to empower yourself with self-criticism. Besides learning where most of your control lies, you'll discover a three-step process for using your energies productively to propel you forward.

For starters, we take the advice of Connie Mack, the famous baseball coach: "I guess more players lick themselves than are ever licked by the opposing team. The first thing every man needs to know is how to handle himself."[2] Throughout this book, I have stressed the importance of self-knowledge. After all, you are your own most valuable resource. You are the one who knows yourself best, and you are the one who is responsible for setting the strategy and taking the necessary actions. If you don't know how to be honest with yourself and believe in what you are doing, you will find it difficult to muster the fortitude and conviction necessary to plunge forward in the face of tough odds.

That's not to say that you won't seek assistance from others. Everyone operates with blind spots, so the viewpoints of others can be helpful in giving you an alternate view of a situation and filling in the gaps. The point here is that you must first seek to understand yourself, before reaching out to others. After you get advice from others, you once again look to yourself to think through what has been suggested, and take action on the basis of what you consciously decide to do, as opposed to what others have suggested. After all, you understand and accept control and are willing to accept the consequences of your actions.

> *Self-criticism doesn't have to be destructive.*

The people I've worked with over the years typically view self-criticism as a destructive exercise that occurs privately within. This is an extension of the myth that criticism itself is destructive, a myth that was dispelled earlier. Like criticism from others, self-criticism can be used destructively or it can be used to encourage personal growth. Carrie and Phil illustrate the difference.

Carrie walked away from her self-criticism feeling terrible about herself. She was embarrassed to show her face to her boss, because she convinced herself that he would never give her another high-profile assignment. Carrie viewed the situation as a personal assault and she dwelled on how her boss's comments threatened her self-image. She emotionalized the experience and thought, in a reactionary way, that she was totally at fault. During the private conversation she had with herself, she focused on rationalizing her failure, rather than paying attention to what was happening in the broader picture. Most important, Carrie walked away from the inward exchange not knowing her next course of action.

As many as 30 to 40 percent of the people in my seminars on criticism resemble Carrie. Like Carrie, they fail to benefit from their internal dialogues because they don't get past berating themselves. Interestingly, their criticisms sound very much like the ones they used to get from their parents, teachers, or coaches. They tell themselves, "I never want to see myself doing that again" and "How could I have been so stupid?" The implication is that by lecturing themselves, they can avoid making the same mistake in the future. That assumption, however, is falsely grounded and it fosters the illusion of control. When people think that yelling at themselves ("Don't ever do that again") is all they need to do to change, they are operating in the blind zone.

Carrie's husband, Phil, was clearly disappointed and upset with himself too. But unlike Carrie, Phil got beyond his emotions, put his hurt feelings aside, and examined his situation. He thought about specific action steps he could take with his boss to help save the customer and also to avoid repeating the same mistakes in his next presentation. So not only was he doing his best to rectify the current situation; he was also trying to learn from his mistakes and make improvements for the future.

In order to achieve, you must learn to use self-criticism the way Phil does. You need to shift your focus away from yourself and address the situation, investing your energies to decide where your control lies. Consider the control factors you can work with and seek out specific action steps you can take to ensure that you don't repeat the same mistakes. At the same time, you can use the negative experience as a catalyst to help you improve in other areas.

> *Self-criticism is the only kind of criticism that allows you almost total control.*

Although you may not be in control of what sparks self-criticism, you certainly are in control of how you conduct the exchange with yourself, what information you accept or reject, and whether you use it to improve yourself or cut yourself down. Viewing self-criticism as your "honesty forum," where you can look at yourself and the situation at hand objectively and use the information gained to your advantage, is not a skill that comes easily. You have to become consciously aware of what you are saying to yourself, then learn from each experience so that you continue to work with yourself to bring out the best you have to offer in a given situation. When you do this, self-criticism is empowering, and builds your self-confidence.

TYPES OF SELF-CRITICISM

To make optimal use of self-criticism and manage it effectively, you need to become aware of the forms it takes.

> *The Two Major Types of Self-Criticism*
> *• Real-time self-criticism*
> *• Long-standing self-criticism*

Real-time self-criticism occurs before, during, and after specific events. *Long-standing self-criticism* tends to surface without a specific impetus, and it sounds like a tape recording of inner thoughts that have been with you for some time. Examples of long-standing self-criticism include "I'm so uncoordinated," "I'll never amount to much," "I'm no good at math," and "I'm ugly." None of us is without our own little tape recording! Our self-criticism exchanges typically include both real-time and long-standing criticisms.

Carrie's conversation with herself began with real-time self-criticism—the mistakes her boss pointed out to her—but then she threw in some long-standing self-criticism—that she is "not cut out for the business world"—to explain her errors. Since Carrie's long-standing self-criticism went unchecked, her self-confidence was shaken even more than it had been by the day's events.

On the other hand, Phil acknowledged his feelings of disappointment and frustration, but then used his inherent control to step back and examine objectively what he had done and what he was saying to himself. Rather than dwelling on a negative self-image (as Carrie did), Phil recalled that he had made good presentations in the past and that his mistakes were confined to this particular situation—specifically, not allowing time for questions. As a result, Phil was able to validate the accuracy of his criticism and discover ways to improve himself—which, on one level, is both exciting and motivating.

From time to time, our internal dealings inevitably include long-standing self-criticisms, as was the case for Carrie. Trying not to rehash these criticisms is extremely difficult. So rather than investing time and energy trying to erase the "old tapes," we would do better to inspect that critical voice inside.

PATTERNS OF SELF-CRITICISM

People engage in various patterns of self-criticism. You can probably recognize some of them in others or yourself. Maybe you have a friend who likes to talk about how she could be a millionaire by now if only she had had the courage to invest in the stock of certain start-up companies. Or one of your coworkers is a nervous wreck before presentations because he keeps reminding himself about all the things that might go wrong. Perhaps when you are tired, you find that your mind overflows with negative thoughts.

> *If you had a friend who talked to you the way you talk to yourself, would you have a friend for long?*

Learning to recognize the patterns that typify your own self-criticism won't enable you to turn criticism into an asset, but it can prevent the exchanges from becoming exercises in self-derogation that erode your confidence and block your chance of achieving a desired outcome. As you examine each of these habitual patterns of self-criticism, you'll find that hindsight self-criticism has the greatest potential as a learning point: By reflecting on situations that were mishandled, you may be able to learn a better way to handle similar situations in the future.

Public Self-Criticism

> *"I'm terrible at remembering names."*

Public self-criticizers make a habit of demeaning themselves in front of others by saying, "I'm always so slow to catch on—would you mind repeating what you said?" "Gosh, I must be stupid—I just don't see what you are driving at," or "I know this is a dumb question, but . . ."

Fatigued Self-Criticism

> *"You aren't going to get that deal—you're not*
> *as good as your competitors."*

Spontaneous, unsolicited self-criticism is often related to fatigue. Negative thoughts may flow late at night, after a long day at work, or when you haven't had a good night's sleep. One workshop participant demonstrated how fatigue made her focus on the negative: "I'll walk down the street mentally beating myself up for not being productive and putting off things. In the middle of all this, I might remember some important things I accomplished, but the negative thoughts somehow overpower the positive ones."

Hindsight Self-Criticism

> *"If only I had checked with my customer*
> *ahead of time, we could have avoided this*
> *whole mess."*

Jonathan, who owns several restaurants, complains about all the money he would have today if he hadn't managed certain things so badly. Susan kicks herself repeatedly because the project she chose to work on turned out to be a disaster. Tom engages in a boxing match with himself for investing a lot of money in a business venture that failed; he's beating himself up for losing the money, but his toughest punches are thrown for not being able to see problems ahead of time. In each instance, the self-criticism is made possible by hindsight, but the criticizer is angry about not having foresight.

Sometimes we criticize ourselves for failing to act when the time was right: "If only I had bought that property when it first went on the market, I'd be wealthy today!" Even though the consequences of our act or failure to act are not yet clear, the criticism swells. The "I should have" self-criticizer yells at herself for not buying the one-of-a-kind dress at the boutique—even though it might still be there—or beats himself up for saying something that may have offended a potential client—even though he doesn't know if it did.

Pre-Event Self-Criticism

> *"What if I can't answer somebody's question?*
> *It would be so embarrassing!"*

Pre-event criticism is the flip side of hindsight criticism: The event has not yet occurred, but already the self-criticism is taking off. The golfer who stands up to hit the ball and clutters his mind with all kinds of negative thoughts is a classic pre-event self-criticizer; the same is true for any athlete engaging in a competitive sport. Likewise, the executive who takes hours to prepare for an important presentation, all the time feeling anxious and criticizing herself for the things that might go wrong, is a pre-event criticizer.

On-the-Spot Self-Criticism

> *"Your message isn't coming across the way it*
> *was supposed to. You're blowing it!"*

On-the spot self-criticizers sabotage their ability to perform by engaging in self-criticism during an activity or event. For example, a salesperson loses self-confidence in front of a client because he's mentally convinced that he's blowing the whole deal. Or an engineer allows self-criticism to crowd her thoughts during a technical debate so that she can't think conceptually.

A point worth noting is that when criticizing yourself—whether using real-time self-criticism or long-standing self-criticism—you won't get any interference from outsiders. No one has to know about the private conversations you are having with yourself or the actions you intend to take. Self-criticism exchanges offer the opportunity to inspect the motives behind your actions. When you take the time to inspect your innermost thoughts in the hope of uncovering ways to improve yourself, you are using self-criticism as your own honesty forum. Consequently, channeling self-criticism positively leads to increased motivation in the short run; it also builds the belief in yourself that is needed to pursue long-term goals.

BECOMING A REAL-TIME SELF-CRITICIZER

Learning to use the control that is inherently yours when engaging in self-criticism is akin to learning to be "your own best friend," and it's a three-phase process. The phases are listening to yourself, validating the criticism, and assessing action.

Phase 1: Listening to Yourself

More often than not, when you engage in self-criticism, you're not really listening to what you're saying: You may hear yourself, but that doesn't translate into inspecting what is being said. Instead, imagine yourself as having an antenna to pick up on what you are saying to yourself. When you start receiving the signals, pretend you are eavesdropping on a conversation between two strangers. Listen to your inner talk without being judgmental. Just say to yourself, "Isn't this interesting." Taking the time to listen is a worthwhile investment of energy because words are very powerful, and your self-talk can provide you with valuable information. Words produce physiological reactions.

Close your eyes for a moment and imagine yourself taking a big, juicy orange in your hand (pause). Slice it open (pause). Take a bite. As you do this, your mouth will start to water in anticipation of eating that orange. You may also envision picking up the orange and placing it on a counter or a cutting board. Besides reacting physiologically, you are able to see the color and shape of the orange, feel the texture of the rind as you touch it, hear the knife cut through it, and perhaps even smell and taste it as well. All your senses are activated, just by using words.

As another example of the tremendous impact that words can have, consider the times you've said to yourself, "I'm so tired." After saying this, don't you feel more lethargic? If imagining a minor pleasure like eating an orange can trigger your senses so strongly, think about the tremendous impact that calling yourself "stupid" has, especially if you do it again and again! In addition to listening to what you are saying, pay attention to the surrounding circumstances. When you objectify the criticism you give to yourself, you may find certain patterns emerging. For instance, you may discover that a lot of your self-criticism arises when you're tired. In that case, making a conscious decision to postpone your self-evaluation until you are more rested is advisable.

You may also find that self-criticism increases right before an important event. Past failures flood your memory just as you face a new challenge. For example, you are about to make a sales presentation, and just before your opening remarks your mind flashes on your last presentation, when you mishandled various objections raised by the customer. Or you're on the golf course facing a difficult water shot; just as you are addressing the ball, you recall how last week you missed every shot that went over the water. Similar thoughts could enter your mind when looking to return a serve in tennis or when cooking a meal for guests. These pre-event self-criticisms, if not addressed, can quickly rattle your self-confidence.

Becoming aware of your personal self-criticism patterns enables you to recognize your behaviors and simultaneously gives you insights into how you will most likely behave in the future. Remember, the chances are great that you won't be able to stop the criticisms, so it's important to get yourself to the point where you can pay attention to your thoughts, determine when and where you tend to criticize yourself, and look at this information with strict objectivity. When you objectify your self-criticisms, you minimize the sting because all you are doing is "collecting information." To put it another way, the harsh, internal giver is standing aside now and allowing the receiver to take control.

Phase 2: Validating the Criticism

Once you have collected information, you need to start examining its quality and accuracy. Keep in mind that you need to be fair when you are criticizing yourself. Most people expect any outsider criticism to be fair, but that's not always the case with self-criticism. Some people are their own worst enemy; you may be among them.

If you cannot count on yourself to be fair as the giver of self-criticism, then you need to rely on good receiver skills to sort out the quality and accuracy of your statements. To validate the criticism, ask yourself the following questions:

- Where is the information coming from and how old is it?
- Is it accurate?
- Is it specific?

Determining whether the information being transmitted is current, accurate, and specific helps you gain valuable insights into your behavior. Another helpful question is: "Are my criticisms actually helping me in any way?" Considering this question helps shift your thinking to the next phase.

Phase 3: Assessing Action

During the third phase, you ask yourself, "Is there anything specific I can do now?" and "What specifically can I do differently next time?" The purpose of these questions is to determine whether action is warranted and, if so, what type. You may develop a preference for certain questions. The important thing to remember is that asking these or similar questions—and answering them— empowers you to effectively manage the self-criticism process and make it work for you.

Using the 2M simultaneous focus can help you temper your self-criticism. Imagine that you just called someone by the wrong name or spilled some food on your clothes. You might automatically say to yourself, "How could I be so dumb?" Before continuing with your conversation, engage instead in the 2M simultaneous focus. While zooming into the macro picture, ask yourself, "Five years from now, how important will this situation be?" Answering this question may instantly put the situation in perspective and help you realize how insignificant the mistake really is.

In some cases, when you step aside mentally, a situation that at first glance seems terrible suddenly becomes humorous. Once I had my parents over for dinner and decided to prepare a new dish—a fancy soufflé. For what seemed like hours, I kept watching the soufflé, hoping that it would rise the way it was supposed to. It finally did, and as I took it out of the oven, I had thoughts about taking a gourmet cooking class—after all, it seemed like I had the knack! Naturally, I proudly served the soufflé to my husband and parents. When my dad tasted it, he wrinkled up his face, but said nothing. My husband tasted it and blurted out, "Oh my gosh, this thing tastes like the ocean!" I tasted the soufflé, and my thoughts about what a great cook I was vanished. My mother chimed in that it was just inedible, it was so salty. As everyone commented on how awful the souffle tasted, I realized what had happened. As you might have guessed, I misread the recipe, and used tablespoons of salt instead of teaspoons! Thinking about the situation in the macro picture, I began laughing hysterically. Instead of beating myself up, I saw the humor in the situation. Luckily, no one was going to go hungry—we just called out for a pizza! To this day, my family enjoys teasing me about my inedible soufflé.

THE PHASES IN ACTION

Let's watch the three-phase process in action by examining two situations.

> Frank is an editor for a major publisher based in New York. He has a lunch date with his author, Joe, and Joe's wife, Eliza, whom Frank has not yet met. After everyone has been seated, in an effort to be sociable, Frank says to Eliza, "Joe didn't tell me that you two were expecting, Eliza." Eliza simply says, "I'm not pregnant." No one says anything—a chill hovers over the table. Frank launches into a self-criticism exchange, calling himself every name in the book for having made such a terrible error.

To handle this situation, Frank steps back and listens to what he is saying to himself (phase 1). He realizes that although being upset is natural, destroying himself in the process is unnecessary. He then starts to examine the criticism he has been giving himself—statements such as "You are so stupid" and "You don't know how to handle social situations." By asking himself where he is getting this information and whether it is accurate (phase 2), Frank recognizes quickly that some editorial changes are needed. He is not stupid; to disprove that criticism, he needs only to think back to what his boss told him the week before—that Frank is one of the best editors in the company. Also, Frank's supposed inability to deal with social situations isn't a fact: He can recall interacting smoothly with lots of people at business and social functions in the past. He has certainly made a mistake this time, but that's all it is.

Moving on to phase 3, Frank asks himself, "Is any more yelling at myself helping?" Of course, it is not. He also asks himself what action he can take now. First, he recognizes that the damage has already been done, so all he can do is apologize to Eliza. Second, he decides that he will wait until coffee and dessert to bring up any sensitive issues he has to discuss with Joe. That way, everyone will have had some time to put it all in perspective. Can he do anything differently next time? You bet. Frank decides that he will never bring up somebody's weight again—especially if the person seems a little heavy. Occasionally, during lunch, thoughts about his blunder return, causing Frank to get upset all over again. So to ensure that his energies and his focus are properly directed, Frank decides to "absorb the mistake and remember the lesson."

To practice absorbing the mistake and remember the lesson as Frank did, you must analyze your mistake and determine what valuable lessons can be gained from the situation. Once you absorb all that you can, you mentally visualize yourself burying the situation and all the emotional debris that goes with it. When the thought returns—and the chances are great that it will—you simply repeat the process and follow it up with getting actively involved in doing something worthwhile. What's beneficial about this technique is that you're ensuring that you make a point of learning from your mistake, while at the same time you are taking control of your emotions.

The second example is a real tough one. For about two years, Clara has not dated anyone. To hear her tell it, she's not happy about being alone, especially on the weekends. She doesn't date because she is afraid of being hurt. Clara's had some very painful experiences in the past and is no longer willing to put herself on the line. Whenever she starts to play back her inner voice, it dawns on Clara that everything she's saying is self-criticism: "To begin with, men wouldn't be attracted to me because I'm not pretty. Now that I've reached a high level within my company, a lot of men are intimidated by my success. They figure I'm too aggressive, and that turns them off."

Clara and I worked together to sort out the quality and accuracy of her criticisms. She had already gone through a painful self-listening stage (phase 1). Up to this point, all Clara could do when working by herself was get herself emotionally stirred up. She would mentally replay experiences in which she had been hurt, and as she recalled various scenes, her emotions would build to the point where she had to stop thinking and get involved in something else. As we began talking about her situation, the thought occurred to me that not dating anyone was a pretty good strategy for Clara at this point, because if she were to go out with someone feeling the way she did, she probably would get hurt again. Why? Because she hasn't learned from her experiences, however painful they may have been. If you walked into a pit with a snake in it and got bit, you'd be a fool to walk in there again without doing something different to protect yourself!

In phase 2, we examine some of the criticisms Clara is leveling at herself. The first one is that "no man will want to date me because I'm not pretty." She asks herself, "Where is that information coming from? How old is it? Is it really accurate?" In answering these questions, Clara soon realizes that *she* is the one who told herself these things, and that the information is inaccurate because she certainly had been attractive to men in the past. Likewise, when examining her idea about men being threatened by her success, she realizes that it is faulty as well. All she has to do is look at some of her friends who are also accomplished at what they do, and see that they are all dating or in relationships. By taking the time to objectively consider each negative statement, Clara is able to disprove just about everything she was saying about herself.

Now Clara is ready for phase 3, where she is left to figure out "What am I going to do about it now?" To help her decide what she ought to do, I ask Clara to think about her role as a consultant with her business. When she's working in the field, how much time does she invest in helping her customers increase market share and revenues? She replies, "Well, with one client in Atlanta, I spent about 10 days, or 89 hours recently. During that time, I helped Kevin come up with several marketing strategies, and I made sure he had adequate support as we started to roll out the first project." My next question concerns the amount of time Clara spends thinking about what she wants in a relationship, and differentiating between what she *wants* and what she *needs*. Clara smiles and says, "I get the point. Unlike when I'm working, I don't give myself time to really think about dating and what caused me to get hurt before. More important, what little time I do spend on it never ends in a strategy or plan of what I could be doing to change my situation. I guess I've been investing time feeling sorry for myself as opposed to realizing that I do have some control here, and that I can do something about my situation." If the criticisms we give to ourselves go unchecked, they can undermine our belief in ourselves and our ability to take action, as happened with Clara.

ONE MORE EXAMPLE: A WORD ABOUT PERFECTIONISM

There are many areas where we can find fault with ourselves and engage in self-criticism. Many of us grapple with one troublesome area: striving to be perfectionists in all we do. When time constraints become impossible, or when we don't want to settle for anything less than the extremely high standards we set for ourselves, we create conditions that are ripe for self-criticism.

When the deadline is tight and the boss is pressing you to get what you're working on done, the self-criticism starts creeping in. You say things like, "I know I'll never get this done on time," or "My name is going on this project, and it's going to be a mess," or "Anything worth doing is worth doing right, and I don't have the time to do this right." When self-criticisms like these bunch up, they can cause you to lose your focus and misdirect your energies. Most significantly, when you can't live up to the standards you've set for yourself, you fail to realize a sense of personal satisfaction from your work.

Compounding the self-criticisms that come while you are working on the task are those that arise when you've met your personal performance standards and no one says anything complimentary about your effort. You begin thinking, "Why do I keep beating my head against the wall? No one cares anyway," or "Won't I ever learn that no one appreciates quality anymore?" Having these words race through your mind unchecked can leave you disillusioned with yourself and your work. Stop and carefully examine what they mean. The bad feelings you experience are important and need to be acknowledged, but they also need to be set aside momentarily while you take a realistic look at the assumptions and habitual patterns that accompany them.

The performance standards you learned in the past need to be re-examined and adjusted to meet today's workloads. After all, you are in control of the standards you set for yourself. You know that making a valuable difference is what's most important. Therefore, when a task has an extremely tight deadline, or when the amount of time you can devote to it is limited, use your energies wisely by giving yourself permission to work along a performance continuum of acceptable to perfect. If you're always striving to do things perfectly, your focus is directed inwardly only, and you may be satisfying yourself at the expense of making a valuable difference. In actuality, you're engaging in one-dimensional thinking.

Use the 2M simultaneous focus to help you determine, in the macro picture, what is needed to make a valuable difference. From there, you can decide on the performance level required to complete the task. On certain occasions, you may decide that perfection is required; at those times, you need to give a 100 percent effort. Remember, though, that if you think everything has to be done perfectly, you are operating only in the micro picture and demonstrating rigidity. Taking control involves staying flexible and doing what is necessary to satisfy yourself, fulfill a task, and make a valuable difference. It's a multidimensional approach. As one "reformed perfectionist" told me during a workshop, "I found that too much time was being invested for too little gain. The frustration I experienced was certainly not helping me enjoy my job. Little by little, my attitude became more negative. The intense environment wasn't going to change—I had to."

Remember, self-criticism is the only kind of criticism that allows us nearly complete control. We have choices—how we give it, how we take it, and whether we make it work for us or let it drag us down. We can choose to be our own worst enemies, or we can learn to use self-criticism as an honesty forum, in which we gain valuable insights about ourselves and about the things we can do to propel our lives forward. Harnessing self-criticism and using it as an asset takes a lot of energy. Life has many twists and turns that are beyond our control. What's left for us to command is our ability to operate with an achieving attitude and to invest in ourselves to do our best.

Here's how you can take control immediately.

1. **STOP** to listen to what you are saying to yourself, and capture it by imagining yourself taking a snapshot of everything you're telling yourself.

2. **STOP** emotionalizing what happened by stepping aside and considering the situation at hand. Go through the three phases of self-criticism, keeping in mind the following rule of thumb: "Whenever you engage in self-criticism, always walk away with a plan of action."

3. **STOP** where you are, if your information is bad, and use a quick charge to eliminate the worthless thoughts or words.

1. **START** asking yourself on a more frequent basis, "If I had a friend who talked to me the way I talk to myself, would I have a friend for long?"

12

STEP EIGHT

RELAX AND REENERGIZE

A 1996 Wall Street Journal/NBC News survey of 2000 people found that 75 percent of those earning more than $100,000 per year (67 percent of the survey population) say that managing their time is a bigger problem than managing their money.[1] You don't have to be making $100,000 a year to have this problem. Perhaps the reason time is such an important commodity today is that people are plagued with too many responsibilities. Here's how one working father of two describes it. "As soon as I finish work, I'm either rushing to class to work toward my master's or going off to coach my kids' baseball and soccer teams. Then it's running home to have dinner and watch a little TV. Afterward, I look over what's been left in my in-box, and end up crashing either in front of the TV or in bed. It's as if one day blends into the next. There's no stopping, and when Friday finally rolls around, I'm exhausted."

This father's belief in having more responsibilities today is shared by many. In 1995, a national study conducted by the American Management Association and Bright Enterprises found that 84 percent of the managers surveyed indicated that their responsibilities at work had increased in the past two years. In addition, 47 percent reported that they were experiencing more responsibilities at home, too. Therefore, finding time to pull out long enough to practice a relaxation or meditation technique is very challenging these days.

This chapter will remind you of the importance of practicing a relaxation or meditation technique, and it will provide you with some insights into how you can "make" the time—because you'll never just "find" it! You'll be introduced to a practical approach I developed years ago called *Creative Relaxation: The Personal Quiet Time Method*, or the PQT for short. Besides learning the PQT, you'll find answers to many of the common questions asked about relaxation techniques.

WHY USE RELAXATION OR MEDITATION TECHNIQUES?

For years, the benefits associated with practicing relaxation and meditative concepts have been well documented. Recent studies have shown that relaxation techniques can help patients suffering from chronic pain, some types of diabetes, arthritis, cancer, and heart disease, and patients undergoing painful medical procedures.[2]

Eric Small, M.D., of Mount Sinai Medical Center in New York, is a top medical expert specializing in sports injuries. He has found in his practice that people who use relaxation and meditative approaches also experience less frequent and less severe asthma attacks, fewer bouts of high blood pressure, and less frequent bouts with stomach upset and heartburn.[3]

Interestingly, although these benefits are consistently experienced by users of relaxation and meditative approaches, many people still don't practice any of the methods available. So years ago I developed a simplified technique, the personal quiet time method, to appeal to busy professional people. Besides its obvious health benefits, the PQT is energizing and time-efficient. Paradoxically, by stopping and investing time alone with yourself, you will ultimately save time, because your effectiveness at engaging in various endeavors is enhanced.

Feeling more alert and energized throughout the day is exactly what a group of doctors, nurses, and operations people from the Kessler Institute for Rehabilitation in New Jersey found would result from regularly practicing the PQT, according to a recent study. The findings also revealed that after practicing the personal quiet time method, the experimental group at Kessler (the group that received training in the PQT) reported feeling significantly more relaxed, comfortable, and steady throughout the day. People also noted improvements in their ability to deal with worries and uneasiness. In general, the experimental group's collective findings indicate that stress levels, both at work and at home, can be lowered by practicing the PQT daily.

It was interesting to me that the majority (82 percent) of health care professionals in the study had no personal training in a relaxation or meditation technique. We reminded all participants that the PQT is not "an answer to their problems," but rather "a promise." When regularly practiced, the PQT has proved to be energizing and effective for people experiencing a lot of stress. That's why I'm recommending that you add one more responsibility to your daily to-do list.

MAKING THE TIME

To reap the benefits of the PQT, it's best to practice the method twice daily for approximately 10 to 20 minutes. It's very important not to view the technique as a chore, an inconvenience, or another responsibility that you have to add to your to-do list. Your PQTs should become a pleasant habit, just like sitting down to enjoy a meal.

So if time is a concern of yours, my first recommendation is that you shift your thinking from "finding" the time to "making" the time. Schedule the PQT into your day, just as you would any other important engagement. Your day is filled with numerous activities and responsibilities. In order to develop a habit of practicng the PQT twice daily, you'll need to make "appointments" with yourself by selecting times that you can reasonably expect to have available each day.

For example, some people with busy schedules have actually "created" their own consistently available time. They wake up 15 to 20 minutes earlier each morning in order to practice the technique. To help convince people, I introduce the following trade-off: Hit the snooze button and sleep 10 more minutes or get up 15 minutes earlier and practice a relaxation technique that's equivalent to one to three hours of sleep. What's the better return? In addition to scheduling a morning time, many people benefit from "making an appointment with themselves" just before they leave the office or before beginning to prepare the evening meal. After you have become familiar with the PQT, you may wish to schedule it right before a common daily stress situation.

Mary, an administrative support person, told me that she found it hard to switch gears after working all day in the office. As soon as she came home, she was bombarded with her children's demands, with cooking, and with all the other things that had to be done. Practicing the PQT just before going home helped her change roles more easily from career woman to homemaker. In fact, many homemakers find that PQT is a great way to prepare for the kids' coming home from school. On the other hand, a business executive discovered that one of his best times for practicing the PQT was during lunch. He not only felt more relaxed and refreshed as a result of the PQT, he also lost some unwanted pounds. The best time to practice the PQT is when it most conveniently fits into your daily schedule and when it provides you with the most benefit.

> *Practice personal quiet time twice daily.*

The thought of scheduling two PQT sessions every day may seem difficult at the outset. But if you understand and accept control, you will make the time, because you realize that practicing the PQT is a wise investment. It's hard to calculate the value to be gained from feeling calmer, more alert, and more energized when interacting with others and when performing tasks, but that's what you experience with the PQT and other relaxation and meditation techniques. For many people, the PQT has come to symbolize a time in which they "don't have to top anything or outdo anyone." It's a time when people can restore their bodies after having them drained by the day's pressures, and come away feeling more alert. One person described the feeling as "like taking a shower without getting wet." Many people have learned to think of the PQT as a time to calmly take inventory of themselves. The feelings you experience and the significance that the PQT plays in your life are as individual and unique as you are.

LEARNING THE PQT

There are five progressions to mastering the PQT. Progressions 1 and 2 can be called the *physical* progressions, because through them you learn to remove yourself from the stress and activity of your daily routine by concentrating on the various muscle groups in your body. Progression 1 is highly structured; in it, you are instructed on how to tighten and relax your muscles in a particular order. Progression 2 is less structured; although you again contract and relax specific muscle groups, you can vary and select the way you contract them.

Progression 3 can be called the *mental* progression, because it involves more of your emotions and thoughts than progressions 1 and 2. After you have become adept at physical relaxation through first contracting a muscle and then relaxing it, progression 3 helps you achieve the same relaxed sensations in your muscles more quickly, by eliminating the step of contracting them. Consequently, progression 3 focuses on relaxing your mind and expanding your level of consciousness.

Progression 4 is the *creative* progression. At this stage, you create your own method. You learn how to select and coordinate the components of each of the previous three progressions that best suit your needs. You practice varying the elements of your personal quiet time to complement your mood. Finally, you learn to use and benefit from the PQT during those times of day that you have identified as stressful.

Progression 5 is the *advanced* progression. Learning the PQT is a skill and, like any skill, it must be practiced. Over a period of time, you learn to relax your body more quickly and easily. The fifth progression shows you how.

Now that you are ready to learn the PQT, you'll want to follow six basic guidelines:

1. Be alone; do not make any association with anyone or anything else.
2. Establish an ideal environment; choose a place that is quiet and comfortable, and play soothing music if you wish.
3. Imagine an ideal scene; make it as luxurious and idealized as you like.
4. Let your thoughts come and go freely.
5. Be nonevaluative. There is no success or failure.
6. Be attentive after the PQT.

1. Be alone. You should be alone when practicing the PQT. This period is an opportunity to be with yourself, and it is particularly helpful to avoid external associations and disruptions, especially while you are learning the technique. If you can, choose a time when you are not likely to be interrupted. Hold all your calls. Once you have learned the skill, you will find it easier to do the PQT just about any-where. To make your experience more enjoyable, make sure your bladder is empty and the clothes you are wearing are comfortable. Kick off your shoes if you would like, and remove your glasses.

2. Establish an ideal environment. Select a location that will enhance your PQT—for example, a favorite room—and then enhance it further by playing the kind of music (preferably instru-mental) that you find the most soothing. Sit or lie down comfort-ably, and feel free to change positions at any time if it makes you more comfortable.

3. Imagine an ideal scene. As you experience your PQT, allow your mind to create the kind of scene that you find most soothing. For example, you might think of an ocean at sunset, lying under a tree, or being in an elegant and luxurious hotel room. Some people find it easiest to picture a favorite place they once visited. One woman told me that she imagined many scenes with the help of pictures she had looked at in magazines. The point to remember is that the scene you create is your own, and it can be as simple or luxurious as you like, as long as it is comfortable for you. Remember, don't make any associ-ation with anyone or anything else when you place yourself in your scene. It's best to be alone—without your spouse, children, girl-friend, or boyfriend. This is your time to be with yourself.

4. Let your thoughts come and go. As you place yourself in your ideal scene, allow thoughts to enter and leave your mind. Don't deal with your thoughts or evaluate them during your PQT. It is your time to let your thoughts and feelings emerge freely and nonjudgmentally. Don't hold on to them. Whenever you realize that you are concentrating on a thought, easily let it go by returning the focus of your attention to the muscle group where you left off, or to your breathing.

5. Be nonevaluative. It is not necessary for you to evaluate how well you are relaxing during the PQT. There is no success or failure. The 10- to 20-minute period is something you simply experience. Let's say you are working with a particular muscle group and you don't seem to be relaxing it enough. The typical response is, "See, I can't do these relaxation techniques. Everybody else can do them, but I can't." If that comes into your mind, don't worry about it. Interpret it as any other thought, and let it go as you were instructed in guideline 4. Keep in mind that the same thought may reenter your mind, and if it does, follow guideline 4 again. The thoughts will eventually go away. Remind yourself that this is your nonevaluative time, and move on to the next muscle group. You will find that by not dwelling on how you are doing, you can relax more easily.

6. Be attentive after the PQT. You do want to look for positive results, but do it at the end of your PQT experience. Actually, this is an important guideline to follow consistently. The reason is that often the results are quite subtle. Many people misunderstand what they are expected to feel as a result of the PQT. It is not unusual at first to feel like nothing has happened; this is because the feelings associated with relaxation are different from anything you experience on a daily basis. They are not readily identifiable. When you exercise, for instance, by playing a vigorous game of tennis, your body's reactions are apparent. You breathe faster and harder, your heart pumps more rapidly, and you begin to perspire. Afterward, your mind feels clearer and your muscles are tired; you are sweaty and thirsty for some cool liquid to drink.

Your body's reactions to the PQT are more subtle. Notice, for instance, if your breathing is more smooth and regular at the end of your PQT than it was prior to the technique. Also pay attention to your thoughts, and whether they have slowed down. Check your hands to see if they feel warmer and drier than they were before. See if your eyes open up a little wider and you feel more alert. You may notice that a lingering headache has disappeared, or a nagging back ache is suddenly gone. Later, take the time to notice if you are able to listen more attentively to others and concentrate better on certain tasks. If it's evening, pay attention to your energy level. Notice if you are not as tired as you usually are at that time of night.

It's important to look regularly at the effects of the PQT, because spotting these subtle but positive changes will encourage you to keep practicing the technique.

PROGRESSION 1: PHYSICAL RELAXATION WITH SPECIFIC GUIDELINES

Practice progression 1 twice daily, preferably in the morning and afternoon, for five to seven days. I recommend that you not move on to progression 2 until you are thoroughly familiar with contracting and relaxing your muscles according to the instructions below.

1. Lie down in a comfortable position. Close your eyes and feel yourself breathing, inhaling and exhaling smoothly and rhythmically through your nose.

2. While continuing your rhythmic breathing, imagine a scene that pleases you. (In order to illustrate the technique, I will use an ocean scene, but you can imagine whatever is most attractive to you.) Envision the ocean on a late summer afternoon, with the waves gently rolling up the shore, and the beach's silken sand warmed by the rays of the setting sun.

3. As you picture this scene, imagine yourself in it. Feel yourself lying on the luxurious sand. Feel the warmth it radiates, and how it begins to relax you. Imagine the palm trees gently swaying, and feel the gentleness of the ocean breeze as it passes over your body—it is just cool enough to make the warm sand feel even more relaxing.

As you see the waves being formed and shaped, hear the rhythmic sounds they make as they roll up onto the shore, then return to sea.

4. Once you are completely comfortable on your beach, concentrate on the muscles in your left foot. Contract these muscles by pointing your toes down toward the floor, as if you were pointing them into the sand. Tighten them as hard as you can, and hold them for a slow count of 3. Release, and feel the muscles relaxing as you nestle into the sand. As you focus on these actions, say to yourself, "I feel my toes uncurling. I feel the softness and smoothness of each grain of sand between my toes as they continue to relax. I imagine the muscles in my left foot feeling so limp that I have no desire to move."

5. Concentrate on the muscle in your left calf. Contract the muscle by bringing your toes back and pointing them toward your face. Tighten and hold for a slow count of three. Release and let go. As you relax the muscle, imagine feeling the tension drifting off and the muscle becoming loose. The warmth of the sun helps you relax.

6. Concentrate on the muscles in the upper portion of your left leg. Contract them by pushing your heel into the floor as hard as you can. Hold for a slow count of three. Release and relax. Continue to imagine the soothing sensations associated with the ocean, the calm breeze, and the warm sand, and how they continue to comfort you.

7-9. Repeat the same sequence for each of the three muscle groups in your right foot and leg. Contract your muscles each time as hard as you can. Hold for a slow count of three, then release and relax.

10. Concentrate on the muscles of your buttocks. Contract them by squeezing them together as hard as you can. Hold for a slow count of three. Release, and as you relax

the muscles, capture the feeling of lying on that sandy beach. As you perform these actions, imagine and say to yourself, "I am nestling my body into the sand. The sand is shaping itself to the form of my body, and it cradles me as I relax into it." At this point, reflect back on the muscles in the lower portion of your body. Notice the overall relaxed feeling and how you can sense the warm sand. You are aware of having no desire to move.

11. Concentrate on the muscles in your abdomen. Contract them by inhaling and pushing your stomach out as far as you can. Hold for a slow count of three. Slowly exhale and relax. If you hear any rumbling noises in your abdominal area, don't worry. They are an indication that you are relaxing.

12. Pause and enjoy how easily thoughts are entering and leaving your mind. Just like the ocean waves, thoughts roll in and out, with no effort or difficulty. You may find yourself thinking a specific thought connected with your daily activities, perhaps a business worry or a household responsibility. In this case, simply acknowledge the idea and return your focus to the muscle group you have just finished relaxing.

13. Concentrate on the muscles in your back. Contract them by inhaling and pushing your back into the floor. Hold for a slow count of three. Begin to relax, feeling the relaxation rise in the muscles of your lower back. The warmth of the sand helps them relax, and that warmth spreads to the middle portion of your back and then to the upper portion. You can feel each vertebra loosen as the warmth travels along your spinal column.

14. Focus on the muscles in your left hand. Contract them by making a tight fist. Hold for a slow count of three. As you loosen the muscles in your left hand, say to

yourself, "I can feel the smooth sand under my fingertips, and each grain is warm and soothing." Notice how, as your fingers are extended, your entire hand is motionless and feels heavy.

15. Concentrate on the muscles in your left arm. Contract them by opening your fingers and pushing your hand down into the floor as hard as you can, as if you were pushing your hand into the sand to make an imprint. Hold for a slow count of three. Begin to relax, feeling the relaxation rise in the muscles of your lower arm and travel to your upper arm.

16-17. Repeat the same sequence for the muscles in your right hand and arm.

18. Concentrate on the muscle groups in your neck and shoulders. Contract them first on the left side, by lifting your left shoulder and tilting your head toward it until they touch. Push them gently against each other. Hold for a slow count of three and slowly relax. Repeat the same sequence on the right side. The neck and shoulder area is, for many people, the place where the tensions of the day seem to accumulate. Imagine that as you lie on the beach, a wave laps softly against you. As it withdraws, it takes the tension with it. You can almost feel the shoulder and neck muscles lengthening as they relax.

19. Concentrate on the muscles in your neck. Contract them by bringing your head forward until your chin meets your chest. Hold for a slow count of three. Slowly relax your head to a comfortable position.

20. Pause and allow yourself to feel your entire body. It is as if you have settled completely into the warm sand, which holds you so that you have no desire to move any part of your body.

21. Concentrate on the muscles in your face. Contract them by wrinkling your forehead, eyes, and mouth. Hold for a slow count of three. Release and relax. The cool breeze is brushing the wrinkles from your face, and your eyelids are so heavy that you have no desire to open them. All the facial expressions and mouth movements that you make during the day are smoothed away, and your jaw is relaxed.

22. Pause and become aware of your breathing. Continue to inhale and exhale smoothly and rhythmically. Notice the smoothness in each breath of air.

23. Again, imagine the entire scene in which you have been progressively relaxing for the last few minutes. Enjoy the deep sense of overall relaxation that you have been experiencing. Remain still for a few moments.

24. Count to five slowly. As you do, say to yourself, "Now that my journey is nearing an end, I will awaken in the usual manner, feeling more refreshed and revitalized for having done the PQT." Now easily open your eyes.

25. Sit up. Remain sitting quietly for a minute or two. Now resume your daily activities.

Answers to Common Questions

After you have practiced progression 1, you may have some questions about what you have just experienced. Although it is important not to evaluate yourself during your personal quiet time, it is valuable to do so afterward. First, identify your physical responses. Do you have an overall relaxed feeling? Have your thoughts slowed down? Check your breathing. Does it feel smoother, or faster and irregular? Feel the temperature in your hands and feet. Are they warmer or colder? Are the palms of your hands sweaty or dry?

Some responses that indicate you have reached a relaxed state are warmth in your hands and feet, smooth and rhythmic breathing, dry hands, and very few thoughts following the PQT experience; later, your thoughts will be clearer. If you have experienced any of these signs, you are relaxing.

What happens if certain muscles aren't relaxed during the PQT?
When one man said to me, "I was able to feel myself relaxing all my muscles except my thigh muscles," I responded: "That's OK. Remember, you don't have to evaluate yourself during your PQT. The important thing is how you feel now."

Is there something wrong if I feel uncomfortable lying there for 20 minutes?
Several people report that they have an extremely difficult time "just lying there" for 20 minutes. They get *more* tense. If this is your problem, I suggest that you limit the amount of time you practice the progression—let's say, to six minutes. Make an agreement with yourself that you will practice the technique for that amount of time. If you are uncomfortable during the six-minute period, that's all the more reason to continue with the method. By being patient with yourself, you'll find that the anxious feeling begins to subside. Repeat this procedure for seven days. By then, you will probably be comfortable with extending your personal quiet time.

Is there a problem with practicing the technique if I have a heart condition or high blood pressure?
Quite the opposite, actually. If you have hypertension or heart disease, though, I recommend that you continue to breathe at a smooth and rhythmic pace as you contract each of the muscles in your body, paying particular attention to your upper body. According to Dr. Gerard Varlotta of the New York University School of Medicine and the Rusk Institute of Rehabilitation Medicine, holding your breath as you contract your muscles decreases the amount of blood flow

back to your heart. "One of the primary functions of breathing, in addition to bringing oxygen into the body," explains Dr. Varlotta, "is to help the blood back to the heart."

Is it OK to fall asleep?

Some people actually worry that they are relaxing too much. For example, one executive said, "I felt as if I drifted in and out of sleep the whole time. Is that all right?" The answer is that it definitely is, because the PQT is entirely your own, and you should give your body what it needs at this time. However, if you continue to fall asleep regularly, perhaps you should sit up during your session. Furthermore, you should take another look at your daily routine. Falling asleep may be a signal from your body. Are you overexerting during the day, or not getting enough sleep at night? Do not push yourself too hard. One of the first benefits of the PQT is that you will discover whether you have been demanding too much of yourself.

PROGRESSION 2: PHYSICAL RELAXATION WITH GENERAL DIRECTIONS

Progression 2 builds on your knowledge of how to contract and relax specific muscle groups, but in this progression you begin to experiment, incorporating variations on the basic technique outlined in the first progression. The approach described here is only a suggestion. Practice this progression for about five days. Do not move on to progression 3 until you have learned (1) how to tighten each of the muscles in your body effectively and comfortably and (2) how to recognize tension in specific muscles and be able to relax them at will after first contracting them. To customize the PQT method to your interests, consider the following.

1. Vary your position. As you practice, discover the posture most comfortable for you. Most people seem to prefer sitting with their hands resting comfortably in their laps, but you may choose to continue lying down, as you did during progression 1. People who suffer from lower back pain have found that lying on their backs with their knees bent and their feet flat on the floor is a perfect position.

2. Vary your scene. Rather than visualizing the ocean, waves, and a sandy beach, create a new but equally pleasing picture. For example, imagine a log cabin high in the mountains on a snowy afternoon. Place yourself in front of the fireplace, nestling into a fluffy rug and feeling the warmth of the crackling fire. As you proceed through each of the muscle groups, imagine or say to yourself key phrases, such as "I'm letting go," "I'm unwinding," and "I'm sensing a wave of calm," as you use this new scene to enhance your relaxation experience.

3. Vary the method by which you contract muscle groups. As you practice, you will discover that muscles may be contracted in different ways. For example, instead of making a fist to tighten the muscles in your hand, open it and extend your fingers as hard as you can. The muscles in your neck can be tensed differently by stretching them toward the opposite shoulder, causing the muscles to lengthen. You can also vary the way you tighten your jaw muscles. Instead of bearing down on your teeth, open your mouth as wide as possible. Make sure when contracting your muscles that you gradually make them more tense, as opposed to tightening them rapidly.

Answers to Common Questions

Now that you have practiced progression 2, you may have some questions about what you have just experienced. Remember, it's important that you know how to relax your muscles. After you have tightened the muscles, consciously note the tension before you let that tension go.

I'm uncomfortable making a fist when tightening the muscles in my hand. What should I do?

When I hear this complaint, I remind people that they are not doing anything wrong. Go back to the point made at the very outset—that the PQT adjusts with you as you learn to grow with it. In this particular case, it means that you should take what you *don't* like and use it as valuable information to help you discover what you *do* like and enjoy. Recognizing and acknowledging how you feel is a significant part of learning to create your own personal quiet time. By experimenting, one woman found that she preferred tightening the muscles in her hands by holding them together. The one thing I do recommend is that you try a technique several times before you decide not to use it, because each experience will be different. What you dislike during one session may please you the next time.

On the other hand, it's valuable to have insights into what it is you like because it aids you in coping with more stressful times. For example, during your practice you find that contracting your calf and thigh muscles is uncomfortable. Then one night you get into bed, knowing that the next day will be very challenging. You simply can't get to sleep, because your mind is buzzing with thoughts about the coming day. Now is the time to call on those elements of the PQT that help you relax and fall asleep—that means don't try to include contracting your calf and thigh muscles.

If I can't picture a scene, does that mean I can't do the PQT?

Lots of people worry about having difficulty imagining a scene. If this is your concern, worry no more. Not everyone is visual, and it is not a requirement when practicing the PQT that you *have* to visualize a scene. Using myself as an example, I prefer feeling my muscles relaxing, and as I do, I sense warmth and comfort from my scene as opposed to creating an artistically clear scene. In other words, I'm not very visual. If you are not inclined to be visual, one path you can take toward improving your ability to visualize a pleasant scene is to re-create in your mind a place that you once visited. Another thing you can do is to look at a favorite painting or photograph before practicing the PQT. Take a snapshot of it and bring it with you while experiencing your PQT.

Is it bad to experience interruptions when trying to use the PQT? What do you do if you are distracted while practicing your personal quiet time? Suppose the phone rings or someone comes to your door while you are in the middle of your exercise? The best thing to do when this happens is to give yourself a few seconds before getting up. Taking just a few seconds is important, because your body is in a relaxed state. If you jump up too quickly, you may experience some momentary dizziness and sluggishness. As you are getting up, tell yourself, "I understand control, and although I'm being inconvenienced momentarily, I can easily regain the relaxed feelings I had before. Just because I'm doing the PQT, the world doesn't have to stop." Having this type of attitude is valuable, because you want to keep your PQT routine simple. If it becomes too much of a big deal, the chances are great the you'll find it too cumbersome, and will eventually come up with reasons not to do it.

PROGRESSION 3: MENTAL RELAXATION

Progression 3 continues the physical experiences of the two previous progressions, but in it you relax without first contracting your muscles. Practice this progression for about five days. Do not move on to progression 4 until you can easily relax your muscles without having to first tighten them. It's also important for you feel comfortable accepting any thought that comes into your mind, including thoughts arising from stressful situations. This progression introduces the importance of abdominal breathing.

1. After closing your eyes, feel yourself breathing. As you take another breath, imagine your lungs are a glass being filled

with water. As you allow the air to enter into your lungs, as with filling the glass with water, the air will go to the bottom first and work its way up to the top. Then, when you exhale, as with pouring water out of the glass, the air will leave from the top first, going down to the bottom. Allow the air to leave from the top of your lungs before making its way down to your abdomen. Repeat this several times. Each time, as you go to exhale, feel the muscles relaxing from your head all the way down to your toes as they accompany the exhalation. Within a few breaths, you'll feel yourself getting into a nice rhythm.

2. Gradually relax all the muscles as you have done previously, following the same sequence of muscle groups. Once again, you want to create the relaxed feeling in each muscle group without contracting them first. You may find it helpful to repeat details of the pleasant scene you imagined in the first two progressions. Remember, you don't *have* to visualize a scene. Instead, you may want to use key words or phrases that trigger memories of soothing sensations. For example, you might think "I'm letting go naturally," "I'm beginning to unwind," "I feel waves of calm," or "I feel warmth and softness."

3. Open your mind. Because your conscious mind does not have to concentrate on contracting specific muscle groups, it is available to any number of thoughts. Allow these thoughts to enter and leave freely. Some thoughts may involve pending stressful situations or unpleasant ideas. You may even find yourself trying to solve some problem. Whatever the case, acknowledge your thoughts, but don't attempt to control them or to concentrate on any one particular idea. Let them go as you have done previously, by following guideline 4.

4. Focus on your breathing as you complete your PQT for the amount of time allocated.

5. When your "appointment with yourself" is over, count to five.

6. Open your eyes and give yourself about a minute before getting up and resuming your activities.

More Questions and Answers

Is there anything wrong if my mind is cluttered with lots of thoughts?

> *To let go of thoughts, use the audiocassette quick charge.*

No. In progression 3, you can expect a lot of thoughts because there is less to do. One woman said that she had little difficulty thinking thoughts—she considered the various chores she wanted to accomplish, a meeting she was going to attend, or what she wanted to prepare for dinner. Her problem lay in being able to let the thoughts go. I told her that as soon as she realized she was concentrating on a particular thought, she should acknowledge it, but then replace it by focusing her attention on the specific muscle group she had reached in the progression. A good technique for letting go of thoughts is the wastepaper basket quick charge. As you learned in Chapter 10, the technique is practiced by visualizing a posterboard. Write out all your thoughts, then imagine taking a very big paint brush and paint a huge X across all your thoughts. Picture a big wastepaper basket. Take the poster, tear it up into little pieces, and dump it into the wastebasket. Then light a match and burn the whole thing. Remember, the number and kind of thoughts that enter your mind during your personal quiet time will vary. The important thing is that you let them go.

Sometimes my PQT experience goes really fast; at other times it goes slowly. Is anything wrong?

One man explained to me that he glanced at the clock while practicing his PQT, but that after what he thought to be only a few minutes, his time was almost over. I assured him that when time seems to pass very quickly, the mind is probably not thinking on the conscious level. This is good. In that state, the mind is left free to entertain a multitude of thoughts. Always remember that there's no need to worry about how quickly or slowly time passes during your personal quiet time.

PROGRESSION 4: CREATIVELY PUTTING IT ALL TOGETHER

Progression 4 is titled "putting it all together" because that's exactly what you do. You will select and coordinate the different components that have worked most successfully for you as you practiced progressions 1, 2, and 3. As you've been advised, the PQT grows with you, and thus it is entirely open-ended. The approaches presented here are suggestions about the kinds of choices you may make, but the choices you do make should be yours alone.

By making these selections daily, you will invariably overcome any boredom. The PQT will fit your mood and physical state. Practice progression 4 for about five days. At the end of this period, you will truly have reached a new beginning. You will find yourself able to use the relaxed feelings you have created with the PQT whenever you need them to cope with the frustrations and tensions of day-to-day living. Keep the following points in mind.

1. Choose the most effective components of your PQT. As you practiced progressions 1, 2, and 3, you may have found that certain elements always worked well in helping you to relax. Let's say you discover that an ideal combination is lying down on your bed while soft piano music plays on the stereo and you visualize resting in a hammock beside a brook. If you vary just one of these elements—perhaps by substituting vocal music for the piano instrumentals—you may still be able to relax, but not as quickly or as completely. On the other hand, you may prefer to choose among several different positions, types of music, and scenes, according to your mood on a given day. You may also choose to omit one component altogether, such as by experiencing your PQT in silence or choosing not to visualize any scene at all. Varying the components of your PQT, as mentioned, minimizes the boredom that can result from a too rigidly defined program.

2. Choose the most effective components of your muscle relaxation technique. Some people prefer to return to the strictly ordered sequence of contraction and relaxation in progression 1, while others choose to vary the sequence or simply relax their muscles in no particular order without contracting them first. It is especially effective to concentrate on relaxing those muscle areas where you most often feel strain in your daily life. One businessman learned from progression 3 to recognize that the muscles in his neck were always tight, producing a tension headache by the end of his workday. When he practiced the technique at the end of the day, he was able to relieve the headache by choosing specifically to contract and relax his neck muscles.

3. Start transferring your relaxed feelings into your active day. During the day, identify your stress symptoms and try to determine the situations or circumstances that bring about these symptoms. Then transfer what you learned during the PQT to help you better handle these stress-related symptoms.

One man who suffered from tension headaches examined his day. By retracing his steps, he realized that he spent a tremendous amount of time on the phone. By transferring the relaxed feelings he experienced during the PQT to when he was on the phone, he found that the tension in his neck muscles eased, and so did his headaches. A woman was told that she had the tendency to talk down to people. When she examined more closely what her boss told her, she noticed that when speaking to people at work, she tended to tighten the muscles in her face and jaw, causing her to enunciate more abruptly. Her consonant sounds became very strong. To soften her voice, she transferred the relaxed feelings she got from her PQT to those times when she was speaking to people. It took a while to gain this conscious awareness of herself, but once she did, her delivery improved considerably.

A Few More Questions and Answers

Do I have to be alone to practice personal quiet time?

Could you do it, say, on the subway to and from work? Of course. The PQT is *experienced* alone, but it can be *practiced* in the presence of other people. When you are first learning the technique, you will find it easier to practice the preferred 10- to-20-minute period alone and with a minimal number of distractions. As you become more proficient in the skill, you will find that the interruptions and outside noises don't disturb you as they may have in the beginning. For instance, you may be distracted by a sudden noise, but you will easily be able to return to your relaxed state.

What if I don't have the 10 or 20 minutes needed to practice the PQT?

The best answer I can give you is "Do it anyway." Doing something is better than nothing. Most important, doing that "something" keeps up your routine. The easiest thing to do is to let the PQT slip. Before you know it, you are out of the routine. Doing anything is better that just omitting it. To help you, progression 5 is designed to take only 10 minutes. The reason the time has been reduced is that you are no longer learning a skill.

PROGRESSION 5: THE ADVANCED APPROACH

Progression 5 introduces you to a comfortable sequence that involves using the PQT method for 10 minutes or even less. Remember, at this stage your body has learned to recognize the sensations and is familiar with the relaxed feelings of personal quiet time. Since you are proficient at relaxing each of your muscles, you will be able to reach the same relaxed state more quickly. You should be able to relax each muscle in your body, regardless of whether the muscle has been contracted. This progression can be practiced effectively in a shorter time because, in general, you are able to reach an overall relaxed state more quickly and easily. Use this progression whenever your time is limited.

Progression 5 involves contracting the entire musculature of your body at one time instead of relaxing individual muscle groups as you did in the previous progressions. Here is one sequence you can use.

1. Select a comfortable environment. If you desire, play your favorite musical or environmental sounds.
2. Close your eyes.
3. Begin breathing very smoothly and regularly, allowing the air first to enter your abdominal area. As you exhale, let the air exit from the top of your lungs, then gradually down to your stomach area.
4. At any point, start to visualize a very pleasant scene.
5. Maximally contract all the muscles in your body from your toes to your face. Hold for three counts and relax. One PQT practitioner finds it easier to relax if he coordinates his muscle contraction with the scene he visualizes. For instance, the ocean scene is his favorite. When he imagines a wave rolling up onto the shore, he contracts his muscles.

When the wave rolls back out again, he begins loosening them.

6. Systematically relax your muscles, starting with your feet. As soon as they feel comfortable, relax the lower and upper portions of each leg.
7. Relax the muscles in your buttocks. As the muscles loosen, pause and notice how the muscles in the whole lower half of your body feel relaxed.
8. Feel the relaxation in your stomach area as the sensation spreads to the muscles in your back.
9. Relax the muscles in your hands. Feel the warmth from the spot where you lie helping to soothe and relax the muscles in your left and right arms.
10. Feel the muscles in the lower and upper portions of each arm loosening as you absorb the warmth from the spot where you lie.
11. Feel the muscles in your neck and shoulder area join in as your tensions seep away, leaving the muscles relaxed. Reflect back to the luxury of the scene, and the relaxed feelings in your body.
12. Feel each of the muscles in your face loosening as the tensions continue to drift away, leaving your muscles relaxed and comfortable.
13. Pause and become aware of your breathing. Focus on inhaling and exhaling for four counts.
14. Count to five. Say to yourself, "Now that my journey is nearing an end, when I reach five I will awaken in the usual fashion, feeling refreshed and revitalized."
15. Sit up, and remain sitting quietly for a few minutes.
16. Resume your daily activities.

Answers to Final Questions

What do you mean when you say that completing the PQT signals "a new beginning"?

I can best explain it by pointing out the compatibility of the PQT with the quick charges you learned in Chapter 10. In other words, the quick charges are extensions of the PQT. By learning the PQT, you can easily let go of thoughts. So when you make a mistake, whether at work or at home, calling upon the wastepaper basket quick charge or the "So what? What now?" quick charge becomes that much easier. So does transferring the relaxed feelings from the PQT into your active day. Why is that? You are more aware of yourself and you can more readily recognize when your muscles are tense and when they are relaxed.

For example, one woman decided to take up the game of racquetball. Whenever it was her turn to hit the ball, she would become very anxious, contact the ball too early, and consequently give her opponent an easy return shot. She learned how to use the PQT to reduce her anxiety and tension, and now she is able to wait until the ball is at a lower point before hitting it. The consequence is a "kill" shot—and a point won. Another PQT practitioner learned to adopt the technique when he began a new job. Each day, he has a 30-minute subway ride to and from work. He now practices his personal quiet time during the trip, and he both enters his office and returns home feeling refreshed and invigorated.

Do I have to practice the PQT?

The answer is no. You've gone through life for quite a few years without it, and chances are great that you'll live a long life without ever trying it. The issues you want to address revolve mostly around two questions. First, what tools or skills do you have in your personal tool kit for reenergizing? Having a good answer for this question becomes even more significant if you demand a lot from yourself each day and want to enjoy all the activities that you have set yourself up to do.

Second, do you set aside any time each day to stop and reflect on where you're going and what's important to you? Although reflecting on your goals is not the purpose of the PQT, it does point you in that direction. Many people find that the method stays their course and helps them keep life in perspective.

Here's how you can take control immediately.

1. **STOP** and assess what skills you have in your repertoire to reenergize yourself—besides going on a vacation!

2. **STOP** thinking that you have to either exercise or practice the PQT. They complement each other well, so use both.

START▶

1. **START** practicing the PQT twice daily for two weeks, and see if you notice any positive effects.

2. **START** making daily "appointments" with yourself to get in the habit of practicing the PQT. Preferred times include immediately upon waking up and at the end of your day, when your gears are shifting from work or school to home.

3. **START** to use the PQT, but before you do, take note of the following:

   • How many hours you need to sleep each night in order to wake up feeling energetic

- Your energy levels throughout the day

- How many pain relievers you take throughout the day for headaches, upset stomach, or general body aches

- How easily you fall asleep

  After practicing the PQT twice daily for about two weeks, reexamine these questions.

The real contest is always between what you've done and what you're capable of doing. You measure yourself against yourself and nobody else.

Geoffrey Gaberino

References

CHAPTER 2

1. Rotella, Bob. *Golf Is Not a Game of Perfect*. New York: Simon & Schuster Trade, 1995, pp. 128, 220
2. Burns, Dr. David. *Feeling Good: The New Mood Therapy*, New York: Avon Books, 1992, p. 28.

CHAPTER 3

1. Naisbitt, John and Aburdene, Patricia. *Megatrends 2000: Ten New Directions for the 1990s.* New York: Avon Books, 1991, pp. 322–323.

CHAPTER 4

1. *1994 Value Study*, American Management Association and Bright Enterprises, Inc.
2. Traverse, Robert M. W. *Essentials of Learning: An Overview for Students of Education*. New York: McMillan, 1972, pp. 297, 299, 320.
3. *New Catholic Enclepedia*, Vol. A, s.v. "attitude."
4. Sanford, William R., and Green, Carl R. *Sports Immortals: Billie Jean King*. Toronto. Maxwell McMillan, 1993, p. 11.
5. Ditman, Terri. Interviewed by author, December 30, 1997.
6. Hill, Napoleon, and Stone, W. Clement. *Success Through a Positive Mental Attitude*. New York: Simon & Schuster, 1977, p. 7.

7. Morris, Edmund. *The Rise of Theodore Roosevelt.* New York: Ballentine Books, 1979, pp. 40–41.
8. Ibid., p. 63
9. Ibid., p. 77
10. Lazo, Caroline *Martin Luther King, Jr.* New York: Dillon Press, 1994, p. 16.
11. Ibid., p. 53.
12. Lieber, Ron. "Zen and the Art of Teamwork." *Fortune,* Vol. 132, Issue 13, Dec. 25, 1995, p. 218.
13. Ibid.
14. Goleman, Daniel. *Emotional Intelligence: Why It Can Matter More Than IQ.* New York: Bantam Books, 1995, p. 54.
15. Burns, Dr. David. *Feeling Good: The New Mood Therapy.* New York: Avon Books, 1992, p. 41.
16. "Dr. Bernie Siegel Tells Us How to Put Much More Happiness in Our Lives," *Bottom Line*, Vol. 17, 2.
17. Goleman, Daniel. *Emotional Intelligence: Why It Can Matter More Than IQ.* New York: Bantam Books, 1995 p. 152

CHAPTER 5

1. Runko, Paul. Interview by author. November 18, 1997.

CHAPTER 6

1. Glasser, William. *Control Theory: A New Explanation of How We Control Our Lives.* New York: Harper & Row, 1984, p. 26.

CHAPTER 7

1. Curfiss, Larry. Interview by author. May 5, 1998.

2. Predpall, Dan. Interview by author. December 29, 1997.
3. Levit, Robert. Interview by author. December 30, 1997.
4. *1994 Value Study*, American Management Association and Bright Enterprises, Inc.
5. Croft, Harry. Interview by author. May 4, 1998.

CHAPTER 8

1. *1985 National Study*, Simmons Market Research Bureau and Bright Enterprises, Inc.

2. ;Bright, Dr. Deborah. *The Official Criticism Manual.* New York: DB Publishing, 1997, pp. 56–57.

CHAPTER 9

1. *The Emotionally Charged Workplace*, 1995, joint study by Bright Enterprises, Inc., and American Management Association.
2. MacCauley, Clark. Interview by author. January 2, 1998.
3. Angelino, Mark. Interview by author. May 7, 1998.
4. Michmerhuizen, Brian. Interview by author. December 30, 1997.
5. Anderson, Peggy. *Great Quotes from Great Leaders.* Lombard, IL: The Career Press, 1997, p. 51.

CHAPTER 10

1. Morris, Edmund. *The Rise of Theodore Roosevelt*, New York: Ballentine Books, 1979, p. 89.
2. Adler, Mortimer J. *Aristotle for Everybody*, New York: Simon & Schuster Trade, 1997, p. 130.

3. *1992 and 1998 Study*, Bright Enterprises, Inc., and the American Management Association.

CHAPTER 11

1. *1995 National Study*, Simmons Market Research Bureau and Bright Enterprise, Inc.
2. Nightingale, Earl. *This Is Earl Nightingale*, Garden City, NY: Doubleday, 1996, p. 223.

CHAPTER 12

1. Glasser, William. *Control Theory: A New Explanation of How We Control Our Lives*. New York: Harper & Row, 1984, p. 26.
2. *1985 Personal Quiet Time Study*, Kessler Institute for Rehabilitation and Bright Enterprises, Inc.
3. Benson, Dr. Herbert. "The Relaxation response: Lessons learned since its introduction exactly 20 years ago." *Bottom Line*, Vol. 16, Issue 19, Oct. 1, 1995, p. 1.

Index